HISTORY

AS THE STORY
OF
LIBERTY

by Benedetto Croce

GIAMBATTISTA VICO

HISTORICAL MATERIALISM
AND THE ECONOMICS OF KARL MARX

THE POETRY OF DANTE

HISTORY OF EUROPE
IN THE NINETEENTH CENTURY

HISTORY

AS THE STORY
OF LIBERTY

Benedetto Croce

Translated from the Italian by

SYLVIA SPRIGGE

New York · W · W · NORTON & COMPANY · INC ·

FIRST PUBLISHED IN 1941
BY W. W. NORTON, INC.

PRINTED IN GREAT BRITAIN
in 12-Point Bembo Type
BY UNWIN BROTHERS LIMITED
WOKING

Foreword

I PROPOSE in this volume to take up again the subject of the *Theory and History of the Writing of History* which I wrote in 1912–13, and which was continued in my *History of Italian Historiography in the Nineteenth Century* and in several other shorter works. I do not wish to offer this book in replacement of the previous book, but only to add new considerations born of my further studies and stimulated by new experience of life. In conformity with its origin, this book consists of a series of essays which share an implicit unity in the thought which runs through them all, and to which I have given also an explicit unity by means of the first essay, which serves as an introduction. Any slight repetition or infraction of the order of exposition noticeable now and then is a consequence of the literary form of the essay.

Particular emphasis is laid, in this volume, on the relation between the writing of history and practical action; not by way of defence against the attacks which in the name of abstract moral absolutism are nowadays often delivered against "historicism" by people who happen to be anxious to put morality outside the pale of history, and think to exalt it, so that it can agreeably be reverenced from afar and neglected from near at hand: no, not with that motive, but because historical thought is born in an extremely complicated and delicate dialectical process out of the passion of practical life, transcending the latter and getting free of it in a pure judgment of truth. By virtue of that judgment, passion is converted into decisive action.

The problem is difficult. Indeed all the problems of historical thought are difficult when, as in this book it is viewed as the sole

7

form of knowledge, and in writing these pages the author has sometimes had the feeling, in the course of his meditations, of having penetrated into the gruelling depths of Goethe's *Reich der Mütter*.

B. C.

NAPLES

January 1938

CONTENTS

CHAPTER   PAGE

Foreword   7

PART I

I.   *What Makes a History Book History*   15

II.   *Truth in History Books*   19

III.   *The Unity of an Historical Work*   23

IV.   *The Historical Meaning of Necessity*   27

V.   *Historical Knowledge Considered as Complete Knowledge*   32

VI.   *The Categories of History and the Forms of the Spirit*   37

VII.   *The Distinction Between Action and Thought*   40

VIII.   *Historiography as Liberation from History*   43

IX.   *History Considered as a Premise of the Struggle Between Value and Non-value*   46

X.   *History as Action*   50

XI.   *Moral Activity*   55

XII.   *History as the History of Liberty*   59

PART II

HISTORICISM AND ITS HISTORY

I.   *Its Own Character and the Beginning of Its Own Age*   65

II.   *Historicism Complete and Incomplete*   78

III.   *The Anecdote*   118

IV.   *The Imagination—The Anecdote and Historiography*   127

History

CHAPTER		PAGE
V.	Philology, History and Philosophy	133
VI.	The "Philosophy of History"	140
VII.	Philosophy as an Antiquated Idea	147
VIII.	The Identity of the Judgment of Events with the Knowledge of Their Genesis	151
IX.	Objections	154

PART III

HISTORIOGRAPHY AND POLITICS

I.	The So-called Irrational in History	161
II.	Political Historiography	170
III.	Historians and Politicians	175
IV.	Historiography—Partisan and Non-partisan	179
V.	The Preparatory and Non-determinate Character of Historiography as Regards Action	187
VI.	The Need for Historical Knowledge where Action is Concerned	196
	Two Marginal Notes	200

PART IV

HISTORIOGRAPHY AND MORALS

I.	Moral Judgment in Historiography	207
II.	Psychological Historiography	214
III.	Religious Historiography	219
IV.	Ethico-Political Historiography and Economic Facts	223
V.	Political Parties and Their Historical Character	227
VI.	Strength and Violence, Reason and Impulse	235

Contents

CHAPTER   PAGE

VII. *Moral Life and Economic Ordinances*   241

VIII. *Ideal Perpetuity and Historical Formations*   245

IX. *Religious Piety and Religion*   250

X. *History and Utopia*   256

PART V

PROSPECTS OF HISTORIOGRAPHY

I. *History Does Not Repeat Itself and Does Not Preserve Itself Intact*   265

II. *Shades of Agnosticism, Mysticism and Scepticism, and the Light of Historical Truth*   272

III. *Humanity in Fragments and Integral Humanity*   278

IV. *History to be Written and History Not to be Written*   282

V. *Historiography and Naturalism*   288

VI. *Nature as History, not as History Written by Us*   292

VII. *Prehistory and History*   298

VIII. *Chronological and Historical Epochs*   301

IX. *Natural Species and Historical Formations*   306

X. *Poetry and Historiography*   310

XI. *Historicism and Humanism*   315

Index   321

Part I

CHAPTER I

What Makes a History Book History

CRITICISM of historical works encounters the same difficulties as the criticism of poetry, or analogous difficulties. Some critics are simply at a loss, with the one as with the other, to know how to take them, and cannot catch the thread which connects them to their own mind; others set upon them with criteria which are extraneous and arbitrary, multiple, eclectic, or self-contradictory; and only a few judge them honestly by that criterion which alone is in keeping with their character. In Italy during recent years those few have undoubtedly increased in numbers; but when I go back in my mind to the days of my youth, in the 'eighties and the 'nineties, it seems to me that a criticism and a history of the writing of history was even less existent than a criticism and a history of poetry.

Works were turned out about historians all of which were superficial and documentary, concerned with sources, biography, authenticity, and the like. The only, or almost the only work which in so far as it touches these arguments might have given an example and suggested a better method, was de Sanctis' history of Italian literature, and that was misjudged, misunderstood and discredited.

A history book is not to be judged as literature or eloquence in the sense that was customary to the old humanistic men of letters who, when not otherwise occupied, used to translate Horace, or indited some historical commentary or an historical incident to which they were quite indifferent but which they deemed a suitable subject for a pretty and becoming presentation.

When the Abbé de Vertot was presented with some documents designed to correct the current story of a siege, he replied, "Mon siège est fait," my literary page is written. Paul Louis Courier was sure that *"toutes ces sottises qu'on appelle l'histoire ne peuvent valoir quelquechose qu'avec les ornements du goût,"* and that it was really all right to let Pompey win the battle of Pharsalia, *"si cela pouvait arrondir tant soit peu la phrase."* Now it is certainly desirable that historical work should be undertaken in scholarly fashion, but since literary merit is often dissociated from historical thought, the latter, even if it is expressed in a rough or careless literary form, still preserves the virtue of its thought.

Neither is an historical work to be judged by the greater or less number and correctness of the facts it contains, if only for the obvious reason that there are very copious and correct collections of facts which are quite clearly not histories, and others which are sparkling with historical intelligence but poorly equipped with information, or even littered with facts that are unreliable, legendary or fabulous: one only has to think of Vico's *Scienza Nuova.* Anthologies of information are chronicles, notes, memoirs, annals, but they are not history; and even if they are critically put together, and every item has its origin quoted or its evidence shrewdly sifted, they can never, on the plane on which they move, however hard they try, rise above unceasing quotation of things said and things written. They fail to become truth to us just at that point where history demands an assertion of truth arising out of our intimate experience. It is certainly desirable that the facts used in an historical work should have been carefully verified, if only to deprive the pedants of an arm which they insidiously and not unsuccessfully use to discredit vigorous and genuine historical writing; and then also because exactitude is in any case a moral duty. But in theory and in fact the two things are different and they may be and are separate, and neither the dull metal of the chronicles nor the highly polished metal of the philologists will ever be of equal value with the gold of the historian even if that is concealed in dross.

Finally, an historical book should not be judged by how much or how little it stirs the imagination, proves moving, exciting, exemplary or even curious and amusing, because dramas and novels can make a similar impression and a history book need not; it may by comparison appear cold, difficult and laborious work, or even at first to the majority boring (as has been said too of pure and great poetry). There are vigilant custodians of the sacred fire of religion and patriotism who invent history books "for family use," for the Germans, the French or any other people, or "for Catholic families" or "for Evangelicals," which are filled with heroic deeds or pious acts of devotion and uplifting customs, and descending somewhat there are those amateurs and compilers of anecdotal books who are on a spiritual level with dreamers of adventures and love affairs; all these have contributed towards a kind of literary production which is called history and is often mistaken for history, whereas it is, in fact, a thing which sometimes moves and excites, but is not pleasurable to the inquirer after truth, and it is to be carefully distinguished from treatises in which severity of thought and not a pathetic imagination or a didactic purpose, dominates. (Polybius, we may recall, mocked at those who compounded tragedies out of history.)

An historical work should then be judged solely on its historical merit, as poetry should be judged solely on its poetical merit. What constitutes history may be thus described: it is the act of comprehending and understanding induced by the requirements of practical life. These requirements cannot be satisfied by recourse to action unless first of all the phantoms and doubts and shadows by which one is beset have been dispelled through the statement and resolution of a problem—that is to say—by an act of thought. In the seriousness of some requirement of practical life lies the necessary condition for this effort. It may be a moral requirement, the requirement of understanding one's situation in order that inspiration and action and the good life may follow upon this. It may be a merely economic requirement, that of discernment of one's advantage. It may be an aesthetic requirement, like that of getting clear the meaning of a word, or an allusion, or a state of mind, in order fully to grasp and enjoy a poem; or again an intellectual requirement like that of solving a scientific question by correcting and amplifying information

B

about its terms through lack of which one had been perplexed and doubtful. Such knowledge of "the actual situation," as it is called, refers to the course of real life as it has gone on up to that point, and in so far as it does so, it is historical knowledge. Historical works of all times and of all peoples have come to birth in this manner and always will be born like this, out of fresh requirements which arise, and out of the perplexities involved in these. We shall not understand the history of men and of other times unless we ourselves are alive to the requirements which that history satisfied, nor will our successors understand the history of our time unless they fulfil these conditions. It often happens that the historical sense of a book is lifeless to us, and becomes mere literary form or a learned book of reference or an exciting pastime until suddenly it springs to life through new experience gained out of the course of events and through new requirements born in us which have their counterpart in, and bear a more or less intimate resemblance to those of former times; rather like certain images of Christ and the Virgin which are said suddenly to shed scarlet blood when they are hurt by some sinner or blasphemer. Historical science and culture in all its detailed elaboration exists for the purpose of maintaining and developing the active and civilized life of human society. If that impulse is barely present, historical culture is at its lowest ebb, as, for example, among Oriental peoples. When there is a sudden break or suspension in the process of civilized life, as there was in Europe in the early Middle Ages, then the writing of history almost ceases and relapses into barbarism, together with the society to which it belongs.

CHAPTER II

Truth in History Books

THE practical requirements which underlie every historical judgment give to all history the character of "contemporary history" because, however remote in time events there recounted may seem to be, the history in reality refers to present needs and present situations wherein those events vibrate. Suppose that I have to choose between accomplishing or evading an act of expiation and turn my thoughts towards understanding what "expiation" is, what forms and transformations it has gone through—this institute or sentiment—before attaining a purely moral significance. Even the scapegoat of the Hebrews and all the many magical rites of primitive peoples form a part of the drama in my mind at such a time, and as I run over their history in my mind I compose the history of the situation in which I myself am.

Similarly the present state of my mind constitutes the material, and consequently the documentation for an historical judgment, the living documentation which I carry within myself. That which is usually called in an historical sense, documentation, whether written, sculptured or portrayed or imprisoned in gramophone records, or maybe existing in natural objects, skeletons or fossils, these things are not in fact documentation unless they stimulate and hold fast in me the memory of states of mind which are mine. For all other purposes they remain coloured tints, paper, stone, metal or shellac discs and the like, with no psychic efficacy whatever. If I have no feelings (however quiescent) of Christian love, of salvation by faith, of gentlemanly honour, of Jacobin radicalism or of reverence for ancient tradition, I shall vainly scan the pages of the Gospels or the Pauline epistles or the Carolingian epics, or the speeches made in the

National Convention, or the lyrics, dramas and romances in which the nineteenth century recorded its nostalgia for the Middle Ages. Man is a microcosm, not in the natural sense, but in the historical sense, a compendium of universal history. The documents specifically known as such by research workers will loom very small in the total mass of documents if we bear in mind all those other documents upon which we continually rely, such as the language we speak, the customs which are familiar to us, the intuition and reasoning we use almost by instinct, the experiences which we carry as it were in our body. Without these other documents some of our historical recollections would be difficult, nay altogether impossible as is observed in certain diseased conditions from which one emerges with loss of memory and identity, as though wholly new and strange in the world to which one previously belonged. It may be noticed, by the way, that the hint of this truth that history does not come to us from without but lives within us, was one of the motives which led the philosophers of the romantic age (Fichte and others) astray into their theory of a history to be constructed *a priori* from pure and abstract logic and free of all documentation; though they later contradicted themselves (Hegel and some others) when, making an outward show of a synthesis, they sought a collaboration between the supposed *a priori* on the one side and the supposed *a posteriori* (i.e. the document) on the other.

If practical requirements and the state of mind which expresses them are the necessary material (but only raw material) for the writing of history, then neither historical knowledge nor any other knowledge is to be found in the supposed reproduction or copy of that state of mind, for the simple reason that this would be a completely useless duplication, and, as such, extraneous to any activity of the spirit, which has not among its activities that of producing the futile. When writers of history set out to present life as it was lived in an immediate sense, the vanity of their aims (their aims and not the facts which are of course different) is thus apparent. The writing of history on the contrary should get beyond life as it is lived, in order to present it in the shape of knowledge. At the best, and by a muddled process, these writers who think they are working as historians, tend to convert their throbbing material into poetical works. Now even if this particular work undergoes an imaginative and poetical process with greater or less speed (and when it prolongs and widens this process, gives birth to poetry in its true and proper sense), yet the writing of history is not imagination but thought. As such, it not only gives the image a touch of the universal, the way poetry does, but it also binds the image intellectually to the universal, distinguishing and unifying at the same time in the judgment that is then passed.

Now though in abstract analysis a judgment is divided into the two elements of the subject and predicate, intuition and conceptual category, concretely the two elements are one, and in that indivisible truth alone lies the truth of history. So it is a fallacious, or at least a merely imaginative and logically inexact critical process, to certify that an historical work is successful on one or the other of these sides alone, or in a subsequent combination of the two, or that it is unsuccessful on one or the other side alone, or through maladjustment of the two sides: to pass judgment on the basis of whether the image was vivid or pale, the criterion precise or vague: as though an image could ever be historically vivid while falsely interpreted, or an interpretation strong and fair-minded while the image was wan and dead. A vagueness and confusion in the one carries with it a vagueness and confusion in the other.

Some historical works win praise for the efficient and truthful way in which the facts are told, while their lack of important criteria carefully weighed and firmly maintained is regretted, as is also the confusion of mental categories with general images or classifications which have been introduced to qualify or explain facts when they themselves are really groups of facts needing such qualification or explanation. But if these factual accounts were as truthful as they were supposed to be, they would have easily corrected and replaced these improper criteria, and have dispelled the false categories. Whenever a book is said to have both presented the facts in an excellent way, and to have used fallacious concepts, it will be found upon examination that in it two different histories coexist or follow and impinge upon each other, and related to them two different philosophies, one outworn and conventional, the other fresh and spontaneous, one ill-expressed and ill-judged, the other well expressed and well judged. On the other hand, when the criterion is clear and firm yet abstract and one-sided, its far-fetched explanations will be matched by not less far-fetched illustrations, recalling puppets at the end of a string or jack-in-the-box. History written on the so-called theory of historical materialism gives an example of this. The men who appear in it are anti-human to the same degree as the theory which offends against the fullness and dignity of the spirit.

But in those works of history in which the standards of interpretation are fitted to the facts to be interpreted a single life pulsates. The images are clear and persuasive as the concepts are lucid and convincing. The facts and the theory demonstrate each other.

Criticism of history consists in recognizing whether an historical narrative is full or empty, that is, whether or no it has at its heart a motive which links it up with the seriousness of life as it is lived, and in discerning how far in it the intellectual element is united with the intuitive; that is to say, how far there is an exercise of the historical judgment and how far this is shirked.

CHAPTER III

The Unity of an Historical Work

THE unity of an historical work lies in the problem formulated by an historical judgment and in the solution of the problem through the act of formulation. This is therefore a unity of a thoroughly logical kind. The problem may be, and often is, connected with many other particular problems; but since these all refer to and are unified in that single problem which has been set, the logical unity persists.

Because of the literary form which the writing of history takes, there enters, of course, a new and non-logical element correlated with that practical requirement which is the prime mover of historical thought, and is by the virtue of that thought transfigured and fixed into a tendency of an ideal of action. This element will consequently be reflected in the words themselves or in what is commonly called the style. But since this affective element follows upon the logical element, it must, in order to preserve the unity of tone (which is, strictly speaking, the literary unity), be subordinate (as particular problems are subordinated to the general problem in the logical unity) to it. Thus all agree in considering it bad literary taste to indite a history in harangues, exhortations, satires or other oratorial forms instead of maintaining the form of the critic and expounder which, while rising superior to passion and rhetoric, is still pregnant with them, and even when silencing them carries their echo. Thus those great historical works which are also great literary works express the authors' minds and hearts in harmonious and not in discordant terms, in a fusion and not in confusion, welding the steady thought which cannot ever be distracted from the pursuit of truth with the warmth of the feelings.

In contrast with historical works which observe logical unity there are many books which also go by the name of history whose unity lies not in a problem but in a thing, or more precisely in an image. Such are the histories of nations, of a people, a country, a city, a lake, a sea or a single person or group of persons; not, of course, when these images are merely means used as the title of the book and a perfectly innocent means of advertising the contents, but when they are in reality the subject-matter of the book. By reason of these subjects, such books, when coherently written, are not history books: but they may be chronicles, gathered together round an image, or even, when the spirit of poetry illuminates the material, they may be poetry, in this way going back (which may be considered a *felix culpa*) from history to the epic, whence it is said that history originated. When, as in most cases, they are not coherent, they will be a medley or an alternation of diverse themes of historical thoughts with fancies, as (to give an example among many, but an example distinguished of its kind) is Michelet's *History of France*, with its fantastic idolization of France as a physical, intellectual and moral person, with her own private genius and mission in the world, whose present and past may be interrogated for the revelation of her future. It cannot certainly be denied that with this fanciful theme there are interwoven original and acute historical judgments arising out of moral and political problems, which Michelet treated with a profound and noble zeal confirmed by the whole tenour of his life.

The harm begins when such essays seek to become coherent in spite of their continued incoherence, because then they offend logic. In the previous case logic was from time to time left behind in lyrical excursions, but logic was not dragged along or compelled to dance or sing. It is then that those sterile spasms occur, in an attempt to give a logical unity to that which can never enjoy it; and in the wake of authors who may not be solely or strictly historical but are at all events poetical, follow the rhetoricians and the sophists, writers who devise and theorize on the concept of France, of Germany, of Spain, of England, and of Russia, Switzerland and Belgium, which being particular and transient are therefore clearly not definable concepts, but historical material to be discerned and interpreted according to the eternal conceptual categories. It is useless to dwell on this, because even recently in Italy we have been afflicted with a controversy that has neither meaning nor end on the "unity of the History of Italy" in this material sense. And yet if this is bad it is not the worst, because the worst in these matters occurs when substance is given to things, and when they are given a reality and a value which strictly belong to the activities of the spirit, to its political and moral, scientific and artistic works. It is of these last and not of things which are an abstraction, and therefore have no life of their own, that there is a history to be investigated and inquired into. If they are rendered corporeal, and thereby the spirit made matter and its wings clipped, then they necessarily take on an ambiguous shape and lend themselves as receptacles of all the morbid and the monstrous which lies like a coiled serpent in the slimy recesses of the human soul: lascivious and possessive instincts, violence and ferocity and cruelty, and then a weariness of life, despair and the desire for dissolution; all that man represses beneath him when he rises to spiritual activity being now released and permitted to expand and morbidly admired and cherished. According as we examine one group of events or a single individual event, these morbid and monstrous things are turned out nowadays as "nationalist" or "racial" histories or alternatively as "biographies" which because their natures cannot be hidden even from their authors are described as "romanticized," that is, they themselves acknowledge that they are not historical. Nationalist histories are not so-called national histories, which (when they do not serve, as we said above as mere titles for serious and truthful histories) are mere collections of notes about a people, chronicles of its life, or are books of edification and exhortation, or sometimes poetry. The others, however, are really obscure and stupid exaltations of that which our own Carlo Troya, speaking of the ancient Lombards in Italy, used to call "The Lombardic" (or it might be "Germanic" or "Aryan" or "Semitic") "whiff": something which tickles certain nostrils and has no other merit than this, but appears grandiose and incomparable, an object of delirious passion and mystic cult, half-way between the bestial and the divine. How much literature of this kind is produced particularly and almost solely nowadays in Germany, everyone knows.

Sound biography, too, falls always under one of the four types of work which we have distinguished and defined above: it consists of memoirs of the life of an individual, that is chronicles; or texts of reflections or sermons of praise or censure, in a word rhetoric; or of poetry; or finally of history in which the individual is portrayed and judged in that which is, and in that which is not, his activity, in that which he does, and that which surpasses him: these latter biographies do not differ from any other history even in the dominant style of the literary form. But romanticized biographies do not seek to take their place among any one of these four kinds of work; nor are they like the good old historical novels of former times, in which an historical judgment used to be translated into tales of imaginary events which were to mirror and describe them. Instead of that their task is to portray "the essence" of a given individuality: not the poetry and the thought of Dante, but the "Dantehood"; not the religious and political action of Luther, but the "Lutherhood"; not Napoleon in the history of the world, but the world rendered miserable and corrupt in him, the "Napoleonhood," and so on; which things would be of no importance were they not given some consistency by that bad taste for morbid psychological complexities, idolized and worshipped in themselves, outside their relation to the productive process in which alone they are intelligible, and therefore outside their own centre of truth. There are such impurities in the stream which feeds even the most ingenious of these biographies and gives them some sort of originality of character, but for the rest they are just insipidities.

CHAPTER IV

The Historical Meaning of Necessity

WHEN judgment is brought to bear upon an event, the event is weighed up as it is, and not as it might be, if it were not as it is. In the old logical terminology, judgment proceeds according to the principle of identity and contradiction, and thinks out the events as logically necessary. In this and in no other sense can historical necessity be understood. Suspicions and even rebellion are raised against it in the belief that it seeks to deny human liberty, whereas it does not deny anything except logical inconclusiveness. In support of our argument it is to be observed that historical necessity is affirmed and repeatedly reaffirmed, by way of veto against the introduction into history of supposition. By this is not meant a ban on the word "if" as a grammatical particle which is legitimate, nor on "if" used to deduce some general warning or prediction of a general or abstract character, from an historical event, as when it is said that, *if* in July 1914, the statesmen of Germany or of other countries had controlled their nerves, war would not have broken out, which kind of supposition sometimes serves to bring home the gravity of certain decisive actions and to excite a sense of responsibility. What is rejected is the historical and logical "if," which is really anti-historical and illogical. This kind of "if" arbitrarily divides the single historical current into necessary and accidental events (it divides it just because if all the events were considered accidental, the historical unity would remain intact, for it comes to the same whether all are accidental or all necessary). One event in a story is given out as necessary, and another as accidental, and in virtue of the "if" the second is isolated to leave one free to settle how the first would have developed in conformity with its character if the other had not disturbed it. This is a little game we habitually play in our own minds, in moments of idleness, imagining how our lives would have proceeded had we not encountered some person we have encountered, or had we not committed some error we have committed. We coolly consider ourselves as the constant and necessary factor and do not face up to the business of revising our personality, with all its accompaniment of experiences, regrets and imaginations, precisely because we did encounter a given person or commit a given error. If we did face up to the reality, then the little game would be immediately interrupted and would cease. The popular saying that wisdom after the event is as common as ditchwater has for its target that fallacious belief in the little game. But since this game in history is quite out of place, when it does make its appearance there it quickly tires us and we quickly desist from it. It needed a philosopher, and one pretty remote from reality at that, to write a whole book (*Uchronie*, by Renouvier) on "*Le développement de la civilisation Européanne tel qu'il n'a pas été, tel qu'il aurait pu être*," in the conviction that the political victory of the Christian religion in the West was a contingent event, which might not have happened if a minor variation, fraught with such vast consequences, had been introduced at the close of the reign of Marcus Aurelius, altering the fortunes of Commodus Pertinax and Albinus!

Historical necessity within the logical meaning which we have determined, which is thought aware of the gravity of its task and not to be diverted from its course, must be carefully distinguished from erroneous interpretations of the same phrase. One is that history is necessary because preceding events determine those which follow in a chain of cause and effect. The following simple and fundamental truth can never be sufficiently insisted on; many minds lost in the shadows of naturalism and positivism find it hard to grasp: that "cause" (though it may seem superfluous we must here too insist that we mean the concept and not the word "cause" which belongs to ordinary conversation) the concept of cause must and should remain outside history because it was born in the realm of natural science and its place is there.

No one has yet succeeded in practice in relating a fragment of history by matching certain causes with their effects; though some have succeeded in adding to a narrative constructed by a different method (the spontaneous method proper to history), an improper causal terminology by way of "scientific" embellishment. Or they may as a sentimental consequence of the deterministic concept, have set out to relate history in the pessimistic and sceptical vein common to man when history, instead of seeming to have been enacted by him and to be preceding by his own initiative, falls upon him like a heap of stones which roll down from a high mountain to the bottom and pin him down there.

The other false notion of necessity is speciously presented as follows: there is a logic in history; there must be, for if there is logic in man there is also logic in history, and if the human mind thinks history it obviously thinks it logically. But the word "logic" in the above sentence means something very different from the "logicalness" of a design or programme in accordance with which history begins, develops and ends, and which it is the duty of the historian to unravel, so that he may find behind the apparent events a hidden mould giving a true and ultimate interpretation. Philosophers have frequently reasoned on this basis, deducing their design from the concept of an idea or of the Spirit or even of Matter; although Idea, Spirit, Matter were only different disguises for a transcendental God, who could think and impose his thought upon men and have it carried out. This is the naked and bare form to which the design must be reduced, and in that form contemplated: a form which Thomas Campanella in his sonnets with no satirical or burlesque intention describes as a "book of words of the comedy of jesting" or as "a scenario" such as the theatrical managers of his day used to outline the action of the comedy, and to give each actor his part during the rehearsal. Abbé Galiani found another simile for it in the vantage of card-cheats, who play with loaded or marked dice. However that may be, no one has yet written such a history; and the embarrassment of its partisans and adherents has already been shown in their method, by their very request, both contradictory and superfluous, that historical research should reveal a design beyond the range of evidence and documents, and therefore unattainable by those means. They made histories and christened them as such by using evidence sometimes as a symbol, sometimes as a superfluous ornament to decorate the display they made of their beliefs, tendencies, hopes and fears, in politics, religion or philosophy. On a par with causality, the transcendental God is a stranger to human history, which would not exist if that God did exist; for History is its own mystic Dionysus, its own suffering Christ, redeemer of sins.

Another false concept disappears from history together with this doubly false idea of necessity, from which it is derived; the concept of historical foresight. If the last act only in the divine programme was generally revealed (for example the coming of the Anti-Christ, the end of the world and the universal judgment day), yet the rest of the programme from the present backwards, was also—on that view—written in the book of Providence, and one small section might through grace be revealed to some pious man. Similarly with the causal concept the Chain of Cause and Effect proceeded and by calculation future links in it could be foreseen. In practice, however, it became confessedly impossible to predict anything, in the first case because of the inscrutability of the divine will, in the second because of the enormous complexity of the various causes concerned: so that the faithful naturalist behaved like the naturalistic author of the story of the Rougon Macquart family; Zola in that novel worked out their family tree from the trunk to the branches and twiglets, submitting them to the cause of heredity, but then over the niche prepared for a child about to be born had nothing to ask but the ironic question left unanswered: "Quel sera-t-il?" Nevertheless the habit of prediction persists in the minds of many readers of history, and as a dignified duty on the part of many writers, and it gets satisfied in a succession of images which lack substance, except within the personal fears and tremors and hopes of those who collect these images.

The Historical Meaning of Necessity

The defenders of human liberty should boldly oppose both causal and transcendental necessity, so closely bound to each other in many harmful ways, but there is no need to go into battle, as they often do, against the logical necessity of historiography, which is indeed the very premiss of that liberty.

CHAPTER V

Historical Knowledge Considered as Complete Knowledge

IT is not enough to say that history is historical judgment, it is necessary to add that every judgment is an historical judgment or, quite simply, history. If judgment is a relation between a subject and a predicate, then the subject or the event, whatever it is that is being judged, is always an historical fact, a becoming, a process under way, for there are no immobile facts nor can such things be envisaged in the world of reality. Historical judgment is embodied even in the merest perception of the judging mind (if it did not judge there would not even be perception but merely blind and dumb sensation): for example the perception that the object in front of me is a stone, and that it will not fly away of its own accord like a bird at the sound of my approach makes it expedient that I should dislodge it with my stick or with my foot. The stone is really a process under way, struggling against the forces of disintegration and yielding only bit by bit, and my judgment refers to one aspect of its history.

But we may not rest here either, nor renounce further consequences: historical judgment is not a variety of knowledge, but it is knowledge itself; it is the form which completely fills and exhausts the field of knowing, leaving no room for anything else.

In point of fact all concrete knowledge whatever is on a par with historical judgment, bound to life, that is to action, of which it marks a pause or an anticipation having for its function to break down (as we have said) any obstacles barring a clear view of the situation from which it must specifically and with determination emerge. Knowledge for the sake of knowledge, so far from having anything aristocratic or sublime about it (as some believe), would be an idiotic pastime for idiots, or for the idiotic moments which we all have in us; in reality there is no such thing, it is intrinsically impossible and the stimulus ceases with the failure of the material itself and of the end of knowledge. Those intellectuals who see salvation in the withdrawal of the artist or the thinker from the world around him, in his deliberate non-participation in vulgar practical contrasts—vulgar in so far as they are practical—do without knowing it compass the death of the intellect. In a paradisal state without work or struggle in which there were no obstacles to overcome, there could be no thought, because every motive for thought would have disappeared; neither any real contemplation, because active and poetic contemplation contains in itself a world of practical struggles and of affections.

Nor are great efforts necessary to demonstrate that natural science with its complement and instrument, mathematics, is also based upon the practical requirements of life, and is out to satisfy them; Francis Bacon, its great initiator in modern times, taught this convincingly enough. The question is, however, at what stage in its development does natural science exercise this useful office and become true and proper knowledge? Certainly not when it makes abstractions, builds classes, stabilizes relations between classes and calls them laws, gives mathematical formulae to these laws, and so on. All these are accessory labours useful for storing up knowledge already acquired or to be acquired, but they are not the act of knowing. A man may possess in books or by rote all medical knowledge, all the kinds and sub-kinds of illnesses with their characteristics, and so possess "bien Galien, mais nullement le malade," as Montaigne would have said, and he will know as little (or nothing) as another man knows of history, who owns one of these many universal history books which have been compiled, and has furnished his memory out of it. The latter will not truly know anything until under the stimulus of events that knowledge loses its deadly rigidity, and his thought studies some political or other situation: and the same is true of the medical expert up to the moment when he has a patient to deal with and must by intuition and understanding diagnose the sickness of that patient, and that patient alone, in that way and under those conditions, and he grapples not with the formula of the illness but with its concrete and individual reality. The natural sciences have their beginning in individual cases, which the mind does not yet or not fully understand, and they execute a lengthy and complicated series of efforts in order finally to bring the mind, which has been thus prepared, up against these same cases, setting it in direct communication with them so that it may form a proper judgment.

Natural science, therefore, is not seriously at variance or in opposition to the theory that all genuine knowledge is historical knowledge; like history it deals with the actual and humble world. It is not so with philosophy, or, if you like, with the traditional idea of a philosophy which has its eyes fixed on heaven, and expects supreme truth from that quarter. This division of heaven and earth, this dualist conception of a reality which transcends reality, of metaphysics over physics, this contemplation of the concept without or outside judgment, for ever imprints the same character, whatever denomination the transcendental reality may bear: God or Matter, Idea or Will; it makes no difference, while beneath or against each of them there is presumed to subsist some inferior or merely phenomenal reality.

But historical thought has played a nasty trick on this respectable transcendental philosophy, as upon its twin, transcendental religion, of which the former is the reasoned or theological form; the trick of turning it into history, by interpreting all its concepts, doctrines, disputes, and even its disconsolate sceptical renunciations, as historical facts and affirmations, which arose out of certain requirements, that were thus partly satisfied and partly unsatisfied. In this way historical thought did due justice to the age-long domination of transcendental philosophy (a domination which was also a service to human society) and marked its end with a decent obituary. It can be said that once transcendental philosophy was subjected to historical criticism, philosophy itself ceased to enjoy an autonomous existence because its claim to autonomy was founded upon its metaphysical character. That which has taken its place is no longer philosophy, but history, or, which amounts to the same thing, philosophy in so far as it is history and history in so far as it is philosophy: "History-Philosophy," of which the principle is the identity of the universal and the individual, of the intellect and the intuition, and which regards as arbitrary and illegitimate any separation of those two elements, they being in reality a single element. It is a curious fate that history should for a long time have been considered and treated as the most humble form of knowledge, while philosophy was considered as the highest, and that now it not only is superior to philosophy but annihilates it. This so-called history which had been relegated to a back seat was not in truth history, but chronicles and research, superficially considered and based on hearsay: the other kind of history which has now asserted itself is historical thought, sole and integral form of knowledge. When the old metaphysical philosophy tried to lend a helping hand to history in order to draw it out of the depths, it was not to history but to the chronicle that the hand was given, and as this could not be raised to the rank of history by reason of its metaphysical character, a "philosophy of history" was superimposed upon it, a process of excogitation and guess-work, to which we have referred above, a sort of divine programme which history carries out like someone who tries to make a more or less careful copy of a model. The "philosophy of history" was a consequence of mental impotence, or, as Vico said of myths, of bankruptcy of the mind.

Among the various didactic forms of literature there certainly are works which may be classed as philosophy and not as history because they seem to treat of abstract concepts, purged of any intuitive elements. But if these treatises are not mere circlings in the void, if they contain full and concrete judgments, then the intuitive element is always there, even if it is latent to the vulgar eye, which is only on the look out for it when it appears as an incrustation of chronicle writing or of erudition. The intuitive element is there, in the very fact that the philosophical arguments formulated in it answer the need for light on particular historical conditions: the knowledge of these conditions explains the argument just as these conditions are themselves explained by the arguments. I was going to say, to take a living example, that even the methodological elucidations which I am giving here are not really intelligible unless with an explicit mental reference (normally made by me simply in an implicit way) to the political, moral and intellectual conditions of our times, which they help to describe and judge.

Then there are the specialists, or professors of philosophy whose occupation appears to be to act as a counter-weight to the philologists, that is to the erudites who profess to be historians. The latter collect bare facts and produce them as history, while the former marshal the abstract ideas, thus complementing one form of ignorance with another form of ignorance, by which means there is not much progress to be made. These are the natural preservers of transcendental philosophy who even when in words they assert the unity of philosophy and history, deny it in fact, or at the most they descend from time to time out of their super-world in order to pronounce some musty generalization or some historical falsehood. As the historic sense grows more refined and an historical way of thinking becomes more general, the historical-philologists will be sent back to the realm of pure and simple and useful philology and the professional philosophers can be thanked and gracefully dismissed, because philosophy will have found in the true writings of history a scope for its labours which they lacked. They philosophized coldly, shunned the excitement of passions and interests, wrote "without reference to any occasion." But every serious history, and every serious philosophy, ought to be a history and a philosophy "for the occasion," as Goethe said of genuine poetry, though the occasion of poetry is in the passions, that of history in the conduct of life and in morality.

CHAPTER VI

The Categories of History and the Forms of the Spirit

THE arguments against transcendence when they were carried too far led to the negation of any distinction between the different categories of judgment, which were themselves considered transcendental; and it was argued that categories and judgment were one and the same thing, and that categories changed and enriched themselves with every new judgment: so many judgments, so many categories, in fact, past numbering. In truth, the distinction of the categories is far from equivalent to the conferring upon them of an alleged transcendental character. The distinction occurs within the judgment, by virtue of the judgment, is indeed the putting into effect of the judgment, since it is not possible to judge without distinguishing the quality *a* from the quality *b*, that is, according to categories. What kind of a judgment would that be that does not qualify action *a* as a truthful action, action *b* as a beautiful action, action *c* as an action of political accurateness, action *d* as a moral sacrifice, and so on; which would restrict itself to an intuitive consideration of *a b c d*, etc., a process which perhaps satisfies the imagination but certainly not thought?

Categories do not change even in the sense of growing richer, because they themselves are the artisans of the change: if the principle of the change itself suffered a change, movement would be arrested. It is not the eternal categories which change and are enriched, but our concepts of the categories which come to possess every new mental experience; and so for example our concept of the logical act is infinitely sharper and more guarded than was that of Socrates and Aristotle. Nor would these concepts, whether richer or poorer, be concepts of the logical act at all, unless the category of logic was constant and present in all of them. The faulty exaggeration of the views contested in this section is made manifest by the incapacity of those who profess them to give due place to that tendency towards truth which must be sought and brought to light even in the error of transcendence, given that at the heart of every error a similar tendency is to be found. This tendency in the case of transcendental philosophy lay precisely in the need to hold fixed amid the flux of reality the criterion of spiritual values (good, true, just, etc.), each one of them with its proper character, and each one opposed to its opposite (bad, false, unjust, etc.). The spiritual values had to be protected against the confusion and the negation to which men in the bondage of the senses unwittingly subjected them. The error lay, on the other hand, in the attempt to detach them from the stream of reality, and to place them in safety in a superior realm, transcending reality; thus providing a problem in logic with a solution in fancy. As against sensuality and hedonism, the theory represented the general need for a healthy intellectual and spiritual life, and in spite of the error it has worked beneficiently at various stages in the history of ideas since the time when Socrates formulated his definitions against the Sophists, and Plato transferred his ideas to a higher sphere. In recent times in the nineteenth century in Germany the pedagogue Herbart made use of a similar remedy to meet the perversions of the dialectics and of historicism, found even in Hegel himself, but far more in the Hegelian school who appeared by the abuse of fluid and soft concepts to be disintegrating science, and by their compromises and easy transferences from one party to another to be damaging morality. It was a reaction, and by dint of the reaction there came an exaggerated divorce of concepts from mere representations. The contours of the concepts were so strongly marked that each one was self enclosed, and all of them seemed without relation to each other, and not deducible from each other. Nevertheless such a distinction even at the heavy cost of a transcendental enthronement of values over facts is preferable to the hotchpotch of representations and concepts, or pure and empirical concepts which some people wish today to reinstate in philosophical thought, without perhaps any clear idea what it is they ask, and unaware of the great consequent loss of all that which has been laboriously acquired through the work of critical philosophy, which is always both revolutionary and comparative.

If such programmes still, despite all, have a semblance of reasonableness, this is due to the fact that propositions of abstract monist philosophy are not subjected to any test in the field of particular events, or particular and precise judgments of concrete thought such as are needed for composing the history of various human activities; if such a test were made they would quickly and miserably go to shreds. To those men of generalizing talents it seems easier and more prudent to introduce surreptitiously the distinctions denied in their methodology into the little that are obliged to give in the way of historical treatises, and to make use of them while declaring that they are empirical (rather like that Mussalman sent by the Grand Sultan who came to the court of King Charles of Bourbon at Naples in the eighteenth century of whom I happened to read in a diplomatic correspondence that he drank a lot of champagne at the Neapolitan banquet, but called it, and made others call it, "lemonade"). I must ask forgiveness for this reminiscence, certainly unsuited to philosophical gravity, but not unsuited to the case in point.

CHAPTER VII

The Distinction Between Action and Thought

ONCE the strange notion had got about that all the lights must be dimmed if the integrity and purity of immanence was to be assured as though its only worthy abode was the *regnum tenebrarum*, it was not to be wondered at that the primitive and fundamental distinction which humanity's common sense has always drawn and observed and which philosophy has respected, between knowledge and will, between thought and action, should have been attacked and, in the realm of the imagination, routed.

The argument used in this operation is traceable to that single source of every sophism, the giving of two interpretations to one term, demonstrating one of the interpretations, and then taking for granted that the other and different one has thereby also been demonstrated. The conclusions of all modern philosophy, from Descartes and Vico and Kant and Hegel down to contemporary thinkers, are that thought is as active as action, that it is neither a copy nor a recipient for a reality, nor therefore does it provide knowledge of reality by serving such purposes; on the contrary, its work consists in setting and solving problems, and not merely in passively receiving fragments of reality; finally, thought does not stand outside life but is its vital function. But the sophism to which we have referred above maintains that thought cannot be distinguished from will, that each of these is equally active, and it pretends that the distinction of which we have just spoken is identical with that which is erroneously made between the activity of will and the passivity of thought. This argument is a sophistry and therefore invalid; and the ancient distinction between knowledge and will, thought and action, stands intact.

Yes, it is unaltered in its substance although greatly modified

and deepened by reference to the way in which it was previously conceived as a juxtaposition or parallelism or a divergence
of two faculties of the soul, and also as touching the precedence
of knowledge over will and practical action, or inversely of the
latter over the former. For if knowledge is necessary to practice,
practice as we have demonstrated above is necessary to knowledge,
and cannot arise without it. There is a circle of the spirit which,
when recognized, does away with all need of a primary absolute
and a secondary dependent, by continually making the first the
second and the second the first. This circle is the true unity and
identity of the spirit with itself, of a spirit which feeds on itself
and grows beyond itself. Every other unity is static and dead,
mechanical and not organic, mathematical and not speculative or
dialectic.

If the attempt to cancel the distinction between these two elements of the spirit were not puerile and ingenious, its effect would
be to destroy the life of the spirit in a simultaneous destruction
of thought and action. Once identified with the will, and with
the aims of the will, thought would cease to be the creator of
life, and by becoming tendencious it would decay into untruth.
Will and action being no longer illumined by truth, would then
be debased to passionate and pathological fury and spasm.
Nothing of this kind happens because it would be against the
nature of things that it should, and against the life of the spirit,
which continually resists the seductions whereby practical interests try to interrupt or mislead the logic of truth, and labours
ceaselessly to transform blind passion into enlightened will and
action: so that there is no need to fear that the order of things
will collapse or that the world will come to an end.

If there is no fear of this yet there is no reason to believe that
a theory which tries to demolish the "unity-distinction" of
knowledge and action is and remains mere argumentation and
academic chatter. On the contrary, it is stimulated and greatly
favoured by well known unhealthy inclinations of our time, or,
if you like, of all time but especially prominent just now. We
only need to glance round or listen to the voices which come

from intellectual, artistic, religious and political circles—in fact, from every corner of society—to be faced with manifestations of indifference and irreverence to criticism and to truth, of activism overbearing and impetuous but devoid of ideals. In some cases it may only be a question of a mediocre literature which leads nowhere, but in many others it is clear that those who uphold with such ease the static identity of knowledge and action, have mortified in themselves all the vigilant strength necessary for intimate discernment and clarity and pass over to sophism and rhetoric to suit their private convenience in public life, only to swell the ranks of those "traitor intellectuals" against whom a French writer, a few years ago, felt the need of making specific accusations. A bad theory and a bad conscience have the same origin, they rely upon each other and in the end they collapse on top of each other.

CHAPTER VIII

Historiography as Liberation from History

IT is even stranger to find that instead of accurately and profoundly analysing social diseases of the kind we have just mentioned or of other or similar kinds, or isolating them in a sort of ideal hospital, so that they can only harm those who are already incurably contaminated, people commonly turn to blaming historical thought or historicism for the generating of these diseases, by promoting fatalism, by dissolving absolute values, by sanctifying the past, by accepting the brutality of facts as facts, by applauding violence, by recommending quietness, and, in fact, by removing the impetus and confidence from creative forces, by blunting the sense of duty, and by disposing men to inactivity and lazy compromise. All these things have already their appellations in the moral world, they are called spiritual tiredness, disintegration of the will, lack of moral sense, superstition about the past, timorous conservatism, cowardice which knowingly tries to excuse itself by equivocation and by appealing to historical necessity when the need is for resolution and action according to moral necessity—and so on. And, although one or other of these things may sometimes be found as in other men, so also in some historians (as in Hegel, whose error or defection as regards social conservatism and political subjection was thrown into relief by the greatness of his stature as a philosopher and an historian) historical thought as such has nothing to do with them and may be quite contrary to these tendencies.

We are products of the past and we live immersed in the past, which encompasses us. How can we move towards the new life, how create new activities without getting out of the past and without placing ourselves above it? And how can we place ourselves above the past if we are in it and it is in us? There is no

other way out except through thought, which does not break off
relations with the past but rises ideally above it and converts it
into knowledge. The past must be faced or, not to speak in metaphors, it must be reduced to a mental problem which can find
its solution in a proposition of truth, the ideal premise for our
new activity and our new life. This is how we daily behave,
when, instead of being prostrated by the vexations which beset
us, and of bewailing and being shamed by errors we have committed, we examine what has happened, analyse its origin, follow
its history, and, with an informed conscience and under an intimate inspiration, we outline what ought and should be undertaken and willingly and brightly get ready to undertake it.
Humanity always behaves in the same way when faced with its
great and varied past. The writing of histories—as Goethe once
noted—is one way of getting rid of the weight of the past.
Historical thought transforms it into its own material and transfigures it into its object, and the writing of history liberates us
from history.

Only a strange obscurity of ideas could impede us from recognizing the purifying function which both the writing of history
and likewise poetry fulfil: the latter liberates us from servitude
to the passions, the former from slavery to events and to the past.
Only by an even greater intellectual blunder can that man be
called a gaoler who unlocks the door of the cell to which he
would otherwise be condemned. Men with a gift for history (not
to be confused with monks intent on compiling registers and
chronicles, nor with the erudite who collect stories and documents,
and by their industry produce reliable news, nor with scholarly
compilers of historical manuals) have always been labourers in
various fields, inclined to meditate upon situations which have
arisen in order to overcome them and to assist others to overcome
them by means of new activity: politicians who have written
political history, philosophers who have written histories of
philosophy, artistic spirits who have tried by means of their
intelligence to distil from the history of art an enjoyment of
works of art, men of great civil and moral fervour who have

severely scrutinized the history of human civilizations. During periods in which reforms and upheavals are being prepared, attention is paid to the past, to that from which a break is to be made, and to that with which a link is to be forged. During uneventful slow and heavy periods, fables and romances are preferred to histories or history itself is reduced to a fable or romance. Similarly, men who shut themselves up within the four walls of their private affections and private economic life, cease to be interested in what has happened and in what is happening in the great world, and they recognize no other history but that of their limited anxieties.

CHAPTER IX

History Considered as a Premise of the Struggle Between Value and Non-value

THE adversaries of the writing of history, the "antihistorians" (as they boast themselves), do not only accuse the historians of preserving the burden of the past by means of memories of the past while they themselves idealize the beatific condition of peoples who have no history or who have forgotten it: they also still more sharply accuse them of complacently setting down facts where they ought to be passing judgments. How can such an accusation possibly be made when historical affirmation is the quintessence of judgment, indeed is the only true judgment; and if historical works are a web of narrative appraisals which cannot even be narrated unless there be discernment of the qualities to be judged, and appreciation of an event in its political or possibly religious, or again, intellectual sense? "To expound things as they really happened" is, according to the famous formula of Ranke, the sole purpose of history, but either it was left out or he meant it to be read between the lines that facts cannot be expounded as they happened, unless they be qualified and therefore judged, on the basis of the logical principle of the indissolubility of the predicate of existence and the qualificative predicate.[1]

The judgment, therefore, which history is alleged to shirk, is not really a judgment, the only judgment which is an act of thought, but an approval or a condemnation concerned with certain ultimate ideals which are to be defended, maintained or put across, and before which as before a tribunal men of the past are to be called up to answer for their actions and to be

[1] On this matter see the demonstration in the *Logica*, Part I, section II, Chapter V, and compare subsequent remarks there about Ranke.

46

awarded a prize or else the sentence which they deserve for their villainy, their vices, their stupidity, their ineptitude, or whatever else is wrong with them. The accusation forgets the great difference, that our tribunals (whether juridical or moral) are present-day tribunals designed for living, active and dangerous men, while these other men have already appeared before the tribunal of their day, and cannot be condemned or absolved twice. They cannot be held responsible before any tribunal whatsoever, just because they are men of the past who belong to the peace of the past and as such can only be the subjects of history, and can suffer no other judgment than that which penetrates and understands the spirit of their work. They are understood yet not automatically as the motto has it (*tout comprendre c'est tout pardonner*), pardoned, because they now stand beyond severity or indulgence, beyond censure or praise. Those who on the plea of narrating history bustle about as judges, condemning here and giving absolution there, because they think that this is the office of history, taking history's metaphorical tribunal in a material sense, are generally recognized as devoid of historical sense; even if they bear the name of Alexander Manzoni. Such judgments somehow grate upon us: we feel their vanity and incongruity, almost as though we saw a boxer attacking a statue which, of course, would not move or change its expression. Caesar is guilty because he deprived Rome of liberty: even if this verdict is pronounced loudly and with proud and austere demeanour, it has no effect on Caesar and has no sense for us, who stand on an historical plane whence the individual appears not as one choosing his path of conduct, but as one who has carried out his task in so far as the course of events and his private mission dictated: thus we must understand him. We are indifferent to this cloaked figure of a Caesar, dragged in front of the tribunals of the pseudo-historians, stamped with a sentence and condemned to penalties of which we do not see how or where they are to be endured. But our mental interest is awakened when the historians who judge but do not condemn come to us to explain how it happened that Rome passed out of an uneasy Republican oligarchy

47

and civil wars through the loss of sense of political liberty into an empire which lasted for many centuries and fulfilled its own work, transmitting it into succeeding centuries so that it still lives in our thoughts and in most of our institutions.

Only historical judgment liberates the spirit from the pressure of the past; it is pure and extraneous to conflicting parties, and guarding itself against their fury, their lures, and their insidiousness, it maintains its neutrality, and seeks only to furnish the necessary light; it alone makes possible the fixing of a practical purpose, opens the way to the development of action and, in the process of action, to the struggle of good against bad, useful against harmful, beautiful against ugly, true against false, in a word, value against non-value. There, in their own camp, is the proper place for the acceptances and rejections, praises and blames, which are commonly called judgments but are not judgments. For which reason philosophy has found it necessary to define them as judgments not of a thing as it is when its value coincides with its existence, but of what something is worth when it is opposed to other things which have no value. These are called by philosophy "value-judgments," but in this case they should have been called "affective expressions." Among such expressions there are some concerning the substance of history which are formed by raising personalities and actions of the past to symbols of that which is loved and hated in the present. Symbols of liberty and tyranny, of generous goodness and of holiness and diabolic perfidiousness, of strength and weakness, of high intelligence and stupidity: hence the love for Socrates and Jesus, the admiration for Alexander and for Napoleon, the disgust for Judas, the hatred against an Alexander VI and a Philip II, and the useless arguments for and against Caesar and Pompey. These are very natural sentiments, and even if in historical works they are restrained and tempered by dutiful observation of logical unity and of good literary taste, in one way or another they still colour our words, and we need not feel guilty at having thereby revealed something in our minds that it was impossible to hide, something which we need not be ashamed of unless with shame for ignominous affections or for unworthy aversions. But these are not historical judgments, still less are they the object of historiography, as the judge-like historians imagined that they were, the imitators of Tacitus, the Augustinians who lacked the soul of Augustine. They are necessary to the field of action: they are inevitable in the spoken and written vocabulary of those who are perpetually preparing for action: but they are incompatible with the logic of historiography, which does not admit either men or achievements as being totally good or totally bad, and repudiates the question which of these they are, as insoluble, because basically erroneous. Where, anyway, is the man to be found who provided he is not utterly devoid of modesty, can hear a favourable judgment passed upon himself or upon his actions without feeling immediately remorseful, without feeling guilty lest the holiness of truth should be thereby offended, and who does not react with a negation or a protest?

If we tried to find a reason for this useless and yet pleasurable transference of "value judgments" from the things of the present where they fulfil their office, to representations of the past, where they not only embarrass but distract research, we should have to consider how vanity and weakness take refuge from the dangers of practical struggles and the efforts which they require by striking with shattering words at those who cannot retaliate because they lie enclosed in the vaults of the past. The literary hack of former times who flattered the great ones of the day was ever ready and tireless when it came to sermonizing and condemning historical characters. He would assume the dignity of a togaed historian, appear austere and incorruptible except in cases where the reputation of these characters was cherished by contemporary powerful ones, and then he would quickly change his tune. This old type of historian, so suited to servile times, must be prevented from re-appearing in our times, which we may wish to consider un-servile; but the desire shown for a restoration of the court-of-justice type of history certainly favours his re-appearance.

CHAPTER X

History as Action

IN this way we pass from historiography, which liberates us from life as it is lived, to living history, to new history; here the categories which were lately forming judgments no longer operate as predicates of the subject, but as a potentiality for action. We mean action in its widest sense, useful and moral, artistic, or poetic, or any other kind, including philosophical or historiographical activity, which is at one and the same time history of the past, and affirmation in the present of a new philosophy which in its turn will become the object of philosophy.

All these are the spheres of human activity corresponding with the fundamental and original forms of historiography: history of civilization, ethics, religion, art—call it as you will; or of thought or philosophy. The distinction between these four forms of history has often been treated with some diffidence, yet it has not been one single philosopher who has come upon them or distinguished them however intently he may have reasoned around them and promoted their definition. It is rather the conscience of the human race, which has never arrived at any distinctions outside these and has not recognized any others without having first subordinated and resolved them in these: nor has ever set up other standards than those called the beautiful, the true, the useful, and the good, together with their obvious synonyms. If anyone cares to propose or to discover other standards let him say so and have a try. However, besides the authority of the human race, to which we have referred (which may be challenged but not challenged lightly), there is the other difficulty that one or more categories cannot simply be added on, as though the order of these four were merely an enumeration which could be continued in the desultory manner of enumerations, but they would have to be conjoined and "re-thought" in a new systematic and dialectic connection, in a new and necessary order of ideal succession (ideal but not abstract, ideal and not temporal or chronological as foolish misunderstandings and criticisms would sometimes have it). The reply that categories are as innumerable and as infinite as particular actions and judgments is (as we have seen) not a philosophical reply, but a renunciation of judgment which is thought, and a renunciation of activity which is always qualitatively specified activity.

Nevertheless, whatever the spheres of these activities may be, the principle of liberty animates them all: it is synonymous with activity or spirituality, that is, of the creations of life. A forced creation, a mechanical creation, creation to order, or in chains, has never yet been tried and is impossible to imagine: these are, in fact, a series of words devoid of sense.

A further synonym of this same activity is its own peculiar enrichment, the perpetual growth of its own spirituality, so that nothing is lost of that which is created and in no way is perpetual progress arrested. It is quite possible to talk of decadence and we do so, but only with reference to certain kinds of activities and ideals which are precious to us (too often insipid grumblers take leave hence to mutter their laments, *pejor avis, nequior* and *vitiosior*); but in an absolute sense and in history there is no such thing as a decadence which is not at the same time the formation and the preparation of a new life, therefore progress. Yet the concept of progress has very often, and never so frequently as now, been called in question and made the object of satire and contempt; but in reality it was not the spiritual law of progress which was thus satirized and held in contempt and considered as doubtful; it stood far too high and secure to be affected by such jibes or moved by such scepticism. It was only certain illusions and beliefs dear to people who like comfort and ease and illusions and prefer to be rocked in peaceful waters rather than to navigate in storms and tempests. Such folk pictured an age of so-called progress into which one entered and in which one continued without interruption or setbacks right on to infinity; in other words, they located progress within a particular epoch and a particular society and a particular set of habits, thereby materializing and arresting eternal spiritual progress. This last has nothing to do with a vulgar search for pleasure and happiness; so little so that it would be safe to define progress, if we so wish, as an ever higher and more complex form of human suffering. And others who are disposed to save themselves and the human race from pain and from the damage of conflicts and would like to smooth the corners and resolve the conflicts in compromises and mutual concessions and establish perpetual peace in this or that part of life, or in universal life, in reality resemble those of whom we have been speaking, though at first sight so different from them. For a Leo X or a Luther are more real historical figures today than Erasmus, whose amiable ideal of abstention from theological disputes, of reasonableness, and of simple goodness, seemed to come into its own a couple of centuries after, once the great religious struggles which started in his day were ended or exhausted and it became possible to breathe again in an atmosphere of humanity and tolerance. But all the while new and harsher struggles were being prepared on the ground which they had worked over.

Certain transcendental and religious conceptions consider the world and history as being in a state of evil and suffering, which can only be healed and compensated in another world. They deny progress because they deny life itself. This is coherent, but the combination formed in certain philosophies subjected to the influence of theological and religious myth, of the concept of progress with that of a final or paradisal condition of life understood as activity and of life understood as stasis or non-life, is not equally coherent. The most important of these combinations, the culmination of many others of the same kind, is to be found in a philosophy which, more than any other, has sought to interpret reality in an historical light, life as a synthesis of opposites, and being as becoming: Hegelian philosophy. This philosophy, by compromising and contradicting its own principles, sets out to describe the various stages in the progress of thought until it ends its course in the philosophy of the Idea beyond which there is no further progress. In a similar way it describes the path of religion and art until it lands them into the same philosophy, where both find their quietus. Thus, too, it pursues universal history until this receives its crown in the Germanic world considered as a world of full liberty with the Prussian State held up as the consummate and final political form. By far the most widespread theory of this sort in our day is, however, that of historical materialism, due to Marx, an after-runner of Hegel, which describes human history in its progress from the ancient servile economy to mediaeval serfhood and to the modern capitalism or wage economy, throughout its whole course weighted down with the yoke of necessity: then discerns that history, advancing by a new and definite dialectical progress through the negation of negation into a final stage of perfect communist economy, thus institutes the reign of liberty on earth. The Hegelian conception has not only been philosophically confuted by the critics, but completely shattered and broken by enacted history which in the course of a century has travelled beyond all the Hegelian termini; thought has set problems which Hegel never suspected, poetry has not ceased to produce beautiful works, and the Prussian type of State has not withstood the Free States which it despised, indeed, it no longer exists but is even regretfully sighed for in Prussia itself. The Marxist concept, with its coarse economic Absolute (occupying the place once held by the Idea) purporting to manipulate events, has been confuted openly or implicitly by every subsequent economic historical and philosophical criticism. It is belied also by the effectual operation of the Communist system (if that system spreads or becomes general the refutation will be greater still), for nowhere is there a shadow of the promised reign of liberty, while new struggles persist alongside of the old ones, every form of life is violently compressed whether intellectual or aesthetic or political, and beneath all this the other struggles heave and come to life. So great is the disillusion about these things that illusion has rapidly had to be called to the rescue, an illusion which says that that which has not yet been achieved will be achieved in the future. Thus it has been wittily observed that verbs in Russia are always conjugated in the future tense.

In contrast with this idea of a progress towards the terminus of some blessed state of self-satisfaction there has very properly been conceived the idea of the infinite progress of the infinite spirit, which perpetually generates new contrasts, and perpetually rises superior to them. But let it not be lightly supposed that this progress signifies a continual condemnation of men's work to futility and a wild race toward the unattainable: everything is transitory and everything is preserved in progress, and if humanity is untiring and has always something further to undertake, if every one of its achievements gives rise to doubt and dissatisfaction and the demand for new achievement, yet now and again there is achievement; something is possessed and enjoyed and the apparently precipitous race is in reality a succession of reposes, of satisfactions in the midst of dissatisfactions, of fleeting moments spent in the joy of contemplation. The most evident proof of this is to be found in art and poetry which are never self satisfied, but always create new forms whose created works stand there like dieties upon a serene Olympus, abounding in strength and beauty. All through life the historian is moved by an impulse towards the future, he looks on the past with the eye of the artist and he sees the works of man in this light, both perfect and imperfect, both transient and intransient.

CHAPTER XI

Moral Activity

IF we wish to answer the question what is the end of moral activity, and if in so doing we put aside the theological doctrine of obedience to commandments imposed by a personal god, and if we convert into its opposite the doctrine of the pessimists who, denying life, seek the end in mortification of the will to life until they annihilate it in asceticism or universal suicide, then the answer is that the object of morals is to promote life. "Long live the creator of life!" as Goethe sang.

Life is promoted by all forms of spiritual activity with their works of truth, beauty and practical utility. By means of them reality is contemplated and understood, the earth is covered with cultivated fields and industries, families arise, states are founded, battles fought, blood spilt, there is victory and there is progress. And what does morality add to these beautiful, true and variously useful works? It may be said it adds good works; good works, however, in a concrete form can only be works of beauty, truth and usefulness. Morality itself in order to become effective turns into passion and will and utility; it thinks with the philosopher, it shapes things with the artist, it labours with the farmer and the workmen, it generates sons, it operates politics and wars, and it uses the arm and the sword. It may be objected that in all these works morality has an intention which is strictly a moral and not an utilitarian intention. But this would be a vicious circle in which morality was defined as intention and intention as morality, and things are left undetermined: the Jesuits made good use of this indetermination for the most immoral "direction of the intentions"; the utilitarians at the other extreme used the apparent lack of distinction between moral and useful works to deny the originality of morality and to identify it with utility.

Morality is nothing less than the struggle against evil; and if evil did not exist morality would have no reason to exist either. Evil is the continual undermining of the unity of life and therefore of spiritual liberty; just as Good is the continual re-establishment and assurance of unity and therefore of liberty. Good and evil, with their contrasts, the triumph of good and the renewal of undermining threats and danger, are not the efforts of intervention by a power extraneous to life, even though they appear as such in mythological representations of a tempting seductive devil; they are to be found in life itself—in fact, they are life itself, which, to speak in a naturalistic language, demands specification of functions within the single organism—or, to repeat the same thing in philosophical language, life is perpetually distinctive in its forms and within the circle of those forms finds its unity.

Since, however, every organism has a tendency to disorganization, and since health is the balancing of that which is out of balance, dominating and absorbing in itself the malady, so every special form by virtue of its speciality, which is its individuality, and by the impetus of its own activity which cannot be active without that impetus, forces itself towards the whole, still pushing itself forward, even when it is time for it to recede—because it has reached its proper end. This effort and this exuberance would destroy the unity of the spirit and the spirit itself would perish were not each form reined in and confined just like those following upon it and similarly striving. An inquiry as to why this process occurs, or the thought that it might proceed in a different way without struggle, without painful passages, without dangers, without leanings towards and entanglements with evil, is nonsensical, as it would be nonsensical to ask why "yes" should be correlated by "no" or to ponder on a pure "yes" severed from "no," or on a life which has no germ of death in it and had not at every moment to surpass death. The kind of action which sets the boundaries of each separate activity, which makes them specifically fulfil their own proper office, which thus prevents the disintegration of spiritual unity and guarantees liberty, is

the kind which faces and combats evil in all its forms and gradations; it is called moral activity.

In this way we are able to understand how moral activity in
one sense lacks any fields of action, and in another sense operates
in all the fields, sustaining and correcting the work of the artist
and the philosopher no less than that of the farmer, the in-
dustrialist, the head of the family, the politician and the soldier,
respecting their autonomy and giving validity to all their auto-
nomies precisely by keeping each one of them within its own
boundaries. It is hence obvious how inept and presumptuous are
those moralists who attempt to moralize poetry, science and
economics, thereby distorting their nature: for morality only can
properly moralize them by giving them a free place wherein to
express their own nature. For the same reason those things which
a man of taste calls ugly a man of truth calls false, and a practical
man finds ill-suited to his purposes, therefore useless and harmful.
Their respective consciences apprehend the reflection of evil and
feel moral remorse for it: hence the source of theoretical errors
and artistic ugliness has, by deep philosophy, been traced to
moral evil.

Another point is now cleared up: the question why among the
forms of historiography one rather than any other branch of
history should always have been sought and considered as history
par excellence; while histories of art, philosophy, and of various
economic activities have been considered as special histories. There
has been considered as true and proper history, as history of
histories, only the history of the State, viewed as an ethical state
and a discipline of life, or maybe the history of Civilization which
gives a less imperfect outline of moral life by abstracting it from
the political limitations of the concept of the State. The so-called
philosophies of history in some respects themselves aimed at
being ethical history of the sort which by the writer of these
pages has been not unsuccessfully termed (and is now currently
called) "Ethico-political history." The appellation itself makes
it clear that morality is not politics or utility just as it is not any
other form of human activity, but includes them all and converts

them all in so far as they fulfil their special end, into an ethical action.

Thus, this ethico-political history does not stand over and above other histories nor does it resolve them in itself, but it penetrates into them and obtains from them its own concrete quality: as they too do from each other. The solidarity of human life does not allow the thinker or the artist to sunder the links with other forms of activity from which he draws his vital inspirations, by placing himself above or beyond them or by substituting himself for them. Nor may the saint move in a sphere superior to worldly cares, unless sanctity is to become idle and prove a mere mask for egoism. The disdain sometimes felt by the artist for people intent on practical work or which such men feel for him and which is felt by the sensitive for those who fight fiercely in the political arena, is a limitation and not a superiority. To say the least ill of it, it is a *morbus opificum*, a disease which those of each calling can with difficulty avoid. The solidarity of life brings a consequent solidarity in historiography; each special history from time to time distinguishes itself from the others only to be again merged in them.

CHAPTER XII

History as the History of Liberty

HEGEL's famous statement that history is the history of liberty
was repeated without being altogether understood and then
spread throughout Europe by Cousin, Michelet and other French
writers. But Hegel and his disciples used it with the significance
which we have criticized above, of a history of the first birth of
liberty, of its growth, of its maturity and of its stable permanence
in the definite era in which it is incapable of further development.
(The formula was: Orient, Classic World, Germanic World
= one free, some free, all free.) The statement is adduced in this
place with a different intention and content, not in order to assign
to history the task of creating a liberty which did not exist in
the past but will exist in the future, but to maintain that liberty
is the eternal creator of history and itself the subject of every
history. As such it is on the one hand the explanatory principle
of the course of history, and on the other the moral ideal of
humanity.

Jubilant announcements, resigned admissions or desperate
lamentations that liberty has now deserted the world are frequently
heard nowadays; the ideal of liberty is said to have set on the
horizon of history, in a sunset without promise of sunrise. Those
who talk or write or print this deserve the pardon pronounced
by Jesus, for they know not what they say. If they knew or
reflected they would be aware that to assert that liberty is dead is
the same as saying that life is dead, that its mainspring is broken.
And as for the ideal, they would be greatly embarrassed if invited
to state the ideal which has taken, or ever could take, the place
of the ideal of liberty. Then they would find that there is no
other like it, none which makes the heart of man, in his human
quality, so beat, none other which responds better to the very

law of life which is history; and that this calls for an ideal in which liberty is accepted and respected and so placed as to produce ever greater achievements.

Certainly when we meet the legions of those who think or speak differently with these self-evident propositions, we are conscious that they may well be of the kind to raise laughter or derision about philosophers who seem to have tumbled on the earth from another world ignorant of what reality is, blind and deaf to its voice, to its cries, and to its hard features. Even if we omit to consider contemporary events and conditions in many countries, owing to which a liberal order which seemed to be the great and lasting achievement of the nineteenth century has crumbled, while in other countries the desire for this collapse is spreading, all history still gives evidence of an unquiet, uncertain and disordered liberty with brief intervals of unrest, rare and lightning moments of a happiness perceived rather than possessed, mere pauses in the tumult of oppressions, barbarian invasions, plunderings, secular and ecclesiastical tyrannies, wars between peoples, persecutions, exiles and gallows. With this prospect in view the statement that history is the history of liberty sounds like irony or, if it is seriously maintained, like stupidity.

But philosophy is not there just to be overwhelmed by the kind of reality which is apprehended by unbalanced and confused imaginings. Thus philosophy, when it inquires and interprets, knowing well that the man who enslaves another wakes in him awareness of himself and enlivens him to seek for liberty, observes with serenity how periods of increased or reduced liberty follow upon each other and how a liberal order, the more it is established and undisputed, the more surely decays into habit, and thereby its vigilant self-awareness and readiness for defence is weakened, which opens the way for a "recourse," as Vico termed it, to all of those things which seemed to have vanished from the world, and which themselves, in their turn, open a new "course." Philosophy considers, for example, the democracies and the republics like those of Greece in the fourth century, or of Rome in the first, in which liberty was still preserved in the institutional forms but no longer in the soul or the customs of the people, and then lost even those forms, much as a man who has not known how to help himself but has in vain for a time received ministrations of good advice is finally abandoned to the hard school of life. Or philosophy looks at Italy, exhausted and defeated, entombed by barbarians in all her pompous Imperial array, rising again, as the poet said, "in her Tyrrhenian and Adriatic republics" like an agile sailor. Or philosophy contemplates the absolute monarchs who beat down the liberty of the barons and the clergy once they had become privileged, and superimposed on all men their own form of government, exercised by their own bureaucracy, and sustained by their own army, thus preparing a far greater and more useful participation of the people in political liberty. A Napoleon destroys a merely apparent and nominal liberty, he removes its appearance and its name, levels down the peoples under his rule and leaves those same people with a thirst for liberty and a new awareness of what it really was and a keenness to set up, as they did shortly afterwards in all Europe, institutions of liberty. Even in the darkest and crassest times liberty trembles in the lines of poets and affirms itself in the pages of thinkers and burns, solitary and magnificent, in some men who cannot be assimilated by the world around them, as Vittorio Alfieri discovered in the eighteenth century grand-ducal Siena, where he found a friend, "freest of spirits," born "in hard prison," and abiding there "like a sleeping lion," for whom he wrote the dialogue in his *Virtue Unrecognized*. Yes, to the eye of philosophy, whether the age is propitious or unfavourable, liberty appears as abiding purely and invincibly and consciously only in a few spirits; but these alone are those which count historically, just as great philosophers, great poets, great men and every kind of great work have a real message only to the few, even though crowds may acclaim and deify them, ever ready to abandon them in order noisily to acclaim other idols and to exercise, under whatever slogan or flag, a natural disposition for courtisanship and servility. And on account of this, and through experience and meditation, the philosopher thinks and tells himself that if in liberal times one enjoys the welcome illusion of belonging to a great company, while in illiberal times one has the opposite and unwelcome illusion of being alone or almost alone, the first optimistic view was surely illusory, but maybe the second pessimistic view was illusory also. He sees this and he sees so many other things and he draws the conclusion that if history is not an idyll, neither is it a "tragedy of horrors" but a drama in which all the actions, all the actors, and all the members of the chorus are, in the Aristotelian sense, "middling," guilty-non-guilty, a mixture of good and bad, yet ruled always by a governing thought which is good and to which evil ends by acting as a stimulus and that this achievement is the work of liberty which always strives to re-establish and always does re-establish the social and political conditions of a more intense liberty. If anyone needs persuading that liberty cannot exist differently from the way it has lived and always will live in history, a perilous and fighting life, let him for a moment consider a world of liberty without obstacles, without menaces and without oppressions of any kind; immediately he will look away from this picture with horror as being something worse than death, an infinite boredom.

Having said this, what is then the anguish that men feel for liberty that has been lost, the invocations, the lost hopes, the words of love and anger which come from the hearts of men in certain moments and in certain ages of history? We have already said it in examining a similar case: these are not philosophical nor historical truths, nor are they errors or dreams; they are movements of moral conscience; they are history in the making.

Part II

Historicism and its History

CHAPTER I

Its Own Character and the Beginning of Its Own Age

"HISTORICISM" (the science of history), scientifically speaking, is the affirmation that life and reality are history and history alone. The necessary corollary to this affirmation is the negation of the theory which holds that reality can be divided into super-history and history, into a world of ideas and values and a lower world which reflects them, or has reflected them until now in a fleeting and imperfect way, and upon which they must once and for all be imposed, so that an imperfect history, or mere history, may give way to a rational and perfect reality. Since this second conception is known as "abstract rationalism" or "illuminism," the science of history opposes and argues with "illuminism" and rises above it.

The quick of this argument lies in the demonstration that the ideas or the values which have been taken as the measure and the models of history are not universal ideas and values but are themselves particular and historical facts clumsily elevated to the rank of universals. Thus the idea of beauty which once served academic criticism as a measure by which to judge works of art was a grouping of abstract lines from the particular beauty of Virgil or Raphael. The ideas of natural rights were nothing more than the juridical institutions, whether actuated, planned or distantly invoked or foretold in the seventeenth and eighteenth centuries. The moral ideas were but the rules and qualities which had been formed by ancient civilization or by early or later Christian Civilization. Similar final and fixed systems of philosophy or whatever passes as such into common usage and belief, refer, so far as they are alive and true, to certain determined, contemporary and historically definite problems, and therefore have no value with reference to all the other problems of the past and the future. On the other hand true ideas and true universal values possess the power of comprehending all the most varied works of the artistic, moral, juridical and intellectual life in their rawest and most elementary form as well as in their most complex and refined aspects, no matter how opposite they may seem to be or how strongly they may react on each other: so that they are not models or empirical generalizations but pure concepts or categories, the creators and the perpetual judges of every history.

For Meinecke[1], on the other hand, historicism consists in admitting that which is irrational in human life, in holding fast to that which is individual, without, however, overlooking the typical and the general which is linked to it; in projecting this vision of the individual upon a background of religious faith and religious mystery. Meinecke is the faithful and fervent disciple of Ranke, whose intellectual position we have already noted, and for whom he has such an admiration as to call him the very genius of historicism in its most perfect manifestations. But true historicism successfully criticizes and overcomes the abstract rationalism of illuminism only in *so far as it is more profoundly rationalistic than this*. Then, having corrected the abstractions, it accepts and fulfils the chosen task of illuminism, but substituting absolute categories and the *a priori* synthesis of experience for the pseudo-absolute ideas of illuminism, so that it is not constrained to come to terms with the so-called "irrational" as it appears to illuminism which despises it and wants to tear it out and throw it away. Historicism on the contrary accepts the "irrational" and understands it within the framework of its own activity and thereby reveals it in a rational light and defines its peculiar forms

[1] Friedrich Meinecke, *die Entstehung des Historismus*. I. *Vorstufen und Aufklärungshistorie*. II. *Die deutsche Bewegung* (Munich and Berlin, Oldenburg, 1936). Since my way of considering this problem differs for reasons which I give in my text, in several points, and complements that which Meinecke holds, I should like to say at once, that much may be learned by the student of this difficult argument from his book which in doctrine, acumen and thoroughness is altogether worthy of the author.

hitherto misunderstood or only partially understood. Nor can historicism suffer beside itself or above itself either religious revelation, or the adoration of mystery, or agnosticism, each of which is incompatible with its being, for it recognizes no other revelation than that which thought gives to thought by means of criticism, no other mystery than the perpetual conquest of mystery by thought, no agnosticism save by way of convalescence from ignorance, and no reality beyond history which is absolute immanence. That very knowledge of the individual upon which Meinecke so strongly insists and which he justly emphasizes as the characteristic of historicism, is certainly not the double in history of the personal and non-historical vision of the poet in which sentiment is transformed into the pure image. No, it is an affirmation of the reality of the quality of this or that individual form; therein the individual is rationalized and by means of the universal alone it becomes historically individuated. The old illuministic rationalism which separated the individual from the universal and made of them two sterile and empirical abstractions, could never arrive at the individual, but a concrete rationalism or historicism, easily distinguishable from the other by its power of individuation, and more especially because this lies in the logic of universals, could arrive at it there. Once the unjust separation has been revoked, the universal pulsates within reality with the pulsation of the individual, and the more we look into this the more we see, at its heart, the universal.

The definition we have given at the same time indicates the "origin" or "birth" of the historicism which cannot arise through any force of external events but only inside the logical mind, just as the genesis of a poem lies in the poetical imagination. In point of fact, this birth is the resolution of the difficulties which there are in the illuministic solution of the problem of history; and whenever this kind of solution is presented in its substance, however varied and diverse the circumstances may be, there will spring to life through opposition and correction, through antithesis and synthesis, Historicism. It seems, therefore, that there is nothing more to say on this point, unless indeed one were to consider thoughts not as thoughts but as images, sentiments or variously associated impressions, and to try to explain the genesis by giving a psychological description to these facts or groups of facts. What it is worth while further to explore is not the logical origin, but the beginnings of the growth and the spread of it in that age which takes its name from it.

Meinecke's book aims, in practice, at such a history. He presupposes or at least only incidentally touches upon the problem of the logical origin of historicism (as we have seen, in a rather unsatisfactory way); but he inquires fully and carefully into and expounds the historical formation of historicism as a consciously held doctrine which he estimates, rightly as a profound "revolution:" for he shares Lord Acton's well known judgment that the difference between historiography at the time of Gibbon and in modern times was the same as the difference between astronomy before and after Copernicus. It is obvious that, strictly speaking, the urge of historicism has never been absent from historiography, because it has never been absent from the human spirit, and the histories written before that time could not be considered as histories and rethought and readapted and developed as such, had they not already had it in them, either implicit or episodically expressed. Nevertheless the intensity, the continuity and the primacy which it won in the age which takes its name from it, are so great and strong as to allow of describing this wholly new event as the acquisition for the first time of a consciousness of one of the potentialities of the human mind. There is evidence of this in contemporary conversation in the almost proverbial saying about "history which is history," about its "objectivity" and necessity, about the "uselessness of finding fault with what has happened," as though contesting its irrevocable occurrence; similarly we notice the disuse or, if at all, the use only with a smile, of that other saying, once universally accepted and repeated, that history was "life's teacher," whose job it was to reach and exemplify precepts of political acumen and moral rules in other words having an end outside itself: whereas history aims "solely at narrating and explaining what has happened," exactly how it happened, in other words is an end in itself.

But when did this spiritual revolution begin, that is, when did the age of historicism begin? If historicism is criticism of illuminism, its age succeeded the glorious age of illuminism and can only have started at that point when illuminism reached its climax in violent impact upon its own boundaries, and revealed to all men its inherent contradictions and its contrasts with reality. This happened, as we know, as a consequence of the French Revolution and marked off the nineteenth century not as an era in time, but in its conceptions as opposed to the eighteenth. But this intuitive and habitual judgment which corresponds with a critically ascertained and reasoned truth, is fairly frequently contested nowadays, owing to a forgetfulness or half-understanding of the true process by which various characteristics are assigned to various epochs. An historical epoch does not coincide with the character which is assigned to it, in the same way as two words are synonyms of the same concept. It cannot do so, for since the life of an epoch is human life, it enjoys all the forms and all the manifestations of human life and in this respect it calls for no more than the anti-historical observations of the author of Ecclesiastes *Quod est ipsum quod futurum* or *nihil sub sole novum*. The character assigned to an historical epoch depends upon the intellectual interest of the historian, who gives importance to whatever is connected with his particular researches and with his own problems; he has recourse to special classificatory concepts called categorical or functional, and with their help he can distinguish the quality of certain actions from the quality of certain other actions as well as the major and minor importance of these in the various epochs under consideration. When weak and argumentative minds seeks to dispute the characterization of an epoch which has so carefully been constructed they easily fall into Sophistry by adducing events familiar to every epoch, displaying different qualities from those whose predominance has been ascertained; in so doing they think they have illustrated the truth of another interpretative criterion, whose justification, however, would really have to be achieved on the basis of a pure philosophy and philosophical logic. This explains how, even in Italy today we get prodigious theories about the Middle Ages, which are alleged to have been far more civilized than the Renaissance, or of the Renaissance which is supposed to have been Christian, or of Humanism, given out for something like a revival of the age of the Early Fathers, or of the Counter-Reformation, as the principle of a new life, or of Nicolo Machiavelli, who is turned into a moralist, or of Giuseppe Mazzini, who becomes a reactionary, and other such foolishness, sometimes the product of ecclesiastical and political cunning. To go no further than the history of historicism itself, in this doctrinal field Cassirer[1] slipped into the same error, by sheer thoughtlessness, for he wanted to shield the age of Illuminism from the accusation of being anti-historical, that is, from an accusation native to it and to its very name. In doing this, even if he had not mistaken (as he did) erudition and the criticism of evidence for historicism—which in themselves they are not,[2] and even if he had limited himself to finding the rare and really scientifically historical moments in the literature of the eighteenth century, he would not on that account have freed Illuminism from the accusation, but he could only have demonstrated (which is any way obvious) that in the eighteenth century, alongside of Illuminism there were anti-Illuministic motives left over from the past, together with others which foreshadowed the future, that is, the nineteenth century.

[1] *Die Philosophie der Aufklärung* (Tübingen, Mohr, 1932).

[2] Others have made this mistake, for example, P. Hazard, *La Crise de la Conscience Européene;* 1680–1715 (Paris, 1935). Speaking of the historical Pyrrhonism of that time: "il y avait cependant un moyen de refaire l'histoire: par l'érudition"; and, in describing the great labours of the erudites, pp. 65–66, "mais quand, aussi, la besogne sera-t-elle achevée? Combien faudra-t-il d'années de décades et de siècles pour que l'on sâche sans supposer, pour que l'on affirme sans mentir? C'est une tâche presque désespérante que de retrouver quelques pierres seulemènt de la mosaique immense," etc. In order to understand the true state of the spirit of that century, it is essential to realize that unscientific history and erudition not only lived peaceably side by side, but that the erudites when they tried to think did so according to the ideas of the time, that is unhistorically.

Meinecke is more wary and does not fall into these confusions. When he expounds the truth of historicism confining his researches to the eighteenth century and finds there for his purpose a few scattered elements and hints in philosophers like Shaftesbury, Leibniz, Vico and other lesser men and French historians and politicians (Voltaire, Montesquieu, Turgot, Condorcet, Rousseau, etc.) and English Illuministic historians (Hume, Gibbon, Robertson) and English pre-Romantics (Blackwell, Wood, Percy, Fergusson, Burke, etc.), and then Lessing and Winckelmann, and those he considers in this respect the then greatest names, Möser, Herder and Goethe. In the latter, writing at the close of the old century and at the beginning of the new one, Meinecke finds historicism attaining its highest expression. He entirely leaves out any reference to that true revolution which in morals was expressed in a new reverence towards the past, in literature by the new atmosphere in history, and in doctrine by the scientific greatness of such a philosophy as Hegel's who did not simply reject the Illuminism from which he too originated, but resolved it in a more profound and more complex rationalism. Meinecke only gives the prologue of this historical movement; in fact, although it does not seem so to him, he is entirely concerned with the "precursors." Even this concept of precursors and precurrents deserves to be more clearly outlined since it can be understood in an altogether generic and improper way as well as in a specific and proper way. In the first sense, since all history precedes, and flows into the history that follows it, one might say (and it would be tautological) that all thinkers and indeed all men who precede a given event are precursors, and repeat the process from century to century; but in the second sense, precursors are solely those who, in conditions as yet immature or unfavourable anticipate that thought and action which will become widely effective and characterize an epoch. That is in our case, those who criticized the abstractness of Illuministic rationalism and resolved it into the rationalism of historical development. In the strict and critical sense historicism in the nineteenth century has only one true and proper precursor:

Giambattista Vico, whom Meinecke (contrary to Cassirer, who
arbitrarily cuts him out because he was inefficacious in his day)[1]
examines in an accurate and careful paragraph,[2] although he
does not give him the unique position as a solitary pioneer which
Vico deserves. It is almost painful to me to have to insist on this
point, but I recently read in an English philosophical review that
the judgments passed by Italian critics and historians upon Vico
(and endorsed in a recent English monograph) have their origin
in a competition of national sentiments:[3] this suspicion, if not
offensive, is always annoying, not to say unjust for anyone who
knows in his heart the clear difference between science and nation,
science and politics, who analyses concepts and does not open
the door to sentiments which, however elevated they may seem
to be politically, whenever introduced into a different sphere immediately become worse than reprehensible, laughable. It is a
fact proved both in documents and in unquestionable criticism,
that there is in Vico's thought the most conspicuous and conscious opposition to Illuminism, which he studied, within the
limits of his opportunities and functions, in its original aspects of
natural law and Cartesianism and of polemical history based upon
the ideals of modern European society and upon "clear and distinct ideas." In Vico we find all those aspects which intellectual
rationalism abhorred as irrational; he promoted them first to the
rank of special rational forms, which were distinct and opposed,

[1] Op. cit., pp. 379–80.

[2] Op. cit., I, 56–74. I should like to note that Vico attributes the character
of "probability" to historical knowledge (p. 59) only in the first version of his
gnoscology in *De antiquissima*, but in the second and more mature version in
his *Scienza Nuova* he asserts its absolute truth because in it there is fully realized
the interchangeableness of truth and fact, and this is his chief gnoscological discovery. Nor do I believe that Vico's law of historical "courses" and "recourses"
can be called a remainder of natural law (p. 70); so much is this so that Meinecke
himself (p. 91) emphasizes the "marked difference" between it and natural law,
in so far as this is not a law of existence and persistence, but of development. If
anything, Vico modelled it upon the great laws of physical science which were
then being elaborated to explain the revolutions of the world of nature.

[3] T. E. Jessop on Adam's book, in *Philosophy*, London, vol. XI (1936), n. 42,
pp. 216–18.

or bound, to others which had hitherto been alone considered as such (imagination in contrast with philosophy, force with right). Together with this we find a justification of primitive and barbaric forms of society as positive and necessary grades of history and therefore of civilization since civilization in the accepted sense arises out of them. It is a saying entirely in the spirit of historicism that we find on his lips when he says (I recall only a line here and there) that the *generis humani respublica* is not the republic built up from its foundation by Plato, but the whole of history as it develops *per varia utilitatum et necessitatum humanorum rudimenta sive adeo per ipsarum sponte rerum oblatas occasiones.* Vico had very little if any cultural efficacy in his day; and little enough during the greater part of the eighteenth century, but this only confirms the profundity of his criticism and his theory which, in its earliest pronouncements, foresaw and confuted the alterior and extreme consequences of natural law and the Cartesian school, destined as they were to merge in Encyclopedism and Jacobinism. All these he countered with new concepts which were due to arise later all over the place and to gain in strength and authority in the coming century. But this foreshadowing inventiveness in Vico proves also his anachronism and his inefficacy in the social life of his time because (as De Sanctis[1] subtly remarked) the younger generation were, at that time, intent upon shattering the remains of that past which Vico interpreted, understood and historically justified, and which they too, in their turn, would have interpreted and understood and justified, but only after having completely shattered it: that is,

---

[1] *Storia della Letteratura Italiana*, ediz. Croce, II, p. 301: "Speech like this would have seemed strange to those men so full of hatred and faith. And one of them might have retorted to Vico: Keep out of the way and stay in your clouds, don't come down among men for you do not understand them. You have studied the past in books: that is your erudition. But the past is a real thing for us, we feel its pricks at every step. The fire burns us and you try to prove that because it exists it has a reason for existence. You must let us put it out first and then you can talk about its nature. Once we have dropped the burden of this past, this torment of ours and of our fathers, perhaps then we shall become fair and able to relish your criticism."

after the French Revolution, when the Illuminists, the Encyclo-
pedists and the Jacobins had turned into romantics and liberals.

None of the other foreshadowings of Historicism cited by
Meinecke can bear comparison with this of Vico; either they are
weak and fugitive hints merging eclectically into different and
opposite ideas; or they express a certain conservatism or sometimes a political and social sentimentality which is not genuine
historicism; or again they consist of shrewd maxims of realistic
government or reason of state which is not genuine historicism
either. These theories certainly do sometimes touch the fringe of
historicism and come to new life and full truth in it; but when
we come across similar interlacings and relations, we must discern carefully and subtly, remembering that something of the
same kind occurs even with the thoughts and doctrines of authors
who hate reason and are loyal to traditional religious beliefs like
De Maistre[1] and Haller. Neither the one nor the other can be
ranked as cultivators of historicism for the capital reason already
given: that historicism has assimilated and converted Illuminism
into sap and blood (just as Vico absorbed Descartes, and in con-
futing him carried his doctrines further forward), whereas these
authors never accepted it at all, or quickly dismissed it. Thus
while some of the facts they observe and some of their isolated
concepts coincide with those of historicism, the interpretations
and systematizations which they give are as different and alien
from it as the criterions which they use.

Nevertheless, flashes and traits of historicism, some of them
dim and retrograde, others clear and progressive, are carefully
noted by Meinecke in a few of the writers of the eighteenth
century whom he discusses (in Moser, a strong sense of the link
between the higher and lower nature of man, of the organic
development of political institutions, of historical periods determined according to these changes and not according to chronological and extrinsic observations; in Herder an understanding of
primitive, popular Oriental and foreign poetry and such like).

[1] See also for De Maistre on this subject, Omodeo's essay in *Critica*, XXIV–V
(1936–37).

But too often he ranked as historicism mere mental phases which had to be passed through in order to arrive at a conception of life as history, or thoughts which were later corrected and transformed and incorporated in historicism. Why should Leibniz (to give an example), who had a traditional idea of history as merely material for reflection and moral political precepts and who in his historical work behaved like a simple scholar, be considered as a "precursor" of historicism? Certainly not, as Meinecke partly thinks, because he asserted the original value of individuality in his theory of monads, because the monad of Leibniz is exactly contrary to historical individuality, which is an individuality of actions and not at all of soul-substances. Hence it is necessary continually to dismiss and indeed to annihilate the idea of the monad in order to arrive at the historical vision of individuality for ever taking shape and dissolving of life and death and new life which is the course of history. Therefore we shall have to restrict our endorsement of Leibniz's claim within these terms; that, without the dynamics of Leibniz, without his *lex continui*, without his *petites perceptions*, without his *nisi intellectus ipse*, the development which did occur would not have occurred either in pre-Kantian Kantian, or post-Kantian that is particularly Hegelian thought, that which finally took the shape of the philosophy of development and of history. This is very true, seeing how impossible it is to imagine the history of thought in the eighteenth and nineteenth centuries, minus the works of Leibniz; but it is equally impossible to imagine it minus the work of any other thinker not only in that century, but in all the preceding ones even in remote antiquity. The same is to be said of that platonic and neo-platonic conception to which Meinecke gives so great a part in historicism: and which too is only one among all the forms of philosophy, each in some way contributory to modern thought.

This method of considering as historicism whatever led or flowed into the idea of historicism, has resulted in Meinecke devoting the greater part of his treatise and indeed the final and conclusive part, to Goethe; to the man who by common consent has always been considered as only superficially a man of history, intent as he was upon the contemplation of the eternally human, and remembered as having often uttered scornful gibes at history and its vain claims. This commonly held judgment on Goethe may indeed here and there be mitigated and tempered, as Meinecke does by the demonstration that such gibes were often justified and were better intentioned than the words seem to show. And it may be offset too by bringing to light other observations and maxims of Goethe, which are actually important for historical methodology. But however hard we may try, Goethe can never be made to shed his spontaneity, and be transformed into a critic and opponent of Illuminism or into a religious contemplater of history, or judged in this respect as being a superior of Hegel.[1] Yet on the other hand how could the spiritual movements of the second half of the eighteenth century and of the succeeding centuries be understood and expounded in a complete and coherent manner in their advance towards a vision of history and an ideal of life as an untiring effort reaching out even higher, if we overlooked the thought and the feeling of Goethe, great poet and wise man, that thought and feeling which an historical conception of life has accepted and allocated to the place which they deserve in its system? Meinecke is right when he wishes us not to forget how much we as modern men and modern historians owe to Goethe; but he is right in a generic and not in a specific sense, much as if one were to insist on the necessity of remembering Plato, Aristotle, Homer, Shakespeare, Polybius, Machiavelli, who are all alive in us. But if we must explore questions of the greater or the less, the more distant or the nearer efficacy of the one or the other system in itself, then in so doing we cannot escape from a surrender of scientific truth to personal preferences, for it will be for their sake that one element will be isolated out of the sum of elements and predominate over the others. This may be useful at most in order to draw attention to certain unknown or not fully valued elements. I myself personally like to note the efficacious reaction upon the theory of development and of historicism, of the slow formation in the

[1] Op. cit., I, p. 631.

sixteenth to the eighteenth century of the science of poetry or aesthetics on the one hand, and of the science of politics on the other, both of which truly served to recall the mind from the abstract to the concrete and to furnish the means for overcoming the transcendence of values.

CHAPTER II

Historicism Complete and Incomplete

(1) ITS RELATION TO POLITICAL LIFE

THERE is another and not unimportant observation, I think, to be made upon a question which runs right through Meinecke's book and also arises in other such books: In which work does historicism achieve its most perfect and most definite form? To this question Meinecke, as we have said, is led to answer with the name of Goethe, followed immediately by that of Ranke, whom he takes to be a sort of filtered and clarified Goethe in relation to historicism. Of Goethe we have already spoken, and we need not say how unconvincing is the idea that a thought first conceived by the weighty mind of a Vico, then accepted by the sovereign mind of a Hegel, should attain its perfect form in such a minor and philosophically indifferent and inexpert mind as that of Leopold von Ranke.

But we may observe, on the other hand, that the very raising of a question about a perfect and definite form of historicism betrays an anti-historic turn of mind. Historicism is a logical principle; it is, in fact, the very category of logic; it is logicality in its full acceptation, the logicality of the concrete universal, and therefore, as we have already remarked, alive and always more or less at work in the human mind. It was notably alive and at work in the age of historicism. But as it is never altogether absent in any man or in any age, so, too, in no intellect, however hard working, however profound, can it take an ultimate and definite form. It often happens that these very men in their own books and in their own times conjoin it with propositions which ignore it and deny it: this even happens to those who were the creators of the age of historicism. Vico, who allowed no other reality in

78

the republic of men than their history developing in an eternal spiritual rotation from feeling to intellect, from force to morality, yet materialized his ideal circle so that history lost the individuality of its actions with him, actions which are historical because they do not recur. Historiography with him lost its colour and turned to a static sociology, and the concept of progress and of the unity of historical development failed him. Hegel produced the great principle in clear terms that "everything which is real is rational, and everything which is rational is real," but then grew somehow afraid of this phrase which his genuis had dictated, till muddled and bewildered, he began all over again by redistinguishing a rational which is truly rational and necessary, from the real which is bad and accidental.[1] Moreover, he set the categories of his logico-metaphysics in historical epochs, and if he did not conceive of history like Vico as the perpetual repetition of a circle of epochs, he confined it to a definite epoch, enclosing the past in a system and shutting out the future, and, like Vico, he left unresolved a dualism of history and nature.[2] A Ranke would doubtless avoid the risk of falling into these errors of Vico and Hegel; but then he is not master of the truths excogitated by those great men who possessed in themselves the virtue of correcting the grandiose errors into which they had fallen and into which Ranke could not ever fall, incapable as he was of taking Luther's salutary advice to sin heartily if at all. Historicism, like philosophy in general, grows and reaches ever higher by overcoming such errors, the indices of problems that have been badly solved, and must be wrestled with until their exact position is

[1] For these oscillations of the Hegelian formula on the rational and the real see *Saggio Sullo Hegel* (3rd edition, Bari, 1927, pp. 156–58) and *Ultimi Saggi*, pp. 238–39.

[2] This dualism was later shaken by the historical trend of the natural sciences which culminated in the name of Darwin, and which Hegel, from the very beginning, resolutely opposed. But this *de facto* demolition was not enough. Criticism of this dualism had to be conducted philosophically. It demanded the rejection of the old scholastic tri-partition of philosophy, accepted by Hegel (logic-nature-spirit), and a critical revision of Hegelian logic itself. I have set forth this criticism and reconstruction elsewhere; it does not enter in the design of this present book; so that it is sufficient to have drawn attention to it here.

discerned and they meet with a solution. What can one do? Life is in every moment both perfect and imperfect, and so is philosophy and its consort historiography.

Meinecke hails what he calls "the historicist revolution" as the second great revolution due to Germany in modern times; the first being the Reformation. In truth the Reformation in the age which takes its name from it was much more of a great ferment than a spiritual revolution, which in the end is always operated by reason—reason which (as the saying goes) is the very character of man and is the single principle of his progress and his revolutions: neither imagination, nor feeling, nor mysticism, nor blind impulse, nor violence lead or achieve the deep changes in the spirit and mind of man by themselves. In any case, between these two revolutions there supervened the theory of natural law, of natural religion, Illuminism. This last (as has been shown), and not Protestantism, constituted the logical antecedent of historicism. Meinecke knew very well, and notes it in his history, that Illuminism was not German in its origin (its remote origin was mainly Italian and especially Socinian), but above all French and English; and when it became European, Germany too succumbed and took part in it and thereby reformed her Protestantism which could develop the germs of free thought which it contained only by the help of Illuminism. Meinecke himself when he describes the anticipation of historicism ranges through English, French and Italian literature, and he might have wandered further. With these reservations and warnings his judgment on the historicist revolution as an essentially German activity, is to be accepted, but not because Möser, Herder or Goethe (and with Goethe, Leopold von Ranke) achieved it, but because philosophy had then reached a higher zenith in Germany than elsewhere, and had laid down some of the fundamental principles of the edifice of historical philosophy, which was still in construction. The authors of the revolution were Kant and Fichte and Schelling and even more directly and consciously Hegel, together with all their satellites, for example Frederick Schlegel, who reflected the same thoughts.

From another point of view it must be remembered that a truly lively and comprehensive mental revolution is bound up with a moral revolution, with a new orientation and attitude towards the problems of practical life, and that between the two there is a cyclic connexion by which both are strengthened and amplified. The correlative of historicism, the heir to Illuminism, in active and practical life, was a new tendency towards liberty; liberty no longer abstract and atomic, as it had been in the age of Illuminism, but concrete and unified in social and historical life. Now in Germany, owing to the peculiar political condition of the country, which was backward compared to England and France (and in some respects to Italy, which had passed through manifold political experiences and had not altogether forgotten them); the process developed an excessive bent towards theory to the neglect of practice, and there appeared to result a revolution of an exclusively theoretical kind although this could not be and was not entirely so. The Germans themselves, at the beginning and in the course of the French revolution, noticed this severance between thought and action, between this purely ideal revolution and a real revolution. Baggesen, Schaumann and Fichte noted it and Hegel in his history of philosophy have it monumental expression with the words: "the new principle in Germany has erupted as spirit and concept, but in France as effective reality."[1] The same contrast between these two related but separate revolutions was popularized by Heine and is set down by Carducci in those verses in which Kant decapitates God and Robespierre decapitates the king[2] "ignorant of each other, yearning for truth, but of faiths opposed." But as often happens with those contrasts which the intellect divines and a brilliant imagination enjoyably and dramatically elaborates, the terms of the contrast are not expressed with exactitude; for the French revolution was the last phase of the philosophy of Illuminism and historicist idealism confronted this not as a theoretical and philosophical expression

---

[1] *Geschichte der Philosophie*, II, p. 485.

[2] The history of this reconciliation and contraposition was outlined by me in *Conversazioni Critiche*, II, pp. 292–94.

of it, but as a new thought and as a sign of new needs and a new age. Half-way through the eighteenth century Möser, comparing the then histories of France, England and Germany with each other, came to the conclusion that in the first the victory went to the monarchs, in the second to the nobles and free men and in the third to the lackeys of the crown (*Kronbedienten*).[1] Historicist thought was cultivated in Germany in the minds of men who were devoted servants of the king and State, and who took care to set up a clear barrier as best they could between speculation and politics, so that practical conclusions should not be drawn from the first for application in the second.

Hence the inefficacy or the deficient civil and practical efficacy of their historicist philosophy which gradually lost the generous illuministic spirit of humanity by which Herder and other thinkers of the previous century had been moved, and therefore gave no incentive to that small offshoot of the European liberal movement which later did after all flourish in Germany; and even under State influence underwent disturbance and corruption in its own concepts employing them for uses of servility towards the existing powers and the old régimes. Overlooking the Germanic theories grafted by Fichte which can be excused by patriotic anguish and by the impetus of the revolt against the foreign invader, even in Hegel the disturbance is there when he confers upon the Germans a supreme rôle in universal history and in the philosophy of law recognizes an eternally exemplary character in the post-Napoleonic German State.

The Italian Vico, it is true, allowed himself to be oppressed by the idea of "course" and "recourse" as a law of nature imposed upon history, which only within the limits of that law could move dynamically and dialectically; and thereby he shut off from himself the idea of progress. Nevertheless poor Vico in the hardships of his life was inwardly independent and philosophically dignified, and he did not err like Hegel by servility towards his people and his State. But in the historical doctrine of Hegel, the Germans at least always represent an ideal, that of liberty; it was

[1] Quoted by Meinecke, II, p. 353.

much worse when they ended by representing nothing whatever except themselves, when they no longer were bearers of the divine message but became a mere brute family and race, as then happened and as happens even more today under our eyes. We must not, however, forget that there was a German in the other camp belonging to the left wing of the German Hegelian School, Marx, who in that quality and in that school where interest had been transferred from political to economic contrasts, produced a teleological materialistic historicalism without a breath of humanity or liberty: Marx was nearer than one imagines to Prussianism and to its cult of brutal force.

The rediscovery of the intimate relationship between historicism and the feeling for liberty and humanity, the establishment of harmony and unity in the theoretical and practical aspects of a single cycle, the collaboration (if you will) of Germanism and the Latin tradition, the historical liberal conception of life; none of these things therefore were born in Germany, nor had in Germany anything but a fleeting and reflected glory, and then only in the years which preceded and immediately followed 1848. The country and the time in which the fusion happened was France of the Restoration and of the July Monarchy;[1] and it was from France that the new conception spread all over the world and even caused revisions of the old liberty of England and brought to life the Italy of Camillo Cavour—Illuminism was then integrated in historicism, passing into and receiving a practical regeneration in liberalism. A true sense of historicism must be kept alive or restored: this is necessary not only to philosophy and to historiography but also to the cause of a recuperation of the moral and political life of Europe in the future or the present. Fierce protesting voices have often been raised against "historicism," and even Meinecke records some of them. But when we listen carefully to whatever was reasonable in their content, it appears that they were not fighting against historicism

---

[1] I have tried to illustrate this supremely important moment in the history of Europe in *History of Europe in the Nineteenth Century* (Bari, 1932), particularly in Chapter IV.

at all but against very different things some of which were indeed worthy of attack. Karl Menger, for example, was not attacking "historicism" in his book of that title[1] but employing a similar argument to that which was urged against the historical school of Law (which Bentham said behaved like someone who did not give the cook the orders for meals, but gave her instead the cost of the meals for the previous years) when he opposed the mistaken attempt of the so-called historical school of economics to replace deduction and calculation which are the reason and strength of that science, by an historical comparison of events and economic institutions. Nor is it really in contention against "Historicism" that some in Germany used this appellation to denote what is elsewhere called "erudition deprived of thought."[2] Troeltsch[3] did not really oppose it. He wanted to overcome it in order to vindicate the rights of moral conscience, which is really unnecessary, because moral conscience is the basis of historicism. The real modern enemy, not merely its adversary, is immorality or a morality which has developed under sham historicist appearances out of corrupt sections of the great German philosophies and has now assumed a monstrous aspect and proportion. Allied to it is a cowardice which seeks to take the style of acceptance and resignation in face of "historical necessity"—meaning fatalism and inertia, negations of history which is activity, and of historiography the fount of activity.

[1] *Die Irrtümer des Historismus in der deutschen Nationalökonomie* (Wien, 1884).
[2] See Heusser's Essay, *Die Krisis des Historismus* (Tübingen, Mohr, 1932); and my observations in *Critica*, XXXI (1933), pp. 210–11.
[3] *Der Historismus und seine Ueberwindung* (Berlin, 1924).
[4] Meinecke's confidence (op. cit., I, p. 5) that "historicism will heal the wounds it has inflicted by having established the relativity of values, given that there be men who will convert it into a straightforward life," is partially true, but errs in supposing that historicism has in any way damaged the integrity of values, when it has only rescued them from abstractions, and planted them integrally in the reality of history, and has thus assured their inexhaustible vitality. If moral force is not obtained from history, the fault (as Meinecke rightly says) lies solely with the man who does not know how to 'convert' it into the straightforward life."

(2) HISTORIOGRAPHY WITHOUT THE HISTORICAL PROBLEM

(a) Ranke

Undoubtedly there is truth in the saying that in the recounting of history, passion must be surmounted and ideas and precon- ceived judgments be put aside; but it is all too easy to go on from this to say that history must be recounted without reference to any participation in the struggle of life, and without any philoso- phical involvement. The turn of the phrase and the sound of the words being fairly similar in both these sayings, it is easy to be deceived into thinking them similar, yet the two attitudes outlined here are radically different, and the second of the two is in con- trast with the very nature of historiography.

Historiography conceived according to the second attitude prides itself on being, and is praised as, "pure": this is an adjective which in its turn has two different meanings, in the one case: "pure as regards anything that contrasts with or is foreign to the character of the action that is under consideration," such purity signifying the greatest energy and perfection of that action: and in the other case "pure from itself," that is, not having what is essential to it, and being thus deprived of its own proper being. In the same way the "pure poetry" of which there is much talk today is not passion resolved in pure fancy, free of all concepts and intentions, having thus the impetus and abandon which unfold themselves in the genuine poetical creations of all times, but it is a kind of empty production without passion and without fancy, full of something very different from poetry. Similarly "pure" historiography in the second and inferior sense, is of a kind that has no active interest and no thought to enlighten it: it is therefore anything, a chronicle, a poem or eloquence, anything except historiography, because it lacks just precisely its own soul —it lacks, that is, an historical problem.

The most celebrated "pure historian" and the head of the school which followed this course was Leopold Ranke, who seemed the incarnation of an elevated and complete idea of historiography. He has been called the "king of historiography," the man who achieved the *non plus ultra* in this sphere and after whom there was only detailed work[1] left to be done; the most "objective" of all modern writers of history; the "greatest writer of historical works whom the Germans have ever had"; the "vast eye looking upon historical reality,"[2] the "greatest master of objective insight into history,"[3] and so on. His great merit is supposed to lie in his having freed historiography from philosophy and in having loudly proclaimed that historiography could fend for itself, therefore squashing once and for all the so-called "philosophy of history" which had perniciously allowed history to become infiltrated by philosophy.

But this is a matter upon which we must be quite clear. Certainly the "philosophy of history" in so far as it was a logical construction, was a shaky one because it pretended that thought could envisage an historical development outside the study of particular events, envisage it not by dint of thought (which is always thought about events or experience), but by a kind of reflection or a superior faculty of thought, or, which comes to the same thing by thought which is abstractly and not synthetically *a priori*. If it was necessary to reject the philosophy of history in this mistaken doctrinal form which it had assumed—and in which it feebly struggled and ended by dying—it was also necessary to inquire into the motives which caused its birth and might contain some unsatisfied requirement, perhaps legitimate and therefore worthy of legitimate satisfaction. And there was one such genuine requirement, nothing more nor less than the idea of an historiography which should be neither a collection of dates and facts gathered together for the pleasure of collecting them, or for some extrinsic end, nor the mythology of some transcendental religion, nor the repudiation of the past as a haunt of dreams and follies, but a true thought process about the events

[1] Thus in Lorenz, *die Geschichtwissenschaft in Hauptrichtungen und Aufgaben* (Berlin, 1886–91), II, pp. 3–5, and *Passion*.
[2] E. Guglia, *Leopold von Rankes Leben und Werke* (Leipzig, 1843), pp. 2, 364.
[3] W. Dilthey, *Gesamelte Schriften*, XI, pp. 216–17.

of the past in their effective development whereby the positive action of each event is established; a thought process intrinsic and not extrinsic, not a compilation of confirmed news and events, but the relating of those sources to the supreme source, that is, the authority of the human conscience, historically alive and active. People were weary of histories of philosophy which produced names and anecdotes in abundance, which praised or blamed philosophers according as their sayings conformed with or differed from a received dogma, or mocked them for sayings incongruous with the new truths; there was a demand that these histories should be written by men who were themselves philosophers, and who, having progressed further, should yet show a dutiful reverence and piety and illustrate the problems which had engaged the labours of their predecessors, and the solutions which the latter had given or attempted to give, and how they had worked to produce the present. Histories of poetry and of art, mere antiquarian catalogues or anthologies of arbitrary judgments had become insufferable; what was wanted was the writing of critical artists, capable of feeling and thinking in terms of poetry and of art. People were most obviously tired and bored by histories which were just sequences (they complained) of political and military news, or chronicles of negotiations and battles; nor were they very pleased with the "histories of Civilization" which had begun to be substituted for the others and to reinforce them, because these played havoc with the past instead of accepting it with a balanced judgment, and the course of events was made to depend upon the arbitrary will of individuals. Even in this branch people asked for a history of ideals and institutions which would show the reason and necessity of their foundation, a history of contemporary moral and religious life, linked up with modern moral and religious problems, in their similarity and dissimilarity with those of the past by which they had been prepared and conditioned. Is it then to be wondered at if at first, with the appearance of this idea of a more truthful historiography attractive by reason of its beauty but bristling with difficulties and requiring much refinement of thought and subtle methodological inquiry and long study of documents, some tried to get hold of all this, not by gradually laying siege to it, but by sudden assault? Is it to be wondered at if in the course of this precipitate attack there was a measure of relapse into old and rejected conceptions, especially theological ones, even though care was taken to disguise the provident and ruling deity? Whence the basic need for a truer history was not satisfied, but a symbol was provided of the requirement itself, an imagination, a mythology woven into it. And the histories of philosophy composed in that stage were not histories of the development of thought in its indissoluble relation to the experiences of a many-sided life, but histories of a schematic development according to the ideal order of the categories or other similar rules; histories of poetry and art came to be written according to the concepts of "idealism" and "realism," "the classic" and "the romantic," and other concepts which were taken from the speculative and moral sphere; and moral and religious history was made to fit the abstract moments of liberty and of moral life, and of particular religious conceptions and beliefs.

It was not difficult to see that historical narratives like this were artificial, and everywhere the outcry was raised that they violated the facts. But there was needed nothing less than a superb vigour of the mind to follow up this observation and easy criticism by recapturing the good thread which this early philosophy and historiography had misused, and to reveal and operate that unity of philosophy and history (hitherto only foreshadowed) in a new historiography. The occasion was missed, because the inventive power of German thought was just then beginning to diminish and the age of the Epigoni and of the apostates was opening. If the period between 1820 and 1848 is celebrated as one in which the great German science of history was formed,[1] such praise mainly refers to the excellent standard to which editing and criticism of sources then attained, and to the wealth of research which, starting with the history of the State spread to every aspect of society, of institutions and of culture. Instead of forging

[1] Dilthey, op. cit., XI, p. 94.

the link between history and philosophy more firmly so that the identity of the two might become apparent in the act of knowing, the order of the day then was to separate them; and the historians steeped in this doctrine mostly turned back and became either great philologists or tendencious historians or both, even if here and there a few of them showed that they had not altogether forgotten the teachings of deep philosophy. In 1821 Wilhelm von Humbolt read a paper at the Prussian Academy upon the office of the historian,[1] in the course of which he rejected the "philosophy of history," and insisted on the point that "ideas in history must come from the very plenitude of events" (which is just as true as the inverse is), and declared that "the history of the world is unintelligible without a government of the world" (which is vague thinking); yet, survivor as he was of the great age which was just then closing, he aspired towards the fusion of ideas with events, as the artist does in the poetic image, and he was aware and fully conscious of the many difficulties which had to be overcome here. Those who followed on him made of these provisional and groping propositions a definite doctrine, and of his perplexed and cautious start a halting place.

Ranke was of this number. Humboldt had said that the proper function of historiography is "the exposition of what has happened" and "fulfils its task the more perfectly as the exposition is more complete and satisfying." And Ranke echoed that history has no other aim than "simply to explain the event exactly as it happened,"[2] without taking the trouble to demonstrate the origin or the nature of this affirmation of the historical event. Humboldt had raised the problem of ideas in history, though he had not defined it nor incorporated it into a system of philosophy of the spirit and of ideas. Ranke always spoke of these ideas or tendencies of various epochs, but he did not allow himself or anyone else ever to go so far as to define them or elaborate them as concepts: he insisted that they could only be intuited by seeing them in

---

[1] See the translation and comment in the appendix to my *Conversazioni Critiche*, serie IV (Bari, 1932), pp. 365–83.
[2] In the preface of *Geschichten der romanischen und germanischen Völker.*

an event.[1] While Humboldt postulated a divine government in history, Ranke rested content with the religious conception of the Lutheran Church to which he remained faithful. He lacked an awareness of the nature of the universal, and in history he looked out for and enjoyed the particular for its own sake, with no ulterior end, just as (he said) one enjoys a flower without being compelled to refer it to a classification by Linnaeus or Oken; after that he began to look for what he called the "general," the relation of these particular events to each other, and with the complex;[2] that is still with an individual centred upon itself, though a larger and wider individual. For him the coherence of history did not lie in the unity of the spirit but in the reciprocal activity of peoples, and universal history was the history of peoples who had reacted reciprocally upon each other in this way.[3] Even when his criticism seems philosophically apt, and he himself to be grasping an unknown truth, careful inspection reveals that he understands it in an empirical and narrow sense; for example, when he lays down that every historical epoch (and he might have said every work and every single act) is not a stepping-stone to another historical epoch but stands by itself and has its own proper value:[4] this is really a half truth, since every act stands altogether in relation to itself and altogether in relation to something else, it is both a point of repose and a stepping-stone, and if it were not so it would be impossible to conceive the self-surpassing growth of history or progress which is a concept without which no history is thinkable and without which the significance of history for us and our work, resting as it does on past work, cannot be explained. But the concept of progress was denied by Ranke; he understood it in a material sense and criticized it with apposite arguments.[5] Another bright

---

[1] See the lectures *Ueber die Epochen der Neueren Geschichte*, I, in *Deutsche Geschichte*, I, p. 59, and in all the other works; and cf. a section of the article quoted by Guglia on *Grosse Mächten*, p. 183.

[2] See the pages referred to by *Dove* in his introduction to *Epochen*, pp. 3–4.

[3] To take only one of many references, see the Preface to *Storia Universale*.

[4] *Epochen*, I, and passion in the other works.

[5] *Epochen*, I.

shot was the observation that history is the eternal struggle
between State and Church,[1] only we are then disappointed to
find how he reduces this struggle to one in which two institutions
try in vain to outdo each other, and neither ever supplants the
other or "at least" (he says) "in our Western nations this has
never happened," instead of going into it thoroughly in order
to find the antithesis of the two eternal movements of Power (or
Utility) and Morality.[2] He was disposed to naturalize ideal determinations, and although he did not abandon himself to racial
fancies, yet he understood the historical nature of nations in a
naturalistic sense when he said, in opposition to the demand for
liberal institutions, that every people must have the institutions
which conform with its character, and sarcastically despised those
reformers who wanted to "think out the fatherland" comparing
them to those who seek to create a language out of grammars
or poetry out of aesthetics:[3] as though moral ideals were abstractions like grammars or theories like aesthetics, and not
motives of affection inspiring and determining the ethical will.
Even his "ideas" tended to become naturalized in "generations,"[4]
as happens openly in the writings of his disciple, Lorenz the
theoretician of history by "generations"[5] who seemed never to have
pondered the fact that ideas in history qualify or mould generations
and not vice versa. He never quite shed the anti-historical thought
that things might have happened differently if this or that action
had not been accomplished, or if this or that incident had not
occurred; that the French Revolution might really have stemmed

---

[1] Introduction to *Deutsche Geschichte im Zeitalter der Reformation*.

[2] For a study of this observation of Ranke's, see my essay in *Etica e Politica* (Bari, 1931), pp. 339–44.

[3] See *Politisches Gespräch*, Meinecke's edition (Munich and Leipzig, 1924); and cf. Guglia, op. cit., p. 167. An Italian cannot fail to note that Ranke applauds (op. cit., p. 175) the ideas of the author of *Dialoghetti sulle materie correnti* (1831, by Count Monaldo Leopardi, the fanatical reactionary, father of the poet Leopardi).

[4] There is an emphasis on the importance of "generations" in the *Geschichten der romanischen und Germanischen Völker* (3rd ed., Leipzig, 1885), p. 323.

[5] In the op. cit., and in *Lehrbuch der Gesamten wissenschaftlichen Genealogie* (Berlin, 1898).

its course if Louis XVI had not committed the fatal error of doubling the number of representatives of the Third Estate, and that Europe might have presented a different shape if Napoleon had not obstinately insisted on getting lost in a Russian winter.[1] Somewhat oddly in his *Universal History* he put the secret of the primitive world in "The Relation of Man to God and to Nature," and handed over this problem to "the natural sciences and the religious concept."[2]

A deep historical vision carries with it profound ethical and political interest: it is stimulated by this, and in turn stimulates it, but Ranke, although his adolescence was spent in the great upheavals of the Napoleonic wars, confessed that the urge for historical research came to him (his attention having been primarily directed to classical philology) not from the events of the day,[3] but from his work as a teacher. His lack of interest in politics disposed him towards pacifism and quietism and in his *History of Germany during the Reformation* he sighs (as is well known) over Germany's failure to reach an agreement with the Catholic Church, which was so nearly achieved in 1541.[4] He was a timid Conservative subservient to Prussian Government, and in 1832 he accepted the editorship of an *Historical Political Review* in order to defend and propagate its antiquated policy. His fame as a historian stood high, and he was credited with knowing the secrets of the future and interrogated as an oracle on what should be done in the present; for good folk think that historiography can utter oracular replies concerning that which is created solely by the spontaneity of action, whence the insistent demands upon it to prescribe a road for poetry, philosophy and practical action, an outline for the future; to all of which the serious thinker answers *age rem tuam*. Ranke's responses always just echoed generalities or acceptance of accomplished facts, like those he gave to Frederick William IV in '48-'49 on the necessity of granting a constitu-

---

[1] Guglia, op. cit., pp. 63, 138, compare *Epochen*, XIX.
[2] See the Preface.
[3] Guglia, op. cit., pp. 42-43.
[4] Op. cit., p. 240.

tion and on the conduct of affairs in Germany;[1] or to King Max of Bavaria to whom he gave in 1854 an abridged course of history, concluding that it was necessary to know the world, to follow the voice of conscience and to harmonize the opposing tendencies of the modern world towards absolutism and republicanism. In November 1870, when the war was brewing, he met Thiers, who was on a mission in Vienna, together with other politicians: "an historian," he said "among many politicians," and argued that the war was no longer being fought against Napoleon III, defeated and a prisoner, nor against France as such, but against Louis XIV, who had taken advantage of a weak moment in the Empire in order to steal Strassburg: to which one of the politicians present justly observed that if one went ferreting thus among the events of the past, "nothing of the present world order would be left standing."[2] He also maintained at this gathering that according to his historical diagnosis, the German claims should be restricted to Alsace, because Lorraine had always been French in language and nationality; but a few weeks earlier he had said that the annexation of Lorraine was "demanded by historical justice."[3] When he was working at his *Universal History*, he said that without the foundation of the new German Empire and without the military defeat which Bismarck inflicted on the revolutionary force, he could not have undertaken that work, for he would have been unable to examine past centuries in an impartial way, owing to the still undecided contrast between the two great world powers.[4]

Ranke's books are on a level with these theoretical concepts and practical dispositions; they are history devoid of a historical problem or showing the mere appearance of a problem, with here and there a sprinkling of extrinsic and generical reflection brought into service to take the place of the absent historical thought. In his *History of the Roman and Germanic Peoples from*

---

[1] These memoranda are for the most part summarized by Guglia, op. cit., pp. 254–70.
[2] *Zur Eigenen Lebensgeschichte* (Ed. Dove, Leipzig, 1890), p. 591.
[3] Op. cit., pp. 591–92.   [4] Guglia, op. cit., p. 19.

1494–1514, the first book to make his reputation, he wants to show that the six nations—three Latin, the French, the Spanish, and the Italian, and three Germanic, the German, the English and the Scandinavian—make a unity which is not the unity of the State, because as States they have always fought and will always fight each other, but a unity which lies in a more or less close affinity of race, in a similarity of customs and in many common institutions and many common external enterprises such as the Barbarian Invasions, the Crusades and the colonization of the New World. But the unity of development is real only so long as it is spiritual, as it lies in determined ideas and ideals; and a unity of mere events can only be a unity of extrinsic coincidences, not resolved into intrinsic relations. Such coincidences delighted Ranke: synchronisms between happenings very different and incomparable in countries far apart, occurring at about the same time. Thus in the middle of the fifteenth century he finds Colà di Rienzo in Rome, Marino Falier in Venice, Etienne Marcel in Paris, the justicia in Aragon, the Golden Ball of Charles IV in the empire, the growing power of the English Parliament under Edward III and so on.[1] Such considerations are too insubstantial to have deserved attention at a time when Giuseppe Mazzini had already set up the ideal of the union of the peoples of Europe (not only of the Latin and Germanic peoples) living in communities under popular government, and each preserving its own virtues and particular attitudes, and had so suggested a very much more intimate and profound vision of the development of European life. Ranke's explanations of events are also causalistic and extrinsic, as when he links up the loss of Italian independence in the sixteenth century with pederasty, with syphilis, with education to rhetorical modes of speech and gesture, with the effeminate and elaborate dress of the men who played and sang, with the introduction of foreign clothes and manners, and with the unnational character of the Epics of Pulcio Boiardo and Ariosto and others who chiefly celebrated French heroes and the wars of Spain against the Moors.[2] His *History of the Papacy in the Sixteenth*

[1] Op. cit., p. 19.   [2] Op. cit., pp. 263–65.

and Seventeenth Centuries outlines the circumstances in which the
Papacy, decadent and sore hit by the Protestant Reformation,
pulled itself together and gained new strength in a defensive
struggle, so that it not only held dangerous positions but re-
captured many which had been lost in the first encounter. Here,
too, Ranke continually declares that he is examining events from
a "purely historical point of view;" but what in fact happened
to the Catholic Church under the Counter Reformation of the
Jesuits, how completely different it was from the Mediaeval
Church; what happened to it during the spiritual decadence,
after the Thirty Years War and in the second half of the seventeenth century and during the whole of the eighteenth until it
reacted to the French Revolution by a fresh recovery, withdrawing from the upper classes among whom the Jesuits had
worked in times past, to lean on the peasants and on remaining
absolute governments; the character and the significance of the
contrasts which arose within it and the extent of the power which
it still possessed in the present and the rôle which it played—
Ranke does not investigate all this: he seems to be engaged rather
in the fine art of embalming a corpse. In his preface to the latest
edition of his book he was happy to say that the Papacy was no
longer important in the modern world and was no longer a
menace now that the days in which it had instilled fear into men
were over and men were insured against it. And all this just
at the moment when that *Kulturkampf* was beginning in
Germany, which did not end in a victory for Bismarck. The very
construction of the book is defective because it comprehends two
different entities and two different developments: the Papacy as
a universal power and the Papacy as the Sovereign in the Roman
State, two histories which never merge and only alternate or run
parallel to each other. If Ranke was moved by any interest in
composing this work, it was not an historical but a psychological
interest: "es sind einige erhabene Naturen unter Ihnen, es sind
grosse Menschen darunter," he said:[1] "Among the Popes of the
Counter Reformation there are some superior personalities as

[1] Op. cit., p. 62.

great men like Pius V"; and in drawing the portraits of these people he enjoyed himself in this book as in the preceding one, as in all his books. We will not dwell on them—*History of Germany During the Reformation*, *History of France*, *History of England*, *History of Prussia*—because this would not serve our purpose, which is to define his method; it would only confirm what we have already said. We will stop a moment at his last and heaviest undertaking, his *Universal History*, to notice that even in this, there is no underlying problem. The history of all times and of all peoples, or at least of those (to which Ranke limited his task) who have influenced each other, is embraced in a single exposition as a sequence down the centuries: this is not the solution of an historical problem but a literary achievement. So-called "universal histories," if they are alive, are always particular histories, like any other, centred round a particular problem,[1] as with Augustine, Bossuet, Voltaire, and Hegel, but not with Ranke. He tries in vain to revive history with reflections which are always extrinsic, as, for example, when he discusses how Philip and Alexander of Macedon, resemble or differ from Frederick William I or Frederick II of Prussia;[2] or when he observes that Alexander's expedition into Asia repeats the Greek enterprise against Ilium and is consciously connected with Homeric times;[3] or, when having described the discontent and the opposition of Alexander's generals against his assuming the attitude of a Persian sovereign, Ranke set it forth as "a problem of the century," how far the devotion due to a legitimate prince can be harmonized with individual liberty.[4]

Even Ranke's famous criticism of modern historians[5] does not concern their conception of history or the philosophy which is implicit in their interpretations of human affairs, nor the progress which all of them comment on in this sphere. He considers these

---

[1] For a demonstration of this point see *Teoria e Storia della Storiografia* (3rd ed., Bari, 1927), pp. 45–48.

[2] For convenience I quote from the Italian translation of the first volume (Florence, 1932), p. 366.

[3] Op. cit., p. 377. [4] Op. cit., p. 393.

[5] *Zur Kritik neurerer Geschichtenschreiben* (3rd edition, Leipzig. 1884.).

historians solely for their value as sources, to see whether they
give direct or indirect evidence, whether they use just a second-
hand material, what interests drive them to speak out or keep
silence or to temper or alter what they know, in fact, he wants
to know not what kind of historical mind they have, but what
their authority is and what kind of witnesses they are. So he
introduced, according to contemporary judgment, into his treatment of modern history that refined method which Niebuhr
had used in his treatment of Roman history: others, however,
accounted it against him that he relied too much upon certain
kinds of sources such as diplomatic documents. The refinement
in any case was that of technical philology which had already
been carried very far by the scholars and critics of the eighteenth
century, like Bayle and Muratori; it was not a refinement of
guiding concepts. Ranke did not admit spiritual progress and
particularly not intellectual progress and he said that in philosophy
Plato and Aristotle suffice;[1] in other words, that the thinkers
from the fourth century in Greece onwards had lived in vain, a
judgment which cannot but astound us especially when it comes
from the lips of one who makes a profession of history.

The deficiency in Ranke's historical thought was quickly
noticed by some of his contemporary critics, who had not altogether forgotten history in the grand style as it had been conceived and attempted in the German classical age. Thus a reviewer
in the *Hallische Literaturzeitung* in 1828 complained of the lack of
solidity in the *Geschichten der romanischen und germanischen Völker*
and noted how "depressing" the book was, because "everything
is made to depend on blind chance, interests, passions and
crimes."[2] Leo described the author as a "vase painter" and re-
proached Ranke for the childishness of his resorts to "the finger
of God" and for his simpering philanthropy "which does well in
ladies' albums, but not in history," and rebuked Ranke with "the
truth of history lies in the processes of the spirit."[3] Soon after
1830 Heinrich Heine in some of his delicious pages placed Ranke

[1] *Epochen*, p. 21.
[2] Guglia, op. cit., p. 87.   [3] Ibid., op. cit., pp. 89–91.

among those whom the Prussian Government "loved to send travelling among the elegiac ruins of Italy to attain the tranquillizing sentiments that go with thoughts of destiny, so that then, in collusion with the preachers of Christian submission, they might quench the short fevers of desire for popular liberty by means of cold application of newspapers." Heine also described him as having "a fine talent for cutting out historical figures and pasting them picturesquely one beside the other, a good soul and very tender," and so on, in the same tone.[1] Very often he is accused of "moral indifference," which in truth was, with him, derived not from cynicism but only from a certain sluggishness of inferior life.

As against these judgments, which were disdainfully dismissed as malicious or, in the case of Heine, as not to be taken seriously (though that they were serious was shown by the way in which they hit the mark), there was a chorus of "pure historians," whose united laudatory and admiring voices we have heard. The "pure historian," who is usually a professor, specially likes careful research work in archives and libraries; he spares no pains to be in philological matters scrupulously exact, and sometimes even cares for a good literary presentation of the results he has obtained; but he spares as much as possible the hard and painful effort whereby thought can acquire its own conception of the world, its own philosophy, as well as that other effort, so charged with responsibility, of arriving at practical resolutions, which would involve him in dangerous struggles. And the "pure historian" ("pure" even when he is impure through his political servility to Bismarckian or "racial" Governments) flourished especially in Germany and from there gained imitators the world over.[2] Ranke's school numbered in its early days Giesebrecht, Köpke, Wilmans, Hirsch and later others of merit; it had a hand in collective works like the *Jahrbücher des deutschen Reichs*, and from

[1] These pages also are translated in the appendix to the *Conversazioni Critiche*, IV, pp. 384–87.

[2] There is detailed critical information about the first and second generations of the "pure historians" after 1848 and after 1870 in my *Storia della Storiografia italiana nel secolo decimonono* (2nd ed., Bari, 1930), II, pp. 1–122.

1859 it ran the review *Historische Zeitschrift*, in which its methods were propagated and defended, but it has recently been snatched from those who worthily represented its tradition and passed into the hands of the racialists.[1] With this numerous and elect band of disciples, reverenced by his people and honoured by his Government, Ranke was elevated above all other historians and practically placed on the summit of the temple of historiography.

It is necessary to move him from this supreme position not in order to cast him down, as is habitually done with the idols of régimes which have collapsed, but in order to give him the position he deserves, which is still tolerably noble and elegant. We must not be mistaken as to the meaning of the criticism we have been developing; it was our duty and it was necessary in order to reassert the unity of historiography with life and thought, and in order to clear the mind of the comfortable idea, too easily accepted, of an historiography without a problem and without philosophy, decorated with the name of "pure." Our criticism has been directed against Ranke's *forma mentis* and not against the work he undertook or against his books, which are based on good documental researches, abound in sensible judgments and are written in a neat and elegant style, rare enough in Germany, and not one of the least reasons for their success. In connection with this Ranke once said that only the most finely composed historical work would last a long time.[2] The "Lust zu fabulieren," or at least a certain desire to write a story, "zuerzählen," dominates his work, especially when he paints a rich gallery of human characters, with preference for the portraits of clever, prudent and refined men. Among all the admiration and praise which have been showered upon him there is an occasional admission of his inclination to narrate for the sake of narrative, for the sake of good narrative; and Dilthey, who was not among his coolest

---

[1] The new programme of the *Historische Zeitschrift* (1936) reads thus: "Aufgabe der 'Historischen Zeitschrift' ist es, die Geschichtforschung in einer grossen Zeitwende so zu pflegen, dass sie der strengen Wissenschaft und den lebendigen Kräften des deutschen Volkes und Reiches zugleich genügt. Ihr Anschauung ist bewusst gesamtdeutsch."

[2] Quoted by Wetzold, *Deutsche Kunsthistoriker* (Leipzig, 1924), p. 206.

admirers, when he had to qualify him, did not call him a thinker, but an "epic," comparing him to Herodotus.[1] An "Epic" is perhaps going too far, because he lacks the sublimity of the Saga Singers, and Herodotus was far more fresh and original; however, Ranke is a pleasant and easy narrator.

(b) Burckhardt

An altogether different writer who, as a young man, had experienced strong antipathy for the neutrality which Ranke professed, for his soft character as a man, for his lack of artistic feeling, and for a certain insipidity which he noticed in him as a "society man,"[2] was Jacob Burckhardt, who studied history and wrote historical books which differed from those of Ranke in every way, except that they too lacked an historical problem. Burckhardt knew nothing and did not want to know anything of philosophy: he had listened to old Schelling at the University of Berlin and had been horrified; Schelling's "second philosophy" of Gnosticism had excited in Burckhardt such a monstrous impression that it seemed likely to him that at any moment an Asiatic God might rush into the lecture hall, with twelve feet and twelve arms, hurtling and smashing.[3] He ended by smiling at philosophy herself, denied that she could have any efficacy whatever in the world, where her universals cut a pretty poor figure when they came up against individuality and personality. At best he allowed her the vain labours of Sisyphus; an endeavour to throw light on the great "enigma of life."[4]

Burckhardt did not withdraw from the world around him and its practical struggles on account of an inclination for peaceful study, but because of an excess of passion which became an insupportable torment in his brief experience of political affairs in Switzerland between 1840–44; and even more because of the

[1] Dilthey, op. cit., XI, pp. 216–17.
[2] W. von D. Schulenburg, *Der junge Jakob Burckhardt* (Stuttgatt-Zürich, 1926), pp. 32–33.
[3] Letter of 1842 (in Schulenburg, op. cit., p. 129).
[4] *Weltgeschichtliche Betrachtungen*, ed. Kröner, p. 4.

consternation he felt at the great political revolutionary movement in Europe which began in July 1830. He had a sort of apocalyptic vision in those days of the Beast rising proudly in the form of the growing and indomitable impetus of Democracy, culminating in the ruin of Europe and the coming centuries of barbarism. Democracy had arrived with the revolution of '89; he thought it would waver between the two extremes of that revolution, Caesarism and revolutionary radicalism; that it would increasingly centralize the State, give an economic imprint to the whole of society, carry the public debt to giddy heights, give rise to militarism, nationalism and wars among the peoples; that refined habits, religion and science would be sacrificed and that culture would be shamefully calumniated as the ally of Capitalism; until in turn the second of the two extremes, Caesarism, would win the day. Then a new absolutism would arise, no longer so tender-hearted and humane as in the old monarchies, but pursued by hard militaristic men who would make all equal—not democratically equal, as people had dreamed, but equal in their servitude. The constitutional monarchy which had been fashioned out of the revolution of 1830 was not, as people believed, the happy ending of a drama; it was barely the second act and the years preceding '48 were a time of adjustment and preparation. The dominators of the future, *terribles simplificateurs*, would have trodden on rights, well-being, popular sovereignty, and even science. The demand of the Socialists that workers should be free from the subjection of capitalism would come to be answered in an unexpected and even ironic way with "a reduction of the workers to a determined and controlled measure of misery coupled with promotions and uniforms; every work day begun and ended to the sound of trumpets."[1]

It cannot be denied that horror and aversion had made Burck-

[1] The greater part of the extracts which I use here are to be found in K. Löwith, *Jakob Burckhardt der Mensch inmitten der Geschichte* (Lucerne, 1936): so that I hardly need to quote specifically from Burckhardt's works and letters. Löwith's book is as accurate as it is intelligent; but since the interpreter completely agrees with his author's feelings of bewilderment and scepticism, his interpretation and judgment are inverse to those we pursue here.

hardt extraordinarily observant of the inherent tendency and logic of democracy, as it proceeds from consequence to consequence, when unrestrained and untempered by other forces, or that under this influence be depicted a fearful future, in such bold outline that he now almost assumes the aspect of a prophet. His saying that "in the gentle twentieth century authority would raise its head again and a terrible head," has a prophetic sound.

A similar fear caused other spirits at that time to tremble; thus Niebuhr was shaken by the revolution of '30 and died a few months later in an agony of apprehension at the destruction which he believed imminent of well-being, of culture, liberty and science; he seemed to think we were re-entering on an age like that of Imperial Rome, half-way through the third century, after the death of the last of the Severus family, with its wars between innumerable pretenders, its barbarian invasions. The idea of the decadence of Rome and of returning barbarism permeates the thought of the people of Europe, warning them of similar disaster ahead, a warning which has not been, and cannot be, disregarded. The incubus is more or less grave according to the causes which move the imagination; for, in the last analysis, this is a question of imagination, and as such altogether sterile in its effects. A critical mind examines the democratic system and cannot conceal the danger to liberty arising out of it, but it does not, on that account, regard as facts that which has not happened, and that which the forthright will strive to avert by pitting strength against strength. It knows that even were the worst to occur, it would have to be faced in a manly way, with confidence in the inexhaustible and ever renewed virtue of humanity.

Burckhardt, dazzled by the vividness of his imagination, forthwith decided not to fight and embraced that personage so unworthy of his affection, Pessimism. No lover of philosophy, he yet loved Schopenhauer's pessimistic metaphysics, and called him "his philosopher" and even followed that other patchwork and eclectic philosopher Eduard von Hartmann. He said that the "radical sin" of democracy was its optimism, its belief in a perfect and blessed social State, and that in the pursuit of this unattainable and absurd aim it destroys the existing State. He defended the Middle Ages, so vivid in colour, full of true liberty, of variety and graduations in form, free of national wars, industrial masses, deadly competition, banks, capitalism and class hatred; inevitable hardships were accepted and people knew how to amuse themselves and how to enjoy life more than they do or did in any other age. Burckhardt, like all pessimists, had in him a streak of unsatisfiable hedonism.

With this kind of feeling and reasoning Burckhardt wanted to take refuge from the world, from the ugly world round him and from the worse world to come, and for his shelter he chose history, which would offer him an Archimedean point from which to contemplate serenely the spectacle of human affairs. But history is not to be excogitated from an Archimedean point situated outside the world; on the contrary, the need of it arises only in the world, and among its contrasts, and with the need, the research into it and the necessary intelligence. A writer who is much honoured in our day, perhaps on account of his complete obtuseness in the matter of philosophy and history, Kierkegaard, denies that life can be known, as he says, in time: that is, in historical life itself, since a moment of complete calm in which to look backwards can never be found; he does not realize that if such a moment were found there would no longer be any reason for looking back and the very capacity to understand would disappear. Burckhardt, for his part, dreamed that he had got free of the necessary links between thought and life once he had denied the conception of history as a process of continuously novel actions, and had affirmed instead their typical, constant and eternally recurring nature. But this substitution gets rid of history altogether, for history is history just because it does not recur and because every one of its actions enjoys its own private individuality. The invention of the typical, the constant and the recurring is essentially anti-historical, yet even this is not to be achieved at the Archimedean point over and above the world; but must be effected in a small corner of the world where drab psychological and sociological generalizations rule. The same anti-historical motive led Burckhardt to try to substitute for the history of events the history of culture and civilization: not in the plausible sense, that the latter should receive and mature and enhance the former, but in the empirical and static sense of a "history of culture," on the lines which Riehl was then pursuing. Thus his historical works tend not to give the "story" or the drama and dialectic of action, but to give the "picture," the description of a fixed and immobilized reality. His great men did not for him show their greatness by virtue of the historical and ultra-individual missions they had fulfilled, and in which they had risen high, and truly realized themselves, but by their own psychological character; Pericles stood for him over and above Athens, Alexander over and above Greece and Asia, and Caesar over and above Rome. The subject of history was, to him, not the spirit which is always creating new forms, and which he was disposed to scoff at, but "man suffering, aspiring, and acting as he has always done and always will do," and on account of that he did not regret, indeed he desired for his historical work the qualification of pathological. His historical reflections are many and varied and sometimes acute; they are always "interesting" because they are expressions of his peculiar personality: but he himself knew that he could not find the thread by which to develop and systematize them, and that he had to leave them scattered and discontinuous.[1] The trilogy of forces which he distinguished in his theoretical treatment—State, religion, and culture —is not a speculative trilogy, but simply a scheme in which to frame his scattered observations.

That is why the historians of modern historiography are so embarrassed as to what place should be assigned to Burckhardt's books—*The Age of Constantine, The Civilization of the Renaissance in Italy, The Culture of Greece*—and that is why also one of his admirers judges him as "far less scientific than Ranke,"[2] and why the word "dilettante" has been whispered about him. The intimate purpose of these books always lies in Burckhardt's unquiet

[1] See especially his *Weltgeschichtliche Betrachtungen.*
[2] Schulenburg, op. cit., p. 34.

and pessimistic soul which turns to whatever meets its mood, and relieves and distracts that mood by procuring some consolation or some intoxication. His *Civilization of the Renaissance* is quite permeated with Stendhalian love for the Italian people and for the agile way in which, as he imagines, it endures and enjoys and lives life. Hence the importance given to individualism whether in the tyrant, in the *condottiere*, the criminal, the republican citizen, the artist, the explorer, or may be even the adulterer "who turns his love towards another developed individuality, to the wife of his neighbour."[1] Not that Burckhardt was an immoralist, indeed he protested when he saw the violence and the perfidy of the Renaissance growing into an ideal in the hands of Nietzsche; but he felt in sympathy with vitality in its energy and exuberance and he made and cultivated an image of it. This individualism which so impressed him he partly observed in events, but partly produced it in his imagination; he was uncertain and oscillated in his concept of it; but what he did not see, nor ever felt the need to inquire into, was the transformation and crystallization of this individualism into the worldly concept of the Renaissance, in opposition to the asceticism and transcendentalism of the Middle Ages. In his last years, amazed at the wide diffusion and good fortune which attended his writing, he remarked jokingly: "Really I don't believe in individualism at all, but I will not say so because a great many people find pleasure in it and I don't want to deprive them of it."[2] He said that in the Italian Renaissance "modern man" was born, and this was an impression rather than an elaborated judgment, for it called for a thorough inquiry into the relation between the Renaissance and the Reformation and into the ages which preceded and followed them; but he cared not for these things, seeing that he did not believe in historical development. In his book on Greek culture he credits Athens with that same "discovery of the world and of man" with which he had credited the Italian Renaissance,

---

[1] *Kultur der Renaissance* (9th edition, Greiger, Leipzig, 1904), II, p. 177.
[2] This anecdote is in Kaegi's introduction to Walser, *Gesammelte Studien zur Geistesgeschichte der Renaissance* (Bâle), p. xxxvii.

which shows that neither the one nor the other cultural processes was properly allocated by him to its true and unexchangeable position in history, nor did he determine their peculiar and unique character, and the exclusive part played by them in the general development of history. On the other hand, given his pessimistic view of the way the contemporary world was going, the appearance of "modern man" infected by rationalism and French Revolutionism and all the rest, should not have pleased him. In the Renaissance he observed a cultured class in the process of formation and of separation from the popular and uncultivated classes, a scission which cannot be healed and has broken the unity of social life;[1] thus he draws near to, yet passes by, one of the grave problems of modern civilization arising out of the dissolution of the common religious patrimony of the Middle Ages —and that of the obstacles which the religion of educated man, rationalistic or liberal, encounters when it is translated into popular conceptions, the effort made to overcome the obstacles by means of elementary secular education, the spread of scientific knowledge, the exercise of political rights and by similar means, more or less efficacious, more or less durably efficacious, human life being what it is. Morality does not appear to him as a disposition of the Soul, made concrete in actions and in customs derived from them, but as a generic moral force, pitted against a generic egoism; and the questions he thereupon raises—whether and to what extent an age is moral—remain, and could not but remain, unanswered.[2] In his earliest and more conventional book also, *The Age of Constantine*, he is interested in the process of decomposition and decadence in the world of Rome, and in those anchorites and hermits among whom he found many with stout hearts, who, disgusted with earthly life, withdrew (such was his interpretation) far from the world to fight their struggles with God. His hatred of force, of that *Macht* to which Ranke bowed reverently, that force which is "essentially the bad" and of the State which uses it, dominates his book, *The Culture of Greece*, in which the *Polis* is described as one might describe a peni-

[1] *Kultur der Renaissance*, p. 186.   [2] Op. cit., II, pp. 156 seq.

tentiary; and side by side with that hatred one is aware of his heartfelt rediscovery of the true Greeks, fellow pessimists, a suffering and bitter people, not at all like the Greeks vaunted by classical German poetry and philosophy as living serenely and happily in a bodily and spiritual harmony: this is the pessimistic conception with which Burckhardt prepared and instructed Nietzsche.

One is tempted to apply Burckhardt's definition of history as "the most anti-scientific of all the sciences, though it transmits much that is worth knowing" (*Wissenswürdige*) to his own historical books, because his books, unlike Ranke's, are indeed full of lively observations, almost always one-sided, though not on that account conclusive, but always stimulating.

Perhaps to his pessimism is to be ascribed the precocious arrest of his literary activity just after he was forty: He was born in 1818. *Constantine* appeared in 1853, the *Cicerone* in 1855, *Civilization of the Renaissance* in 1860; and then he lived another thirty-seven years, abandoning his chief works to the care of others. He had let them drop, as it were; from time to time and rarely he published other things, but mostly he confined himself to lectures and conversations in Bâle, and out of these from notebooks and notes came the *Considerations upon Universal History* and the vast treatise on *Greek Culture*, which lack the force and splendour of his youthful works.

His works on the figurative and architectural arts, chief among them his *Cicerone*, are particularly important (he does not seem to have had much knowledge of nor any comparable intelligence for poetry), and certainly the history of art might have progressed more rapidly if it had paid more attention to some of his indications, and had it developed and carefully determined some of his leading concepts. Even in this sphere he is diffident of philosophy, but it was a healthy diffidence, since it was directed "against those philosophers of art who speak of the idea of works of art," and was not subject to the arbitrary and conceptual aesthetics which flooded Germany in his day, so that he never lost touch with the reality of art. Together with philosophers he discarded philologists, antiquaries, biographies of artists and all those who introduced matters extraneous to art in their work, or otherwise distracted attention from it or otherwise disfigured it. Burckhardt wanted to be simply (but how difficult this simplicity is!) a "Cicerone," a guide to the enjoyment of art, which is, after all, the real *raison d'être* of criticism and of historiography of art. The single work was the unique object of his observation; instinctively he felt that while customs and thoughts of various epochs could be transmitted in pretentious "evolutionary" histories, art could not; experience suggested incidental aesthetic propositions to him, and they are worth far more than the heavy tracts of so-called philosophers; they themselves are philosophy, a well-bred, as against an ill-bred philosophy, philosophy genuine and not of mere appearance. Hence he affirmed the unlogical character of art and rejected strained attempts to "give a complete verbal account of a work of art," because if such a thing were ever possible "art would be superfluous and the work in question would not have been built or sculptured or painted."[1] He called attention to the absurdity of "classes" of works of art, because "art as an active force takes no notice of the definition and can spring surprises upon the contemplator by its continual variations and lapses which render an exact classification impossible."[2] He could not follow the formal judgments of the devotees of light or colour, declaring it to be false that "the objects of painting can ever be a mere pretext for a single characteristic which is not even among the highest, achieving sovereign prestige."[3] He always distinguished between "the dust which fashion and society impose upon the artist and the gold which the artist extracts from it," and he did not like to see statements about a specific artist referred to the "style in general" of which

[1] In his preface to *Cicerone*, of which we fortunately now have reprints (in the *Gesammelte Schriften* and in Kröner's edition), in the original text unaltered by successive editors who had reduced the work of the original personality to a collective work, and turned it into an information manual.

[2] In the essay *Ueber die Niederländische Genremalerei in Kulturgeschichtliche Vorträge* (ed. Kröner), pp. 41–42.

[3] In his essay on Rembrandt, vol. cit., p. 133.

that artist might be a representation or exponent.[1] He felt how important it was to concentrate on the unmixed and lively impression made by a work of art, and how it could be falsified by the very search for explanations in its particular aspects and qualities; and he said that here one reached a locked door which no key could unlock and upon which was written: "Du sollst das Verhältniss zwischen dir und die Kunst nie ergründen!" ("You shall never fully explore the relationship which exists between you and art").[2] His taste was excellent, classical and Goethian, directed towards beauty and harmony and firmly set against the seductions of the curious, the strange, the colossal, and the morbid, to which his German co-nationals so easily yielded. He took no part in the fanaticism or in the romantic caprice for the Gothic; but he gladly defended the much maligned Italian Gothic. He penetrated the Baroque in all its most intimate deceits; after his day it was to enjoy great fortune and to become so inflated into a powerful form of the spirit and of art, above all as the result of the work of German historians and critics.[3] He thus did not allow himself to be dazzled by what he called "the false dramatic life of Bernini." His judgments may be contradicted here and there, and there is room for much amplification and inquiry into his concept of art, but he took the royal road of the history of art, which is the history of single works of genius and not of anything else. Here his historical inquiries dealt with true and real historical problems, whereas in civil and political history this was excluded by his dismay and pessimism and by inertia of the will into which he had lapsed. It is indispensable in order to understand and pass judgment upon the historiography of the nineteenth century that we should be clearly and con-

[1] H. Kaufmann in the appendix to *Erinnerungen aus Rubens* (ed. Kröner), p. 134.

[2] In the essay on Rembrandt, p. 113. One of his pupils in Bâle records that he sometimes stopped in his lectures "while talking of Raphael's painting, or of the erma of Pericles in the Vatican, his voice, suffocated by tears, ceased, so that in the great silence, one heard the Rhine flowing" (R. Marx, in the appendix to Kröner's edition of the *Weltgeschichtliche Betrachtungen*, p. 286.

[3] On this point and in defence of Buckhardt's judgment, see the notes to my *Storia dell' età barocca in Italia* (Bari, 1929, pp. 490–96).

tinually aware of the kind of crisis which followed on the hurried
and unconsidered amalgamation of history and philosophy in the
ill-famed "philosophy of history," and ended in producing not a
greater and better method but a renunciation. Nor can it be said
that the assertion of the individual against the universal, bringing
with it the separation between history and philosophy, is a thing
which belongs to the past, because the ideal of "pure historiography" still persists widely in the historiography of our days,[1]
and especially in the historiography, which is in certain respects
laudable, cultivated in universities and schools, institutions which
should—if such a thing were possible—be awakened to consciousness of the unity of historical thought with the actuality of
life, and to the tasks which that awakened conscience imposes.

(3) CERTAINTY IN HISTORICAL TRUTH

It is the not infrequent and always possible falsification of documents and evidence which furnishes the main argument for a
scepticism which is specifically historiographical, because even
when these falsifications are unmasked they suggest to the mind
so many others which no one has yet succeeded in unmasking,
and throw a shadow over the whole mass of documents and
evidence, destroying faith in history and producing doubt about
historiography as such, so that the conclusion is reached that
historiography is an illusory and conventional science.

As against this, the fact remains that everyone, including the
sceptic, goes on calmly distinguishing between what has happened and what has been imagined, while general consciousness

[1] I have come across a pamphlet by a writer who, although he makes much
of philosophy, especially of Kant and Hegel (W. Schornfeld, *Der deutsche Idealismus
und die Geschichte*, Tübingen, Mohr, 1936), is completely unconscious of the
fundamental problem, and still endorses Ranke and Burckhardt, and concludes
that "history manifests its reality existentially not ideally, personally and not
systematically, practically and not theoretically, *a posteriori* and not *a priori*,
materially and not formally, just because it is history and manifests itself historically. In a word: history to the historians! Briefly, this is the sense of the whole
discourse: in this simple, and perhaps for some too simple, knowledge, historiography reaches its highest point" (p. 43).

indisputably holds that we move in a world whose past is present in our memory and that by the industry of research students and historians we get to know it better. Scepticism, however, here as elsewhere, is hasty and lazy; it lingers and willingly dwells upon the contradictory and the irrational for lack of the vitality necessary to pass on from the initial promptings of a reasonable scepticism to that speculative inquiry which it stimulates and demands.

False evidence and false documents are manufactured by specific practical interests, which do not consider them as either false or true, but as means, as good as any other, to achieve specific ends; and often the rival factions vie with each other in the cleverness or brazenness with which they manufacture them, as we saw in the last war and as we see still today, now that we have taken to making war in peace time as well: indeed, one of the most painful sensations of our time is that of living in a welter of ever-renewed lies served up to us daily in proclamations, newspapers and books. Yet practical interests of no less importance are served by the labours of those who discover and demonstrate these falsifications: such labours serve not only opposing interests on the same plane, but the superior moral interest which aims at introducing and preserving as far as it can a loyalty notwithstanding inevitable conflicts in human relationships, thus saving the critical capacity from eclipse or decline, and upholding the honour of the cult due to sacred truth.

Since some falsifications of documents and evidence are punished by law, the discovery of falsifications occurs, to a considerable extent, in courts of law; and the criticism of evidence and documents, the refinement in methods of apposite inquiry, the establishment of rules, and the compilation of relevant treatises have been carried on both in the forensic world and in schools or erudition and philology, and theory makes no account of the difference in quality of the conclusions: of the fact that in courts of law the sentence is executive and leads to judgment with consequences which are practically or anyhow partially unalterable, while philology when it demonstrates errors always allows of revision, and this unlimited possibility of revision gives force and authority to these demonstrations. Philology has, indeed, especially during the last two centuries, accomplished great and good work in ruthlessly dealing with false documents, chronicles and histories! The most abundant crop has been found in ecclesiastical and conventional archives, because such forgers as are to be found among church people, void of scruples and confirmed in their activities by the concept of *pia fraus*, are not to be found in lay society, and it is not without significance that one of the first classical examples in which historical forgery was discovered and demonstrated was Lorenzo Valla's dissertation, *De falso credita et ementita Constantina Donatione*. Still there are thousands of counterfeited Roman inscriptions and hundreds of town histories and family genealogies and biographies forged for reasons of national or civic or family arrogance or to satisfy the vanity of learned persons filled with the ambition of discovery; not to mention all the Greek and Roman fakes for which factories sprang up in the Renaissance, which have not closed down since, and have indeed been supplemented by *objets d'art* of other ages and other artists, mediaeval and modern, who have since been prized. Innumerable volumes of memoirs of the eighteenth century, and of collections of letters of Marie Antoinette and Napoleon, were forged in the nineteenth century, especially in the first ten years of it; and nearer to our times there are the *Protocols of the Elders of Zion* and the *Chronicle of Ura-Linda* regarding Germanic origins, which have been used by the Racialists. Criticism has acquired so much acumen and experience in this field that it can proudly review the defeat of masses of forgers, who have tried from every side to attack and to overcome it and to deprive it of its vision of truth; it can almost smile at these vain efforts, armed as it is with its infallible methods.

But just as sometimes the criminal evades the law or the innocent is punished and the criminal goes free, it also happens that, in spite of the prompt exercise of criticism, there are still forgeries to be found in museums which pass for being authentic, and in our histories there are statements born of fanciful and credulous imagination or of conscious forgery. Even the best critics sometimes go wrong in condemning the false when it is genuine and vice versa, and so give rise to that sceptical doubt which we have been examining. Will it ever be possible to make history radically immune from forgeries and to establish truth securely? Who can protect it from all the clever and coherent and seemingly true fables based on witnesses who are supposed to be trustworthy? Who can summarily dismiss the doubts which can surround every document and every narrative just because they are practical things and may have been tampered with by someone for a particular purpose? And supposing that all evidence and all documents become suspect and are outlawed, what material will be left for the reconstruction of history? Perhaps we must be satisfied, in the making of history, with statements which do not exceed the limits of probability, of that probability which is so fragile and which often in everyday life shows up so poorly when confronted with the reality of facts. That would be a fine result and a fine advance on the part of modern historical thought, whose pioneer, Giambattista Vico, prided himself on having left the realm of the merely probable and reached "the certain" and "the true!"

If we are to find a way out of this perplexity[1] and clear up these doubts we must be quite clear and firm about the nature of documents and of well-founded facts, and about their place in historiographical work.

---

[1] It is a perplexity only for him who feels the intolerable sting: others get used to the idea of the probable and seek no farther. In the days of my youth the latter was the general state of affairs: there was a well-known book, *The Methods of Historical Study* (London, 1887), by an undoubtedly estimable historian, Freeman, who after describing all the traps into which history can fall, said: "We cannot reach mathematical certainty, we cannot reach a degree of certainty a good deal lower than mathematical certainty. But we can reach that high degree of likelihood which we call moral certainty, that approach to certainty on which reasonable men are content to act even in the gravest concerns of life. You believe that I am Regius Professor of Modern History; I believe it myself. But you have no proof of the fact, neither have I. Yet I did not decline to act because it is possible that what I believe to be Her Majesty's sign-manual appointing me may have been a forgery, for I certainly did not myself see Her Majesty sign it"; and so on in this vein (pp. 151–52).

First of all a vigorous definition of documents includes all the works of the past which can live to us through handwriting, musical notations, in pictures, in sculpture and in architecture, in technical equipment, in alterations of the crust of the earth, in profoundly spiritual transformations, in the changes suffered by political, moral and religious institutions, in the growth of virtues and sentiments which have gradually been formed in the course of centuries and are still alive and active in us. These are the documents which as they are gathered from time to time in our minds unite with abilities and thoughts and sentiments we have acquired to make possible a knowledge of what has happened, by means of a sort of platonic anamnesis, or rather by virtue of Vico's principle of the interchangeableness of truth and fact through which man, who has created history, eternally recognizes it and recreates it in his thought. Each single sort of historiography is based solely on this, and not only, as has often ingenuously been believed and said and is still believed and said, the historiography of poetry and art whose works are supposed to have the privilege of being always alive—no, for the works of the mind and of practical action are just as alive as these others; it is a question of re-discovering the freshness in them. Burckhardt noticed this without being fully aware of it when he read the literature of the fourteenth and the fifteenth centuries and remarked that if he still felt doubts about certain political facts, yet the moral life of those days was present to him and the *Kulturgeschichte*, as he called it, proceeded on no uncertain ground. The word "documents" is by historians usually confined to diplomas, notaries' acts, administrative acts, diplomatic papers and such-like, and these are certainly on the one hand remaining vestiges of the works of the past, but on the other hand they are evidence about facts and as such have to be classed among the assertions of witnesses: narratives themselves have a double face and however much discredited as narratives, by this very fact they acquire the value of documents. Those who have worked on research know how the merely stimulating character of documents, understood in an extrinsic sense, is proved by the fact that there comes a time when any further documents, already possessed or newly found, serve no useful purpose in the inquiry that is being undertaken, because the resuscitation has already occurred, and these documents do not add to it but only impede it.

Now if the true and genuine document is the work of the past, can such a work ever be faked? On this showing, in order to fake it is necessary to create, and the faker is a faker and not a poet or a painter or any other artist, nor an institutor of customs or religion. What can he do therefore and what does he, in fact, do? He works on what has already been created, he co-ordinates, copies, and gives his manufactured article the lustre of a new thing; but his work is empty. He may with artistic objects, which adorn certain houses and are exhibited in museums, deceive certain antiquarians, even some of the alert ones, though he mostly deceives those who are not expert or overtrustful, but we can never strike a new note in our hearts or enrich our historically formed consciousness. Take a sonnet written in the style of the fourteenth century, attributed to Petrarch and so well done as to persuade the expert of its authenticity and to be placed among those of Petrarch which it resembles: there it will remain for a shorter or longer time without offending, because among Petrarch's rhymes there are some of little value in which the author repeated himself working at them mechanically, just as today his forger worked at them, and though incapable of emulating Petrarch in his moments of genius is very capable of resembling him in the others. Take a brief philosophical treatise, a perfect imitation of Renaissance Latin, into which certain later philosophic concepts have been introduced, so that the man who has been taken in is amazed and confused to find that already in the fifteenth century there were people who thought in terms of "Cogito ergo sum" and of the *a priori* synthesis. There is confusion and astonishment, but the object of it in no way widens our thought, since the "cogito" and the *a priori* synthesis are already familiar to us in the names of Descartes and Kant, which are as extrinsic and indifferent to these concepts as the names, for example, of Ficino and Pico. The impossibility of artificially creating an original work is proved by a little noted fact: that whenever in dramas and in novels an artist, a philosopher, an explorer, a conqueror, or a statesman, are as *homines novi* brought into the story by an author, not being characters taken from history and introduced into dramas and novels called "historical" with specific references to history, the narrator or dramatist seems to be moving in a void and the reader feels it too, because the great works attributed to these heroes are but adjectives without substance, and they necessarily become fatuous and move jerkily like marionettes.

For this reason forgeries have never had any effective value: their only value has always been conferred by fantasy, just as a forged autograph only has a value for the superstitious cult around the name which has been forged. If an author of a really beautiful and therefore original and new poem or of a profound and new philosophic concept pretends for the sake of eccentricity or for any other motive that the work was by another or produced in another time, it is obvious that there is no forgery in the work, but only in the name of the author (as happens with supposed names and pseudonyms)—in other words, a forged testimony.

The importance, in the economy of knowledge, of well attested information explains the care with which it is collected and examined and passed through a critical sieve and protected against alterations, confusions and disposal. But in the limit of this importance, in the externality that must cling to it and the exactness which can never quite become truth, there lies an assurance that even if one or other piece of information is lacking or fallacious, history remains what it was. Thus in the history which more personally concerns each one of us, our diaries are arranged according to the years, the days and the hours referring to the information about our actions and our labours, and the figures of our accounts are a record of our credits and debits, and our legal papers are a record of our obligations and rights, and if one of these documents gets lost we are undoubtedly in for trouble, complications and losses. But we do not on that account lose consciousness of ourselves, of our intellectual and moral being, of that which we have been and of the reality of that which we now are; and every action and every cycle of actions in our past is outlined according to our knowledge of it, separately from actions which have preceeded or followed it: and this happens even when the day, the month and the year in which the action took place is doubtful. Our history is the history of our Soul and the history of the human Soul is the history of the world.

CHAPTER III

The Anecdote

Now that we are familiar with the clarifying concept of history as an act of consciousness arising out of a moral need which prepares and invokes action, it seems that all the descriptions and narrations of facts and of human passions born without this stimulus, void of this fundamental intention, and not answering to any special demand for action or education or preparation for action, are colourless, frivolous and empty: such are all those books called "memories," "reminiscences," "diaries," "chronicles," "anecdotes," "profiles," "portraits," "intimate and private lives," "curiosities," or whatever, of which there have always been, and still are, a great number, almost greater than the number of historical works.

And yet, once the reflection of this clarifying beam from without has been curtained off, all these reprehensible tales and stories immediately take on their vivid colouring and many-sided attractiveness again; they speak to our hearts, the heart which beats for all the imagery of power and greatness, and shares now with trepidation and melancholy, now with indulgent smiles, in every human affection, revolutions and despair and dreams and follies, yes, all of them, from the stories and descriptions in the lives of Plutarch to those very different lives of the Holy Fathers and the ascetics, the biographies of a Cromwell, a Napoleon, a Goethe, a Byron, a Foscolo, a Columbus, a Galileo, a Bruno, a Vico, a Voltaire, and a Kant down to those depictions, which win so much favour, of the gallant society of the eighteenth century, of the Marie Antoinettes, the Pompadours, the du Barrys, and the Casanovas, of the characters and incidents of the great Revolution and of that period which was afterwards called and idolized as "the Romantic," and so on. Who will have the heart to deny

the title of history to that which provides the chief or the sole
food to lovers of tales of the past who are convinced they can
learn and know "history" by that medium?

Truth to tell, not much courage is wanted to deny it, because
there has always been a distinction—it is even found in ordinary
treatises on the elements of literature—between history and
memoirs, history and chronicles, history and anecdotes; history
has always been considered as something that was more severe
—more elevated, compared to the others, compared to "the
anecdotal," which may serve to cover all those kinds of work.
"Anecdotal" not in the etymological sense, which means "un-
edited information," but in the other sense which the word has
come to take on, and which is only barely connected with the
former, of information upon particular, separate, unconnected
events, which therefore stand in no relation to any superior
event: lights which blaze and fade out one after the other and do
not light up the landscape, but are fitful fires.

However, we must even here beware of believing, and even
more of acting, as though that which is distinguished or excluded
from a particular form of spiritual activity need or ought to be
excluded or thrown out of the life of the world, dispersed and
annulled. The anecdotal is not history, but it has good and
intrinsic reason for existence, and love of it is not at all illicit.
It only becomes so when it seeks to supplant history. "j'aime bien
autant," Montaigne said (II. 10), "veoir Brutus chez Plutarch
que chez luy mesme"; but the "autant" then changed to a
"plutost"; " je choiserois plutost de scavoir au vray les devis
qu'il tenoit en sa tente à quelqu'un de ses privez amis, la veille
d'une bataille, que les propos qu'il teint le lendemain à son
armée et ce qu'il faisoit en son cabinet et en sa chambre que ce
qu'il faisoit emmy la place, et au sénat;" whence the descent is
easy to the saying of Prosper Merimée: "de l'histoire je n'aimé
que les anecdotes": which is certainly liking too little, and liking
nothing that is historical.

The anecdote is born and bred out of a need to keep alive and
increase the experience of the most diverse and varied mani-

festations of the human soul; collecting into a sort of herbal more and more new specimens from ever new places. Just as the need for knowledge of a given historical situation arises out of deliberation about an action which has to be undertaken now, or about a point of view to be taken in the continual and urgent battle of life, so the desire to know about the manifestation of the human soul arises out of life in general, the generic human drama which accompanies the specific historical drama. That is why information of this kind is often called "common" or "vulgar." History searches out the special and peculiar character of institutions and customs which men of action jointly set up; of the concepts and systems elaborated by philosophers, of the poems and pictures which the artists create; because all these spiritual facts are premises of new facts which are in preparation. The anecdotic recalls to the man of action in what way, and in what circumstances, other men of action braced themselves for their work; the difficulties, often very prosaic, which they had to overcome, their errors, how they loved and hated and were loved and hated, their torments and consolations, their despair and their rejoicing; similarly it speaks to the philosopher about philosophers, to the poets about poets, to the saint about saints, and to the more humble who are concerned with less dignified affairs about those who were like them, and whom they would like to resemble. The principle behind the anecdote departs from that gravity of history which is its serious practical interest; it was called in antiquity by Flavins Vopiscus, a writer of anecdotal biographies 'curiositas,' which might (he added) seem "frivola," but which 'nil recusat,' because "minima quaeque jucunda sunt et habent aliquid gratiae cum legunter."[1] The selection of one or other of a series of anecdotes and the sentiment which the narrator or the reader lends to one or the other, depends on the elevated or mean quality of the initial need; but from the formal point of view the genesis and nature of the anecdote is always the same.

[1] *In Script. Hist. Aug.*, ed. Peter: see the lives of Carus XXI and of Probus II: compare that of Aurelius X and of the tyrant Firmus XII.

The Anecdote

Since these anecdotes are pictures of the human in the widest
sense, one might be led to think that the need referred to could
be equally well satisfied with ingenious depictions of the possible,
in fact with novels, which represent the most varied situations in
which a man may find himself and his most varied reactions, and
themselves, too, have their effect upon attitudes of mind and
practical action, since novels of various sorts excite and sharpen
the attention not only of lovers (love stories), but of warriors
(books of chivalry) and men of adventure (adventurous tales).
But it is not so, and everyone knows it: we have all had occasion
to see the changed force and the disillusionment of children when
they are told that the story they have been listening to wide-
eyed "is not a true story," and one remembers the poor story-
teller who went blind, but continued holding the book in his
hand as though he were reading out of it, but was deserted by his
listeners once they discovered his infirmity and saw that he was
not reading any more out of "the book," that book which was
for them the guarantee of reality. The characters of novels
inasmuch as they contributed to experience and to practical
example, are at that moment believed in and thought of as men
belonging to the reality of events. The information in anecdotes
must refer or pretend to refer to things which have happened, for
only in this way can they satisfy the need they have described.

This peculiarity of theirs, which is indispensable, certainly does
not make them "historical"; events are only historical in so far
as they are thought of within an historical development, and this
information is in no way so connected. Although this information cannot rank as historically understood and versified, yet
it is ascertained information because it is certified with good
testimony that has been checked and approved by the criticism
of evidence and documents; it has been coloured by imagination,
but only within certain limits, and it claims belief as being true.
To withhold belief on the strength of a hypocritical scepticism
would be as imprudent as is the extreme opposite, of a foolish
credulity. One should be "in lectione historiorum" (as Francesco
Balduino, the tenth-century pamphleteer, said) "neque pueri

121

neque senes, ad credendum neque nimium faciles neque nimium difficiles." The need for the truth of the events in anecdotes lies in the very nature of the need for anecdotes which is the desire to know not possible but effectual occurrences, in fact to know what has been the real capacity of humanity for action and suffering in good and evil conditions, and thence infer in the future what can be done and suffered or reasonably expected. In this way the objection, so often made about certain tales and certain ideals that they are "poets' dreams" is parried. They are not poets' dreams like those of the golden age, or of the Knights of the Round Table, for while ascertained knowledge of human life through the centuries discourages us from believing that men, however great they may be, can ever be free of weakness and mistakes, it also shows that there have always been and always will be sublime sacrifices and deeds of amazing goodness and beauty and men of generous heart and courageous spirit, so that (as in Goethe's lament for the Death of Euphorion) hearts regain confidence, and there is the refreshing thought that "the earth will bring forth those again as it has always brought them forth."

For these reasons the anecdote persists and will persist side by side with history, each serving diverse and complementary purposes in the harmony of the spirit. In periods when intellectual and moral life is active each of the two advances with equal strength, and more intense development of the most vigorous and philosophical historiography will not take the place enjoyed by memoirs, lives, and all the other anecdotes. The most severe historical thinker and craftsman will from time to time read or even write this kind of book, and not only as mere *levamina mentis*, nor only because the mind refreshes and comforts itself by passing from one form of spiritual activity to another and continuously reintegrates its harmony by relaxing the tension of historical thought in favour sometimes of the different tension of poetry, and sometimes of the anecdote.

The relation between the two, however, is not one of matter as compared to form as Montaigne held; Montaigne, whom we will go on quoting since he noticed, and for all practical purposes distinguished, between the two different treatments of occurrences, calling the one *simple* history and the other *excellent*, and saying that he loved either historians who were *fort simples* like *le bon Froissart*, or historians who were *excellents*. But then he went and overloaded the definition of the one kind, which was so pleasing and attractive to him, describing it as *"la matière de l'histoire une et informe,"* while he left to the other *le jugement entier pour la cognoissance de la verité*. What does correspond to the relation between form and matter is the relation between history and erudition or philology; philology, which has characteristics of exactness, but can never have those of truth as history has, nor those of a probable human reality as the anecdote has. The erudites and the philologists are and must always be arid, cold and indifferent (and that is the duty of their office), compared with deeply stirred historians and intimate writers of anecdotes. On the other hand, the history which Montaigne hated because it stood *entre deux*, and which was, he said, *la plus commune façon*, the work of writers *qui nous gastent tout*, because they want *nous mascher les morceaux*, and claim it as their function to pass judgment, *et pour consequent d'incliner l'histoire à leur fantaisie*; this is not an intermediate form, but is the premonition of true history itself, which dissatisfaction at what is dispersed and not-thought-out in the anecdote has rendered distinct from anecdotal narrative; and thus severed, pursues its path as best it can. It may be rough, awkward, bestrewn with explanations which do not explain, with arbitrary judgments, inadequate and confused concepts; but it will no longer be anecdotal. And it is this, and not the anecdote, which enters into the history of historiography, enters with its positive moment or moments, and also its negative moments upon which further progress depends. The histories which are *excellents* are just those in which the positive moments follow each other more continuously and more comprehensively, although they, too, must at some point break down in negative moments, if only by reason of the circumscription and limitation of the spiritual interests which inspire them and make them appear unsatisfactory to anyone who studies the material with new questions, and correspondingly new concepts in mind.

Finally, the problem which worried above all the romantic age and is not dead yet today, of the linking of history and anecdote in order to make a complete work and a really perfect history, to which the former would contribute a philosophical interpretation, and the latter a vividness in the presentation; the former the design and the latter the colour; this problem is non-existent. The distinction between design and colour is metaphorical in any historiographical discussion; it is as fragile as in painting, where design and colour in an ultimate analysis are one. In truth, historiography has its own design-colour, and so has the anecdote; the one and the other, each in its way, are thought and presentation; each has its own vividness of style. Any attempt to merge them would only make a hotchpotch, a muddle in which history and anecdote would be at loggerheads, each of them fighting against different interests and spiritual attitudes. If the question then arises as to how historical and anecdotal narrations can eventually be included in a single exposition, the problem set in this way is not, like the former one, of a logical nature and logically ill-founded, but of a purely literary nature and well founded in this respect because we cannot deny that it may sometimes, for certain purposes, be useful to unite history and anecdote in a single whole with a literary subordination sometimes of the one and sometimes of the other, treating now the one and now the other as a running aside, and finding a style to match both. But the art of literary composition has nothing to do with scientific methodology, which is here under discussion.

In quite a different way, historiography borrows from historical collections of anecdotes when it likes, not to supply any integral parts of its thought, but solely for image-forms of "expression"; and it idealizes the anecdotes so used in relation to its concepts and judgments, so that they become mere symbols of the latter. As far as possible only those anecdotes which are supported by critically examined evidence are used for this purpose, but if there are mistakes, and if criticism, as often happens, changes its mind and regrets what it had just accepted, there is no substantial loss or change in the true history itself, because the anecdotes had not been used for the purpose of proving anything. It may be that Madame Roland did not exclaim, as she went to the guillotine: "Oh Liberty! What crimes are committed in thy name!" or that her Neapolitan co-religionist, Eleonora de Fonseca, did not say, when preparing for a similar fate, "Forsan et haec olim meminisse juvabit"; it may be that both sayings were fashioned by their admirers or friends, or that they arose of their own accord out of a series of mistakes and misunderstandings. Nevertheless these sayings are very truly symbolic of the stout hearts and high purpose of those intellectuals, the dreamers of liberty and humanity who incited the French and Neapolitan revolutions and represented them and died in them. The symbolic idealism of the anecdote in history explains why philologists meet with so much impatience and annoyance when they scrutinize evidence and then destroy legends. Although they cannot do otherwise, and their profession must be exercised by someone, their activity seems almost to trample on and to mock the ideal significance of the legends that have been criticized. Among others, Goethe used to call down damnation on those who said that the stories of Lucretia's and Mucius Scaevola's heroism were spurious and false, because he was quite convinced that the false and spurious could only be absurd, void, obtuse and unfruitful, and never beautiful or inspiring, and that "if the Romans were great enough to invent things like that, we at least should be great enough to believe in them."[1] Burckhardt,[2] too, defended the typical or mythological which is so common, and indeed interwoven in the stories of ancient Greece, a sort of *historia altera*, an imagined history which tells what people believed these men capable of and what their most characteristic features.

Although the anecdote as such cannot be converted into

---

[1] *Gespräche mit Schumann*, October 15, 1825: cf. March 11, 1832.
[2] *Griechische kulturgeschichte*, section VIII, chap. 6.

historiography, and therefore cannot be resolved in thought, yet thought can very well afford its company to anecdote and give rise in such narrations to moral, political and aesthetic observations and to references to history.

That is what the best writers of anecdotes do; and intelligent anecdotes are thus distinguished from vulgar ones, just as the moral affinities of the spirit draw a distinction between frivolous and serious anecdotes, between noble and ignoble, and between those which speak to man of man and those which discourse to him of all that is animal and bestial in him and mislead him into favouring and cultivating it.

CHAPTER IV

The Imagination—The Anecdote and Historiography

HISTORICAL writers and research workers on the one hand protest that history has nothing to do with the *folle du logis*, fancy, but on the other hand they frequently allow that historical construction cannot be achieved without the aid of fancy. It is odd to see how this second opinion is not spoken by them with the humility of one acknowledging his own limitations or impotence, but with a kind of complacency as of one who says "I'm a painter, too!" These writers are angry when accused of being arid pedants, as they hoped to find they, too, possessed the divine gift of the Muses and fancied themselves to be among the inspired prophets and poets.

We must disenchant them about this, because the faculty which they observe in their works is not poetic fancy, but the associative imagination. These are two different gifts which the highest aesthetics and the highest criticism of art have always kept quite separate; they cannot be united even empirically because there are men of the most fertile imagination, but almost wholly deprived of poetic fancy, and there are poets of slight imagination who yet excel in the vividness with which they endow their phantoms. Neither can the associative imagination be interchanged with the imagination which thinks out the conjectures and hypotheses for the purpose of giving direction to research which completely fulfil themselves in that task of discovery. That of which we are speaking, though, intervenes directly in historiographical work in order to fill the gaps left in the series of images arising out of information which has been attested and critically verified; which intervenes sometimes more and sometimes less, but always (provided the writer is not restricting himself to copying or summarizing his sources) does intervene to overcome the interruptions in the information and to weave the thread of the story with complete perspicacity, and "imaginative persuasiveness" as the ancients said (they spoke of a φαντασία πιθανή). The sources say that a certain personage famous already for his ability and eloquence went one day to confer with another personage and signed a pact with him, but historiography will say that owing to his ability and eloquence he persuaded him to sign the pact. Documentary sources say that a man who was a noble knight found out that his wife was unfaithful, and killed her: the historiographer will add that he killed her not in a rage of jealousy and hatred, but because of his intransigent feeling of honour. The documents say that Francesco Petrarca came to Naples from Marseilles at the end of March 1431, and was examined there by King Robert for three days before he went to Rome to receive his laurels: the historiographer will colour this story, showing how Petrarch crossed the piazza delle Corregge with its princely Angevin houses, walked into the new castle where the king lived, and how those three days were spent in discussions of problems by the king and the poet, both equally intent to make a show of doctrines and subtleties. This is what Ernest Renan called "Solliciter doucement les textes," although his own solicitations were not always so mild as those we have quoted as examples. Whether mild or brusque, careful or bold, these solicitations are the work of the imagination; they can all be disputed, because in the first example the pact could have been signed not on account of the ability and eloquence of the able and eloquent man, but because of the astuteness of the other man who let his interlocutor believe that he had won, calculating the while how best he could serve his own ends. In the second case the noble knight might have killed his unfaithful wife for a less honourable motive, that of ridding himself of a wife who was a burden, and in the third case Petrarch, when he crossed the square, might not have seen the princely Angevin houses, and Robert of Anjon (for example) might have received him in one of his other Neapolitan castles or houses and not in the new castle, and the three days' exercise in scientific discussion might have consisted not in competition between two vanities, but in boredom of one of the parties at having to sustain and feed the vanity of the other.

Some writers of treatises on historical methods like Bernheim, try to keep that dangerous ally, imagination, away from the process of integration by insisting that the associating faculty is clearly and sufficiently distinct from the imagination. Since the former "does not create and does not want to create anything new," but "only tries to re-establish the connecting links which have disappeared, and does not thereby lose itself in arbitrary associations of ideas and representations, but binds itself rigorously to the real data of historical tradition and to effectual analogy, drawn from experience, of the course of human affairs in general and of historical affairs in particular," and that, in fact, if the integrating connection "needs the imagination, it is nevertheless not a function of the imagination."[1] And indeed in this case it is not a legitimate function of the imagination to succumb to the stimulus of whatever is pleasing, and to paint great heroes and evil spirits or loving and beautiful creatures or scenes of grief and horror, the way novels do. When history writers let themselves go in this way they are blamed and soon neglected on account of the discredit attaching to them. The end historians have in view when they use, must use such expedients, is to get as close as possible to that which occurred, and the principle which guides such work is that of "verisimilitude" or "probability."

The associative capacity or the "gift of attachment" ("Verknüpfungsgabe" Wilhelm von Humboldt called it), seemed profoundly mysterious at first, and almost like an inspired and prophetic manifestation,[2] seemed so for want of an analysis of the reasons why the likely or probable are so often made to play a rôle in past events. The principle of probability belongs primarily to

---

[1] *Lehrbuch der historischen Methode* (5th–6th ed., Leipzig, 1908), pp. 614–16.
[2] Bernheim, I. C.

considerations not of that which had happened and is over, but of that which has to be done and belongs to the future. It is simply a drawing upon our experience of how things usually worked out, of what have been reckoned to be the regularities or propensities of nature. Correlatively our experience is also, it is true, experience of the unusual, of the diverse and of the interrupted habit. When, however, discussion takes place upon action about to be undertaken, the former aspect weighs more heavily with anyone who does not conceive of his actions as a continual reckless gamble. Thus one who wants to undertake a pleasure trip will fix the date for the month of April when spring is pleasant and temperate, or if he wants to marry he will choose a bride from a family where the women have been models of every virtue for many generations; or if he wants to acquire a car he will buy it in a factory famed for the solidity of its products. It may, of course, happen that the season, the wife, and the car chosen by him will be disappointing and give him some unpleasant surprises, and then he will face the unexpected situation and get out of it as best or as worst he can. In any case, however, if he behaved wisely in making his choice he will not be obliged to utter that bitter reproach addressed to himself by George Dandin, "Tu l'as voulu George Dandin!" Now why does this scrutiny of the probable which happens and can only happen when action is under consideration, get projected back into the knowledge of the past, where it does not seem to refer to any need or use? That the fancies which fill the lacunae of verified information are probable is a matter which is of no practical consequence, and does not shed any new light or knowledge—cannot do so since they are fancies and not affirmations of reality. The scrutiny of the probable has only one justification, and that a true one: that it should satisfy a practical need for the exercise of sentiment, judgment and action through the imagination, which wants living, coherent and harmonious images, and will not be content with odd pieces and scrapheaps; and thus, when it meets with an able and eloquent person (well certificated as such), demands that he shall have conformed to his type even in the cases in which it is not possible to know whether these gifts served him well. And when it meets with a chivalrous man, it attributes chivalrous sentiments to him even when he may have harboured much lower sentiments; in fact, when it has to deal with an unfinished picture it completes it in order to enjoy the completed picture better.

And thus we once again come up against the idea of a history doubly enslaved to imagination and probability, because first the documents on which it is based are only "probably" trustworthy, and secondly the stories told, whenever they go beyond what is vouched for by the probable sources, only "probably" represent things as they happened. We are back indeed at the idea of history as the meanest form (if it can be called form at all) of human knowledge, its foundation unstable, and its walls cemented by imagination.

But that which is here conventionally called "history" only deserves, as we have already shown, the name of "anecdote" which naturally deals with affairs in a generic and abstract way and never reaches the concrete and historical in human affairs, and by its method of ascertaining and of exposition reveals that it verges on the confines of the historical novel. By the best authors the anecdote is firmly restrained from straying from the sources, yet it must so stray in order to tell its story, even though it keeps close to experience (in any case variable) of the usual and the normal. And since experience includes also the opposite, the discontinuous and the extraordinary, it is easy to become ever bolder with these integrations until, from hardihood to hardihood, the most imaginative of imaginative historical novels is reached. The distinction between the anecdote and the historical novel is not absolute but empirical, approximative and gradual, and we must accept this situation which nothing can alter. The call that the events recounted shall be real and not imaginary can only be satisfied within this framework in so far as the element of imagination which cannot be completely annulled, is reduced to a minimum.

History, true and proper historiography, which stands not in the lowest but in the highest, indeed exclusive rank of knowledge, these are not subject to such anxieties and spasms, because they are not "anecdotal," so that they exclude imagination altogether, and are solely explained in thought. Not of course in thought arising out of a spirit, void of imagination and fancy and desire and passion, for all these things thought feeds on and they burn in its flame; but in thought whose flame shines by its own light. The assistance of the connecting faculty or of imagination would be superfluous, because "the fact" is vital and active in true historiography, and is converted by it into "the true."

CHAPTER V

Philology, History and Philosophy

DROYSEN is the writer who has most clearly perceived and resolutely affirmed that historiography consists of the "Frage," of putting the historical question. This is a fertile concept which he sets forth in the definition that the aim of historiography is "to understand by inquiry" (*forschend zu verstehen*),[1] though he did not elaborate it with sufficient emphasis or depth or application. His concept liberates the mind of the fallacious belief that historiography is, or must be, some sort of copy or imitation of reality, and admits of viewing it as the true and unique form of knowledge, that is: as the answering of those questions and the resolution of those theoretical problems which the reality of life continually raises.

But the formula of the "Frage" remains generic and vague unless the character of the historiographical question is now strictly determined and distinguished from the philological question with which it is often confused. There is, for example, a great difference between asking what are the series of authentic documents, or what is the chronological succession of the facts of the Lutheran reformation, and what, on the other hand, was the nature and office of the Lutheran reformation. The first question arises out of the technical need of the erudite who want to collect and arrange the materials for the history they are writing; the second comes from the moral need for intelligent orientation. The first, therefore, does not lead to direct knowledge, but to the practical preparation for a future knowledge; the second is this very knowledge itself. How peaceful, how restful, and how leisurely is the labour of the erudite who are

---

[1] J. G. Droysen, *Historik. Vorlesungen über Encyclopädie und Methodologie der Geschichte*, ed. Hubner (München-Leipzig, 1937), p. 34, cl. n. 22, et passim.

not drawn in to the human drama, nor into difficult comprehension and judgment of the human drama, but like the Goethian
Wagner, find heavenly pleasure in scanning and consulting
books and in fingering a grand old parchment; and how tormenting, on the other hand, and charged with responsibility is
the fate of the historian "mid mournful cries, still studious" (to
use Thomas Campanella's saying), as he meditates upon the
course, the tragic course of human affairs, in which we are both
spectators and actors! If the two kinds of questions or inquiries
are not kept distinct, it usually leads to a compounding of
historiography with simple erudition, or the mortification of the
very virtue of historiography.

Another consequence of the confusion between the tasks of
philology and of historiography is the all too simple belief that,
because the collecting and separation of philological material
happens without direct philosophical elaboration, therefore
philosophy (the critical use of categories whereby reality is
perceived) is not necessary, indeed is harmful to historiography.
Instead of these categories empirical or representative concepts
are considered sufficient for historiographical research, and it is
recommended to keep them flexible, fluid, light of form, apt
to relax some of their determinations, and to receive new ones,
so as not to do violence to the individuality of events, but to
accompany them discreetly.

There is no point in tarrying here to confute such an ingenuous
logical and gnoseological theory, nor to point out that it lacks
even a hint as to what are pure concepts, without which no
historical knowledge and no historiographical proposition is
born, but instead of that emphasizes the classificatory and pseudo-
conceptual concepts by means of which historical knowledge
is more easily grouped for exposition and attention. It is more
important to single out a graver and more immediate error in
the matter of those classificatory concepts. Their various origin
and quality is often misunderstood, and with that the different
ways in which they can be used and be useful.

In controversies among historians the flexibility and fluidity and lightness of form which are rightly commendable in empirical concepts are frequently upheld as desirable for other concepts which are not empirical: like, for example, "Renaissance," "illuminism," "liberation," "classicism," "baroque," "romanticism;" of which it is urged that they are not strictly capable of definition, and that any definition of them would prove to be arbitrary; that therefore the reality to be kept in mind and considered is that of epochs, of individuals, and of societies as they are directly and immediately apprehended.

Very recently in a lecture by one of the most thoughtful students of our contemporary history, dealing with the concepts of classicism and romanticism, I read that he considered the attempt to reach definite clarity and precision in these concepts as "hopeless (*aussichtlos*), as was apparent from the endless and ever new criticisms roused by the efforts to define the essence of romanticism." The mental sciences (Meinecke adds) "cannot elaborate these concepts in such a way as to give them the exactness of natural science: and, I dare to say, that they must not do so, because what is most precious and refined in spiritual life would be in danger of being lost in the *caput mortum* of a definition. Because of this we do not wish to reject the efforts made to arrange spiritual phenomena in concepts, which would only precipitate the mental sciences into chaos. But such definitions can only claim a provisional value since the life of the spirit and of historical configurations so produced is of a fluid kind and capable of multiform changes, and can only be known in ever new aspects and movements."[1]

On the contrary, there is need for a rigorous and correct definition of "romanticism," "classicism," "the baroque," and similar terms in the history of art, just as for "monism," "dualism," "materialism," and "mysticism," and similar philosophical terms, and for "absolutism," "democracy," "Renaissance," and "reformation," and similar terms in political and civil life: because, failing such definition, one might as well never

[1] F. Meinecke, *Klassizismus, Romantizismus und historisches Denken im XVIII. Jahrhundert* (Cambridge, Mass., 1937, pp. 1-2).

use words which become empty and void of meaning. All these concepts refer to the dialectics of spiritual forms or categories, within which they find their balance, and when resolved their complete truth. They are consistent in thought, and not merely in imagination: whereas empirical or representative concepts are only consistent with the image which has suggested and represents them. But the true concepts are not in themselves provisional and approximate, nor to be taken as in themselves corresponding roughly or broadly to the reality of events; they become so (and this is a point which must be kept in mind), only when used like classificatory concepts for ordinary and classifying purposes. They will not be available for this office at all if they have not previously been formed, that is, if they have not previously been well defined; but for the purposes of classification they naturally take on quantitative determinations of "more" and "less," and their classification must, by implication, always be merely a guide to the summing up of facts in the mass. For example: the baroque is a vice of artistic expression, which substitutes for beauty an effect due to the surprising or the unexpected; and this definition, just because it is precise, assists judgment. When, however, an attempt is made to classify a work, an artist, or an age, according to the same concept, it is understood that in that work, in that artist, and in that age, there will be non-baroque elements, because in every man there is the whole man. The same can be said of political absolutism which is the substitution of the will of one man for the actions arising out of the will of single individuals which are in contrast, and yet thereby became harmonious. There is no completely absolute age, just as there is no completely democratic age, and the necessary use of a concept to classify certain régimes and certain ages does not exclude the existence of liberty in absolute régimes and absolute moments in régimes qualified as democratic. If then we do not boldly refer the distinctions between epochs to the concepts which underly them, and do not reduce these in turn to their philosophical terms, we shall always find historians struggling with the clay into which they have plunged their hand. . . . (What is "Christianity"? What is the "Reformation"? What is the "Renaissance?" What is "Romanticism"?, etc.) and unable to elaborate a single constructed or formed object, nor even to get their hands out of the mess.

Such anxiety to avoid the logical duty of defining classificatory concepts of non-empirical origin or, as they are now called, functional concepts (serving the classificatory function) is perhaps one of the last manifestations of the reluctance and the fear (or reluctance due to fear) felt by the historiography of the nineteenth century towards philosophy, with which it had previously boasted itself on good terms. At the same time there was a demand for a theory and a methodology of historical studies which should not be a particular philosophy or philosophy in general. "Sociology," then much vaunted and recommended —Dugald Stewart called it "theoretical historiography"—put the historians instinctively on their guard partly on account of its trivial and superficial sponsors, but mainly on account of the confused perception which they had, that sociology, if it was to be more than a sequence of generic classificatory schemes, tended to issue into a naturalistic positivism, the enemy of everything spiritual and historical. Unintentionally, and often in opposition to its own firm intentions and explicit protests, the new theory, under the name of "History," took a dangerous philosophic turn, so much so that the timid shunned the word with its pretensions and wrote "manuals of historical method." In fact, under the name of "Historics" nothing less was attempted than to provide historical studies with an implement analogous to that which Kant had provided for the physical and natural sciences in the *Critique of Pure Reason*; philosophical tendencies and attitudes appear in those who sought to discover or tried to use this instrument, like Humbolt, Droysen, and Dilthey. Droysen, who gave the very first schematic treatise on this subject, thus defined the new science: "Historics is not an encyclopedia of historical sciences; it is not a philosophy (or teleology) of history; it is not the physics of the historical world; still less is it poetics for historians. Its object is to construct an implement for historical thought and research."[1] The four negative definitions can be fully accepted, and so can the fifth and positive one derived from Aristotle and Bacon, because all the concepts which are abstracted from concrete judgment or historical knowledge can only serve as an implement or instrument for that knowledge. But what is this theory, which is neither an encyclopedia, nor a fantastic and arbitrary philosophy of history, nor physics, sociology, or aesthetics, and which is said to be an implement of thought and historical research?

There can be no doubt about our answer: in this much involved theory we can only discern philosophy, the whole of philosophy, which is always intrinsic in historiographical statements; philosophy which can be formulated abstractly or methodologically only in so far as it can clear away difficulties and bring strength to judgments, that is, to effective thought and historical narration. If further proof were needed, Droysen's own treatise would supply it, wherein not only are serious logical problems perforce dealt with, but the universe is surveyed and the concepts of nature and of man, of the aims of man and of society, of language, of art, of the sciences, of religion, economics, law, politics, and so on[2] are defined: in fact, all concepts may from time to time require a new and more particular elaboration, because all are necessary to the historian.

The conclusion that philosophy serves no other purpose than as a "methodology of historical thought" has often been formulated and doctrinally demonstrated by me to the great displeasure of the so-called pure philosophers. Sometimes, where certain fundamental yet particular truths are concerned, one feels strongly disposed to throw off doctrinal armour, and, in the belief that philosophy is good sense, to turn straight to good sense and ask it briefly in the present case—whether there is anything else to be known in the world other than the events

---

[1] In the *Grundriss der Historik* (reprinted in the recent edition of *Historik* 16).

[2] See especially the second part "Systematik," in the *Grundriss* and in the *Vorlesungen*.

among which we live and have to work, and whether philosophic
reflection can ever be justified as anything but a way or method
by which to achieve this sole effective and useful knowledge.
Perhaps good sense which usually wears a smile may reply that
philosophy pursued for its own sake and outside historical knowledge, is only to be found as a profession among others by which
man earns his living, and as such is worth little because it has
been removed from its live source whence it arose and in which
it can renew itself.

CHAPTER VI

The "Philosophy of History"

As we have noted, "philosophy of history" used to mean in the primitive sense which it had in the eighteenth century, "considerations upon history," or else just history conceived in relation to the concept of humanity and civilization, conceived therefore in a more philosophical manner than it had been by historiographers who obeyed the rule of old religious beliefs or by mere erudites, chroniclers, diplomats, and narrators of military affairs. It was an unceremonious and quite innocent use of the term. But when it is taken strictly within the terms in which it is enunciated, then it contains a strident, though not universally evident, incongruity and superfluity because the conception of history already involves philosophy, nor can one philosophize without referring to events which are history.

It is just in this excess, and therefore in this defect of philosophers, in this shooting beyond the mark into a theoretical void, that the "philosophy of history" consists, in the scientific sense in which the formula recurs in methodological discussions; and in this sense it is nothing less than a particular case of a false theoretical position; it belongs to the phenomenology of error.

Understood in this way, it could not even have an appearance of solidity or an illusory existence if it had to do without the partitions according to time, space and the classification of events by which historical narrations are usually schematized and ordered for their better recording and transmission; if it could not lay hold on these representative fictions and raise them to spiritual categories, converting them verbally (since it is not possible to do so intellectually) from empirical and material into speculative and formal: in which process correlatively the categories of the spirit are materialized and made empirical, and each corrupts the other.

This process of caprice and confusion can be observed in the works of "philosophy of history." In one book the Orient will be identified with "immediate consciousness," Greece with the "liberty of the individual," Rome with "abstract generalities" or with "the State," the German world with the "union of the individual and the universal," or "union of worldliness and spirituality." In another book the Orient will be identified with the "infinite," Greco-Roman antiquity with the "finite," and the Christian era with the "synthesis of the finite and the infinite." In yet another ancient history gets identified with the idea of "destiny," the Christian age with the idea of "nature," and the future is envisaged with an idea of "providence." The philosophers of history who use materialist concepts or pseudo-categories like the Marxists proceed in the same way when they identify ancient times with the concept of "slave economy," the Middle Ages with that of a "serf economy," the modern age with "capitalistic economy," and the future with the "socialization of the means of production"; it is the same with the racialists who are concerned with geographical and linguistic groupings of peoples, converting them fantastically into pure races with a perpetual and constant existence, then dividing them into inferior and superior races identified with ideas of virtue and vice, of spiritual forces and their contrary defects, of heroism, prowess, religious speculative and artistic capacity as opposed to baseness, vileness, irreligiousness, mental weakness, lack of genius, and so on.

When classificatory representations have been thus idealized and ideas have been thus personified in hybrid forms which clutter up the field of the mind in its various attitudes and combinations, the reflection of all this is to be found in the diverse theistic, pantheistic, materialist, monist, dualist, and dialectic philosophies, and in the opposing and combining feelings of optimism and pessimism, from which they draw their elements. There are philosophies of history which start from a primitive condition, from a state of spontaneity and innocence, from a sort of terrestrial paradise, which are then lost so that, passing through the hells and purgatories of succeeding ages, they regain paradise in a higher form with no further risk of ever losing it. This is the most common type, and is to be found in historical materialism with its Eden, half blessed, half brutish, in primitive communism, with its hard historical intermezzo and its rationalistic and most blessed communism of the future. There are others which describe the struggle between two principles of good and evil, and happiness and pain, with the final victory to the principle of good and happiness, accompanied by a paradise on earth or in heaven. But there are yet others which outline an irreparable and even more disastrous decadence following upon the exit from Eden, and who see a liberation in the painful acquisition of a growing knowledge of invincible human unhappiness which will conduct society to an ascetic annihilation of the will and to a deliberate universal suicide. Philosophies of history, like religions, tend to make themselves transcendental and so come to be possessed of the evil consequences, more or less material and materialistic, of transcendental ethics.

The confusion of concept and imagination is the very constructive principle of myths; this mythological character of philosophies of history is self-evident. They all want to discover and reveal the "Weltplan," the design of the world from its birth to its death, or from its entry into time to its entry into eternity, and they take on the shapes of theophany and cacodaemonophany. Indeed the relationship in this case is not only ideal but historical: the philosophy of history which the Germans claimed for a thoroughly new and thoroughly German science grew to its full stature in an atmosphere prepared by Protestantism and the Bible with that never-forgotten dream of Nebuchadnezzar interpreted by Daniel about the successive kingdoms of gold, silver, copper, iron and clay: the scheme of the four monarchies which the Renaissance had evicted from its historical books and expressly criticized and rejected.

Vico's historical thought in these matters belongs neither to the Protestant Reformation nor to the traditions of the Catholic Church, but solely to the Renaissance. Philosophizing and the making of myths about the chronological course of history is quite extraneous to it. It seeks on the contrary to find the categories (or as he calls them the modifications of the mind) which must always govern history even if (as he says) there are infinite worlds. According as they dominate or preponderate they outline the various historical epochs. It is a gross error against which I have often protested, but which still persists, or is often restated in treatises upon the history of philosophy or the philosophy of history, to place the work of Vico in the vanguard of that Germanic "philosophy of history." The latter was substantially a mythological formation, even though philosophers of great merit played with it, whereas Vico's work was a genuine philosophical inquiry, born of critical thought, developed by subsequent criticism and still alive today and in a flourishing state.

Since the philosophy of history does its work or plays its game, if you like, upon the divisions and subdivisions which are the usual groupings of historiography, it is not concerned with the original thought or construction of history, but deals with it ready made, thought out, recounted, and provided with headings, summaries which are then used as a foundation. By refining or rather contorting these it is said the "inside" history, the true, underlying the apparent, history is produced; and this is simply the mythology already referred to. In this way we get a duality: on the one hand historical accounts constructed by way of criticism, on the other hand interpretations which lie beyond criticism being the result of revelation or of ulterior vision, of a faculty which cannot be described or find any relationship or harmony with the other faculties of the human spirit. This duality takes practical shape in the dualism known as "allegorism";[1] which explains why the old critics of Hegel and of the other philosophers of history could not make head or tail of the method followed by these writers, which was not (they said)

---

[1] For the concept of the allegory and for its history see my remarks on the subject in *Nuovi saggi di estetica* (Bari, 1926), pp. 329–40.

either induction or deduction, but a poor mixture of the two. The allegory does not establish a superior unity; it is a writing between the lines of other writing; a speech added or interpolated in another speech; a book added to another book, a book which may be good or bad, reasonable or unreasonable, and which in this case utters wholly unreasonable matter, but is in any case intrinsically different from the book with which it is conjoined in an exterior way. The so-called "philosophers of nature" are similarly allegorical and badly allegorical; they flourished at the same time as the philosophers of history and enjoyed the same method and fate.

Notoriously when allegorical dualism appears in the field of poetry the law holds good that the more perfect the allegorist the less is he a poet, and the greater the poet the more incoherent and fitful the allegorist: poetic genius gets the better of the allegorical intention, and irrepressibly pursues its work, taking no notice of these intentions or breaking out through them. But when, as in our case, the process takes the form of an arbitrary thought, which is not really thought, being superadded to an effective and critical thought, then though not wanting to destroy the latter completely because then it would destroy the very materials necessary to the game, yet it stunts and weakens it and injects as it were a poison which chokes it. This fully explains the intolerance, the fierce hatred felt by the students of history against philosophies of history; under which condemnation they became prohibited books—and a far more effective prohibition it was than any noted by the congregations of priests in the index published by the Catholic Church. Thence the aversion spread to philosophy in general, to that philosophy which is not only not the philosophy of history, but opposes to the philosophy of history a radical criticism, shattering its very foundations by showing up their illogical character; grave harm was certainly done, the effects of which are still felt today, but the blame (if it can be so called) must not rest with the historians, who reacted, but with the philosophers of history who provoked the reactions.

Yet every absolute prohibition is perilous, every encourage-
ment to unawareness and neglect may become an incitement to
ignorance and laziness, so that it is advisable to read even prohibited books, and in our case philosophies of history, not only
in order to keep one's conscience aware of an error which may
always crop up again in new and harmful ways, and not only for
the evidence they give of political and moral tendencies of their
times which are worthy of attention, but also for whatever
effective historical thought they do contain. It is true that such
thought is scarce and hardly original in most of these books;
their authors lacked the preparation and the discipline and the
interest of the historian; they re-told by means of the allegory
and with the aid of current history books and scholastic text-
books their abstract philosophical concepts, expectations, hopes,
despairs, and consternations. But one great exception has to be
made, at least for one of these authors: Hegel, the profound
renovator of the philosophy of the spirit and the profound
reviver of historiography in those fields to which he mostly
brought his speculative innovations; these fields were above all
in the history of philosophy, and more particularly in the science
of logic with its innumerable conclusions in the matter of ethics,
of the science of Rights, and of the State. His limitations are the
limitations of his philosophy: such as that in the history of
philosophy he held that systems developed following the order
of the categories of logic; in the history of art he held fast to
aesthetic conceptualism, in the history of the State he let himself
be continually obsessed by the part Machiavellian and part
theocratic idea of the State as the supreme instance, and by the
notion of the dialectical opposition of peoples attaining its
resolution in the German people. And if his direct knowledge of
original documents was unsurpassed in the field of the history of
philosophy, it was far less in that of political and civil history,
in his lectures on which subject, as we see from the notes of his
hearers, much that he said was hasty and provisional. But in every
field he discovers deep relationships and flashes out brilliant
comparisons, and even when, as is frequently the case, his interpre-

tations and historical dispositions do not satisfy us, and we feel something too forced and rigid, due to his habit of introducing thesis, antithesis, and synthesis into relations which cannot stand them, yet he always carries the mind into those sublime regions in which historical thought should move, even if it moves there differently, or in an opposite way from the way he has marked out.

Those who are acquainted with physical and natural sciences, who also have a humanistic and philosophical culture, ought to be able to tell us (if they will forget or suspend their first contempt and facile mockery) whether there are any merits still to be gleaned from the "allegories" in the old books of "Philosophy of Nature," sister to the "philosophy of history." We cannot allow that all that speculative fervour in which even an Oersted, the inventor of electrodynamics and author of the *Spirit in Nature*, took part was quite barren of every thought and every ray of truth, until a thorough and methodical review of those works has been once again undertaken.

CHAPTER VII

Philosophy as an Antiquated Idea

THE new relation—of identity—which has now been established between philosophy and historiography seems to alter the customary image of the former much more than that of the latter.

Historiography, once it has been distinguished from the anecdote and achieved its own appropriate character as the work of thought, and not of sentiment and fancy, leaves the anecdote in its own peculiar field, and recognizes it there as useful and necessary. Philosophy, however, having become identified with historiography or historical thought, eliminates and annuls the concept of philosophy as something outside or above historiography. Philosophy is the consciousness of historiography, and thus inseparable from it just as moral consciousness is inseparable from moral action and aesthetic consciousness from artistic creation, or (as the doctrinal formula has it) as taste is from genius. When philosophy has been defined as I have defined it as the "methodology of historiography," we must still not forget that methodology would be abstract unless it coincided with the interpretation of events, that is, unless it renewed itself and continually developed at one with the intelligence of events; thus a partition between philosophy and historiography only has a practical use and a didactic purpose. A philosophical problem can be resolved only when it is set and dealt with in relation to the events which have made it arise, and which have to be understood in order to understand it. Otherwise the philosophical problem remains abstract and gives rise to those inconclusive and interminable arguments which are so frequent with professional philosophers that they seem to have become a natural element in their lives, where they come and go lazily and in vain, always agitated here, there, and everywhere, but always at the same stage of development. If philosophy has been and is the subject of a special mockery which has never been aimed at either mathematics, physics, natural science, or historiography, that mockery must have a special motive which is the one we have described. If we can seriously render it historical we shall win respect and, if we like, fear for it.

The concept of a philosophy which is outside and above history is often hidden under the formal distinction of thought problems as being some "chief," "supreme," "universal," "eternal," and others "minor," "inferior," "particular," and "contingent." This happens irrespectively of the description thereafter given of the former series of problems (which were once associated with God and immortality and suchlike, and are today usually associated with the relation between thought and being, or with gnoseology and phenomenology), and irrespectively of the relation established between these of the former series and the others of the latter, whether, for example, these are considered as empirical and not philosophical, or as not soluble unless the first, which give them their necessary premise, has been solved. But the effect is always the same: the arguments are developed inconclusively. If the light of truth occasionally shines through these arguments it is due to the intervention of good sense which will not for ever be intimidated into silence, or of some flash of intelligence which almost unwittingly discovers in the shapes of history the true significance of the problem that is being debated and the road to its solution.

Much the same happens in the case of the problems which have been called inferior or particular or contingent; deprived of philosophy or eternally awaiting the arrival of philosophy for their clarification, they become dim and confused, being abandoned to the most varied caprices of feeling and imagination, unless the authors resort to self-help, and to a philosophy far simpler than that ordained by the proud philosophers, namely to serious thought and criticism which can render their work fruitful. It is in that way that special theories are formed in

various historical fields, which not rarely have a higher speculative value than those of the scholastic and tedious "sublime"
philosophies. Specialists must be encouraged to reach out towards
philosophy, while generic philosophers, who are occupied with
major problems, must be urged to study the minor ones in which
alone the major ones live and are to be re-discovered and solved.
This is the double and convergent action which should be
impressed upon thinkers, not, however, with too much hope or
expectation of success. For here, too, it is a question of arriving
at the middle point, that of virtue, which, as Aristotle knew, was
the point of excellence and the most difficult and the highest to
reach. In other words, philosophic historians and historical
philosophers will always be rare, and will always be a restricted
aristocracy.

Among the regrettable consequences of philosophy, when it is
considered as being outside and above history, and connected
with so-called supreme problems, are the pretensions boastfully
advanced by adherents of this theory, of being directors and
reformers of society and the State. Historical philosophy or
philosophical history is modest because it continually brings
man face to face with reality; having made him achieve the
catharsis of truth it leaves him free to seek and find out what
his duty is and to create his activity. But the other is made bolder
perhaps by a vague memory of its derivation from theology and
the Church; perhaps without being so, it seems bold through
the antics it goes through within its own void, from which it
tries in whatever way possible to extract itself. Practical action
inculcated by it may be noble at least in its intention, or ignoble;
it may want to "réorganiser la société," as with August Comte,
or it may want to revolutionize and rationalize society, as with
Karl Marx, or it may want to use its means to keep the peoples
quiet and servile, as with other philosophers: but the incongruity
is always the same. If some weighty thinkers to whom we owe
new philosophical concepts sometimes usurped an office which
was not theirs and deduced arbitrary programmes from their
abstract philosophy, this is the ruined and dead part of their work.

Once this desirable dissolution of philosophy into historiography has happened we may say, if we like, that philosophy is dead. But since that which in this form seems to die was never alive, we must be more exact, and say that it is the antiquated idea of philosophy which dies and gives place to the new idea of it arising out of the profound thought of the modern world. Ideally it dies, though materially it will drag on its life like so many things which are ideally surpassed, and it will serve (as we have hinted above) to support a trade among other trades in the world: reducing to mere trade the task of the philosopher which, in its real being, is no more a tradesman's business than is the task of the poet.

CHAPTER VIII

The Identity of the Judgment of Events with the Knowledge of Their Genesis

THE concept that concrete and true knowledge is always historical knowledge has the obvious consequence that the knowledge
or qualification or judgment of an event cannot be separated or
distinguished from the knowledge of its genesis, nor can that
which is a single act be made to appear as two successive moments,
still less as two divergent and separate acts. To know (to judge)
an event is to think of it in its being, and therefore in its birth and
development among conditions themselves altering and developing, since its being can only lie in the course and development
of life. It would be useless to try and think of it outside this life,
for once the spasm of this impossible effort was over not even
the shadow of the event could be traced. The more profoundly
we can penetrate into its proper character, the more we feel
ourselves to be moving with it within the confines of its proper
history.

For all that, we may find not only among the illiterate but
among men of science and learning and letters the principle and
the practice of separating judgments from the history of events.
It is suggested that an event may be historically ascertained while
judgment upon it is reserved, or that historical confirmation of
an event is objectively and historically possible, while judgment
belongs to an arbitrary subjectivity to which it should rightly
be abandoned. On such a method political history, the history
of poetry and art and even the history of philosophy, is attempted.
This method of treatment can, in practice, at best only produce a
sequence of chroniclers' notes unconnected with any theoretical
or historical problem, which being unconnected with thought

take on an objective but stupid appearance like certain people one sometimes meets in real life, whose words and behaviour are solemn and grave and cannot be otherwise because they have nothing to say.

Turning our backs on these couplings or makeshifts of arbitrary judgment and unhistorical history so courted and praised especially in those academic circles where histories of politics, of philosophy, and of poetry are composed without any political, philosophical, or poetic intelligence or passion, or love, we must mention another fallacious idea connected also with a kind of separation between inquiry into historical genesis and inquiry into events. Judgment which makes history of an event, and history which by virtue of this determines the character of the event; this unique act of thought which ever and anon clears up the historical problem and fully satisfies the mind, does not satisfy certain insatiable people for whom the act seems always to remain superficial and disintegrated. They seek a further elaboration—another history which alone is worthy of the name —which will supply the links between single representations and judgments. In truth these single representations and judgments are so little disintegrated that they can already, without having to be asked or constrained to do so, forge the links or the relationships between themselves, since the process of judgment always implies the formation and growth of an interior mental order. In the request for some higher unity in which, as we have said, it seems that true and proper history should operate, we legitimately recognize, in a more or less attenuated or conscious form, the familiar features of the old philosophy of history with their two-fold expression, the one materialistic, deterministic, and causal, in which everything was to be deduced from a cause, and the other dialectically abstract. Such requests are therefore to be left aside, as being either beyond the scope or beneath the notice of Science. A new treatment, demanded in this manner, easily yields to fanciful visions and to "brilliant" expositions which may have and have their transitory admirers, but which remain foreign here, where we are dealing with history and criticism. How many such "brilliant" histories appeared in Europe in the first thirty years of this twentieth century! And how quickly after briefly dazzling and exciting they were forgotten!

This demand for a higher inquiry into genesis and a superior history to confront existing histories which need no such elaboration, and cannot stand it, is frequently due to a lack of intelligence about the nature of the material under treatment: this is noticeable in the efforts frequently made to reduce political and moral history to a history of philosophical and doctrinal problems, or the history of poetry to a history of similar problems, or to that of political and moral development. This latter perversion is very common owing to the common lack of any vigilant poetic and aesthetic sense in the common histories of poetry. It has been indicted and fought by the writer, who has called upon the history of poetry to do no more than portray the character—that is, the genesis and the history—of particular works of art and poetical creations. This has raised the hue and cry that in this way the history of poetry and art is destroyed, although it should have been clear that a confusion of the history of poetry with other historical series which have nothing to do with it, is all that has been vetoed. Whoever overlooks or in the grossness of his mind denies the peculiar quality of each such history, falls back into finding and imposing on them a quite superfluous connexion, one therefore arbitrary and fanciful.

CHAPTER IX

Objections

ANY proposition that is put forward may arouse the most varied objections according to the intellectual rank and capacity and the moral attitude and the degree of education of the hearer. Therefore vulgar objections (the infinite "vulgus" of them) are usually ignored in scientific treatises; these usually deal only with objections representing ideal and historical positions, or those maintained in not yet obsolete literature on the subject. As for all the other objections, however often we may hear them vexatiously made, we can only repeat half-resignedly and half-impatiently: *qui vult capere capiat*; let each one unravel his own difficulties by meditation and by entering into the thought of the author and into intimate relations with the subject of research. Nevertheless among vulgar objections there are some which frequently torment even intelligent readers, and when psychological experience makes them known to us, it is really a kindness on our part to assist in their removal with little trouble to ourselves and much benefit, if not gratitude, from others.

One of these objections is that the idea of historiography, as we have described it, is like the Arabian phoenix; no one knows where, if anywhere, it is to be found, since historiography so defined excludes from its realm all or almost all of the works of the most famous and significant writers of history because it cannot find any work that is fully adequate and truly distinct from history of the chronicles, or philosophic or tendencious or literary history, to all of which it should be opposed. Here our difficulty is due to our not having looked out for things in themselves, in this case the real problems of thought, but for classifications and labels which describe things in a completely extrinsic way, and often place side by side things which disagree completely with one another. So that this objection must be firmly eountered by the statement that only those historical judgments and narratives and works are true which conform to a reasoned definition; such may be found scattered haphazard without prominence in a given history book; or dispersed in philosophical or scientific treatises and in political or actively polemical pamphlets; or may even occur in a novel or a play. Poetry likewise is only found in small doses in those innumerable books of so-called poetry, which are usually mostly filled with mental productions that are of a different or alien nature, and sometimes poetry is found where it was least to be expected, in the pages of a philosopher or historian or in a letter or an epigraph. The greatest poets have not always been the purest poets as the works of Dante prove, and if William Shakespeare has by comparison been rightly considered as a pure poet even his Shakespearean purity must be understood in a relative and approximate way. True, the development of culture tends towards the greatest possible external distinction between the different qualities of the works of the human spirit: and just as poetry has broken its one-time literary alliance with theology, philosophy, ethics and politics, so also it is to be hoped that historiography, once it has become aware of itself, will in the future, in the composition of its books, make the distinction ever more clearly between historiography and the anecdote, historiography and the chronicle, and historiography and philology. But what we must never lose sight of is that, whatever the literary and didactic forms and combinations may be, the true difference is to be found and always has been found in the existence of a strictly historical judgment: this is the only thing of any value in our case.

The second objection, or a second cause for torment to amateurs and novices, is the paradox they seem to find in the statement that true history is generated by the need for a clear perception of practical and moral problems, that it is born in the consciousness of man, historically formed, and that the evidence of events which have occurred is either valuable as a basis and a stimulus which can excite or reawaken such a consciousness (which alone has the authority to make statements), or remains a mere "it is said," or "it is written," upon which fancy may work while it remains extraneous to thought. Now, in order to understand this doctrine considerable knowledge and much philosophical meditation is certainly necessary: but something can be done towards rendering it persuasive and towards relieving it of the aspect and the suspicion of being a paradox.

For this purpose I should like to use an address which Sybel,[1] another prominent historian of the same school, made in 1867 in honour of Niebuhr (the man hailed by German philological and anti-philosophical historians as their master and guide, who was opposed by Hegel). Sybel, a few years earlier, had argued for the truth of history being founded solely on the criticism of evidence and on sifted separate documents,[2] but in this discussion of Niebuhr he was unconsciously led to consider a different and more profound basis for the truth of history. He noted that in the eighteenth century in Germany there were collections of accurate and erudite researches made in the service of the Empire and of various states, uninspired works: but on the other hand there were, he found, far from uninspired books of so-called philosophy of history which has not, however, penetrated into concrete history; they stopped short of a critical study of the particular, and of any integration of this into the Whole on the basis of a positive national life. We must not lay too much emphasis on the word "national" here; which comes so easily to German lips, but here (if we examine it carefully) corresponds to the "practical and moral" problem to which we have referred. In fact Niebuhr, who was (as Sybel records) a *Fachgelehrter*, a specialist of considerable profundity and precision, but gifted also with insight and imagination, passion and inventive spirit, had had much experience of life when he underwent a crisis and

[1] *Drei Bonner Historiker* (in Heinrich von Sybel, *Vorträge und Aufsätze*, Berlin, 1874).

[2] In his essay in 1864: *Ueber die Geseteze des historischen Wissens* (included in the volume quoted).

found his measure as an historical investigator; led thereto by heartfelt participation in the great movement of the German war of independence against Napoleon. At that time he became aware that knowledge such as can be gleaned from maps and landscapes without calling to mind the images of the objects themselves, could no longer satisfy him as a student of ancient history. That history needs must be treated in such a way as to attain an equal clarity and distinctness with contemporary history, and Niebuhr formulated the principle that the historian fulfils his task with more power in proportion to the greatness of the contemporary events in which he has taken part and experienced pain or joy. Criticism of evidence should "lead to the event itself, not merely viewed through the eyes of ancient interpreters or attestators, but with an imagination that is at once creative and orderly, like an eyewitness or a participator." This process, so described, is certainly more obscure and mysterious than the process described by the present writer because it introduces "creative imagination" which belongs to the poet and then, strangely, requires this to be "orderly," and asks it to make a leap in order to reach the "event" which is placed somewhere outside the observer and ourselves, no one knows quite where; but the obscurity, the mystery, and the extravagance is lost when we realize that here, in a somewhat mythological guise, it is a question of the process of penetrating and recapturing ourselves in ourselves, and that it is we ourselves who are the "event" in our historical ontogenesis. But Niebuhr and his panegyrist had need of even more than this direct participation in the event or this interior revival, or whatever one calls it; for, in order to see the event alive before them it was necessary (said the latter) to "understand its real quality," just as one cannot say that someone has seen a machine who is unacquainted with the construction and the purpose of the machine. Thus he found astonishing that while a history of medicine can obviously not be written through pure erudition and without understanding of medicine, yet histories of peoples get written without serious study of religious, economic, and philosophical questions, and great political events are treated without a knowledge of law and of the State, and complicated conflicts and great passions are judged without knowledge of the human heart: all this with consequences, as anyone may see, which are deplorable. Niebuhr came to his definitions and his historical expositions of the Roman "plebs" not by the path of erudition, but with a statesman's intelligence ripened by the knowledge of different nations and by his own political career, so that his quick eye discovered connections and vitality there where his predecessors had only seen incomprehensible fragments. Finally, his historical vision was animated and warmed by the energy of moral feeling so that Niebuhr, among his Romans—said Sybel—is always the same, with his conspicuously and fundamentally German character, enthusiastic for all the greatnesses of other peoples the more he feels love for his own country.[1]

The moral urge, the finding of truth not in external evidence but in internal and intrinsic reconstructions, thought in terms of concepts or categories and therefore philosophical thought: these three moments which we have reasoned out were enunciated by Sybel when he studied Niebuhr, and he found them all three necessary to historiography. He enunciated them almost as they were imposed upon him by reality itself, in the way that truth shines through, though dimly, and sends out its rays. But he did not systematize them in the philosophic conceptions to which they belong and which belong to them; he did not define them exactly, nor did he draw the inevitable consequences which they imply, nor did he foresee that by virtue of his discovery he should have reconstructed his justification of historical knowledge, which he had previously based solely on the criticism of sources. But this doctrinal imperfection is useful to us now, because it prepares the way for the theory which we have outlined and relieves it of that paradoxical aspect which can never match with the truth, for truth is naturally simple and alien to all that is unilateral and exotic.

[1] Op. cit., pp. 24–28.

Part III

Historiography and Politics

CHAPTER I

The So-called Irrational in History

INSISTENCE upon the following point is not, though it may seem, superfluous: history is about the positive and not about the negative, about what man does and not what he suffers. The negative is certainly correlated to the other, but just because of this it does not enter the picture otherwise than through this correlation and in virtue of this office, and may never become itself the subject. Man's action combats obstructing beliefs and tendencies, conquers them, overcomes them, reduces them to be mere stuff for his handling: and on this man rears himself up. The historian never loses sight of the work achieved among these obstacles and with these efforts and with these means. Even when some work has completed its life cycle and becomes decadent and dies he gazes not upon the decadence and the death, but upon the new work that is being prepared within this decadence where it is already sown and will grow in future and bear fruit. The history of historiography continually offers examples of the progress achieved when the negative considerations are turned to positive, and there is ascent from the first to the second. The Middle Ages, long and dark according to the judgment of the generations that followed each other between the Renaissance and the eighteenth century, began to find historical treatment when emphasis was laid upon the new spirituality achieved by men through Christianity and the Church, and upon the peoples who gradually were called to the deepest life of the soul, and upon nations then in the process of formation, with their languages transmitted or formed by Rome, upon liberties won by the Communes as they rebelled and fought, upon chivalrous customs which engendered the idea of a supernational, and in some respects super-confessional, human society, upon art, which was no longer Hellenic and yet had its charm and its beauty, upon poetry which sounded such new notes as the ancients would have heard without understanding them, and upon philosophy itself more varied than it seems at first sight, and which even among the scholastics could not but strain the Aristotelian shell and here and there penetrated outside it and presaged the future. The history of the decadence of ancient Rome was found to be wrapped in mystery, although its causes had so long and so variously been the subjects of research; and it remains and will remain a mystery so long as the point of view of "decadence" obtains, and so long as the historiographical subject of the decadent Empire is not replaced, as it is now tending to be by another subject, that of the Christian society and civilization which was then rising and growing, in which the Empire sometimes played the part of a more or less involuntary and ignorant co-operator and sometimes that of a vanquished opponent. Both the natural disasters which fall upon human communities, like earthquakes, volcanic eruptions, floods, and epidemics, and the disasters men inflict upon men like invasions, massacres, thefts and plunderings, and the wickedness, treachery, and cruelty that offend the soul of man, all these may fill human memory with grief, horror, and indignation, but they do not merit the interest of the historian (who, in these matters, verges always upon the epic, and the heroic), except as they provide the incentives and the material for generous human activity in which alone he is interested. This activity protects itself from hostile nature, by inventing contrivances, by making repairs, by sending out observers, and by making use of hygienic methods; it protects itself against man, who is a wolf as regards other men, by founding cities, by making arms, and by instituting courts of justice; fleeing from evil appetites to cultivate goodness it forms religious associations; and from grief, horror and indignation, and all the similar affections comes the inspiration for fine works of poetry and of other arts and for philosophical meditations. All this creativeness, and it alone, is the true and sole subject of history.

In conformity with this, historiography, which is generated

by a need for action, must be aware of the activity which has taken place for to this, and not to inactivity and the void, to the living and not to the dead, will the new activities be related which historiography prepares through its inquiries and meditations. When history came to be called for in the shape of "the history of civilization," or of "knowledge," or of "progress," its active character came also into evidence, or was at anyrate perceived; and these formulae (whatever their defects and misunderstandings in other respects) were formulae of activity, conceived by active men.

As against historiography defined in this way, there is another historiography which strings together sequences of misfortunes, disasters, and villainy without even being able to find so much justification as these spectacles hold for ascetics, for whom earthly life is an accumulation of errors and troubles by contrast with the heavenly life which is the only true one. Such negative histories today rarely exist in the pure state, yet the taste for them is still fairly widespread and the sentiments behind them fairly often replaces any other directing sentiment or concept in historical narrations and portraits. Sometimes there is even talk of an historical pessimism upholding its rights against the optimism of histories of civilization and of progress, but the question here is not really one of optimism or pessimism but simply of an historiography which is either conclusive or inconclusive, intelligent or unintelligent, useful or useless. There is talk, too, of the need for allotting an important part to the "irrational" in history: as though the irrational were an element of history and of reality and not merely the shadow projected by the rational, the negative aspect of its reality, intelligible and capable of representation only in so far as the rational is represented and understood.

That which seems irrational and therefore an object of regret is, when considered in itself, fully rational, as may be seen by the following: no sooner is the historical point of view shifted from moral or civil subjects to strictly military, economic, natural and vital subjects, than the shadow becomes solid and the negative takes on the positive character, in other words, it receives that positive treatment which historical thought always gives. When thoughts on military art reign highest in the mind, there is understanding for the way in which Attila and Genghis Khan collected and led their hordes into battle and how their mamalukes and janissaries were chosen and disciplined, and appreciation and admiration are given to the particular efficacy of these achievements without wasting thought on the devastation and barbarity which such virtues carried with them in the east and the west. He who studies the art of political negotiation can similarly reconstruct and estimate the shrewdness and the cunning of the Ambassadors of Florence and Venice and the firm coherence of English and French political traditions, without any profound examination of the aim involved, and without having to find out if and when such policies helped to raise human standards. He who turns his mind to economic production watches the prodigies of gainfulness, the boldness of enterprises, the multiplication of wealth and the financial power of states and of individuals without paying attention to the disturbances and the confusion which such giddy movements produce in families and in societies, or to the accompanying business and utilitarian imprint on social customs to the loss of nobility and refinement. Even among bands of political adventurers and of brigands and of other criminal associations one looks to find where they have recruited and how they have administered their forces, and how their rules of life are related as means to an end, and how rational within these terms the relation is. As to so-called natural disasters they are, in the eyes of the physicist and the naturalist, found to be none other than the process of the earth putting itself in order with earthquakes and calming itself with eruptions, and of the struggle for existence among various species of living organisms which leads, as was once said, to the survival of the fittest.

All these histories are to be distinguished from history of an eminently civil, moral, or ethico-political character as specialized histories each with its own technique (military, political, indus-

trial, etc.); thus they must still be regarded in their relationship
to civil history, as in some sort histories of the obstacles which
have to be surmounted by the latter, of the requirements it has
to satisfy by absorbing them, and of the means obtainable and
used. But when they are considered separately as they must be,
the concept which unites all these groups and distinguishes them
from history is that of life or vitality. They are all histories of
vitality and of the various manifestations of vitality as of the
so-called inferior or natural reality of the human species: manifestations of a vitality which surges up and spreads impetuously,
suppressing other lives and taking their place or insinuating
itself cunningly and obtaining the means of enjoyment through
industry or exchange or such like. Vitality is not civilization or
morality, but without it civilization and morality would lack
the necessary premiss, the vital material needed to give moral
and civil form and direction; without it ethico-political history
would come to lack its proper object. And vitality has, as well as
its requirements, its own reasons which moral reason does not
recognize. Hence the apparent reconditeness and mystery of its
processes, the unexpectedness, the confusion and the perversion
of its manifestations, and its imposition like an independent force
beyond moral good and evil. It is not only the pious believer
who bends to the will of God and to Providence which has so
disposed when he sees the triumphant and unrestrainable out-
break of vitality, but every serious mind aware of the laws of
reality disdains useless regrets and abstains from undue judgments, because no one can say that things would have turned
out better if such an event, painful and destructive as it was,
had not happened. We ourselves, who suffer from it, would not
be what we are without it, and we would not necessarily be
better, purer, more intelligent and quicker at our work. Then,
when the cycle has been completed, and the sky is more serene,
the mind tries to find out whether, in all these raptures, follies
and childish vanities and naughtiness and mania of destruction,
if there is no human and moral reasonableness, yet there may be,
as Kant said, a concealed intention on the part of nature (*eine*

Naturabsicht)[1] : in fact the history of it is made, that is, the history of that which has been newly created through or by means of this vitality.

When we recognize the necessity and when we understand the purpose of this overbearing and eruptive vitality, or estimate or otherwise admire its vigour and coherence and consider it as a weighty power to be educated and not merely to be restrained or suppressed, it is not the same as liking its roughness and violence or as exalting those who have embodied it and venerating them as the highest lights of humanity. They were instruments of a vital necessity; they possessed the will and the corresponding shrewdness required for the impulse by which they were obsessed and as happens with all specialized beings, they were lacking in, or deprived of, other gifts; in this case just those to which the human heart goes out; and when one of them fell or outlived his days of greatness, he appeared as Caesar Borgia appeared to Machiavelli, vague and irresolute and almost out of his mind, a poor fellow, who had seemed wonderful to him at the height of his fortune. Even Napoleon, who had learned the art of administration from Talma, does not appear as great on the rock of St. Helena as Socrates does under sentence of death in his prison, or as Dante does in exile. Hegel called them "the errand-men of the spirit of the world," but the errand was not always of a very high quality, more often it was of the kind that God gave to his servants, Satan or Mephistopheles. The faults we notice in them in the midst of their usually dazzling brightness are silenced in so-called idealizations due to a conscious adulatory process, or to a credulous and ingenuous imaginary beatification, whence the myth of their magnanimity, their pity, their generosity, kind hearts, mildness and sweetness arise, so that they would listen as under a charm if they opened their eyes again on the world and would immediately feel wickedly ready to seize upon and use these idealizations just as they had once done, using similar means for attracting the vulgar crowd. They would hardly enjoy the serenity, not exempt from sadness, of Cosimo, the

[1] In *Ideen zu einer allgemeinen Geschichte in weltbürgerlichem Absicht.*

first Grand Duke of Tuscany, the destroyer of ancient Florentine liberties, who said to Bernardo Segni, when the latter praised him for his goodness in one of his writings, that he would have liked and ought to have been good if he had been a private individual, but that being a prince he was obliged to exercise very different qualities.

For the last fifty years European literature has idolized these men of unbridled and impetuous vitality, valuing them almost more highly than those who contributed ideas to humanity, or forms of beauty, scientific discoveries, the institutions and sentiments which have gone to make its civilization and mark the difference between human and animal life. This idolization is unfortunately the mark of moral abasement; herein lies a bad ideal, a confused and corrupt sensibility, an unworthy relationship of admiration and love, like that of women who fall for scoundrels. While the historian understands the part played by these men and the destiny they fulfilled, he cannot on that account forget that they spread terror and hatred in the human heart and tortured the body and soul of men: and he stands on his guard lest his historical justifications lapse into moral justifications and so become perverted by supporting perverse dispositions. The adoration of the State or of "might" (*Macht*), born in Germany and introduced among other peoples, is nothing more in a final analysis than a base affection, not of citizens, but of liveried servants and courtiers, for might as such which is vainly adorned with sacred and moral emblems. The opposite judgment of a few noble German spirits of a better age—Herder, Humboldt, and Goethe—even if it is somewhat unilaterally or exaggeratedly formulated is valid: that culture or civilization are always superior to the State.

It is, in fact, stupid to exalt the State, which can only provide the necessary condition of stability for the developing of the highest spiritual achievements as if it were the supreme end of these: it is as though one were to say that the end of thought and art and morality was to assure a good digestion to the human organism. The fact that the safety of the State becomes the *suprema lex* in difficult moments of war or upheavals tallies completely with the suspension of higher human activity on occasions when the stomach is upset and must be attended to. On the other hand, we must note that those practical or technical forms belonging to moral, or religious, or intellectual, or aesthetic, or other creations prove to be both the fixing and the solidification of those creations and their death. One only has to think of the churches, the rules of cults and hierarchies, in which religions become fixed, of the schools which fix philosophy, the rules and fashions which are the fixation of the works of poets and other artists: in all of which the life of art, thought, religion and morals is menaced and brought nigh to annihilation until new and personal religious movements arise, which are notoriously heretical even when they seem to arise within the churches themselves; similarly with new and revolutionary philosophic concepts and new poets who break the rules and modify habits and fashions. All this, however, does not alter the fact that the unceasing sequence of these arrangements and the unceasing solidification of the creations of genius, the conversion of that which was spiritual into nature or "second nature," does fulfil a vital purpose by serving and continually increasing the supply of dispositions and attitudes in the shape of latent forces to be rekindled in new geniuses and in new artistic, philosophical, and religious moments of genius.

Finally, we have to consider that close relationship which occurred so spontaneously to us between so-called "natural" acts—the slow, secret, labour, the explosions, the revolutions, the adjustments of nature—and those actions which belong to what we have defined as the sphere of vitality, which used to be called in the schools a sphere of *facultas appetitiva inferior*, inferior to ethical activity, but not at all irrational, having indeed its own rationality in itself. And we must demonstrate that if human personality in this sphere seems to touch and mix with nature that is because elementary spirituality takes chiefly the form of a vitality which opens out a path for itself and creates the subhuman or natural world, as it has been called, and goes on creating within the confines of history, laying the foundations and preparing the material of what is more specifically human or civilized. A demonstration of this has been given elsewhere,[1] and can only be presupposed or remembered in this connection.

[1] See especially *Filosofia della Pratica*, and cf. *Ultimi saggi*, pp. 43–58.

CHAPTER II

Political Historiography

THE equal rank which we have hinted at assigning to purely political history together with military history, economic history and others which are only concerned with the utilitarian aspect of the course of history, raises some doubts and difficulties when we recollect how the histories which were and are still called "political," arising in contrast with the histories of civilization, by their very appearance and also by explicit argument, accused these latter of insufficiency.

It seems improper to include "political histories" within the concept (which covers the military and economic histories) of histories shaped by the purely technical needs of statesmen and diplomats, or of soldiers and economists. Neither the works of Machiavelli and Guicciardini, nor those of Thucydides and Livy among the ancients, nor yet the many other works of this type which were afterwards called "political" or "of the State," were designed in this spirit. But our definition does not really refer to them; it originates from the effect of the polemics to which they were subjected and of a new and more ample idea of "civil history," and it bears witness to a more precise awareness of that which merely political history can and ought to be: such an awareness could not be displayed until the principle which disintegrated the old form and made necessary its new reconstruction had been established.

Those old histories, on the other hand, were designed as nothing else than history *par excellence*, history itself, in other words as histories of man engaged in his chief and predominant activity. It was very natural that in a first consideration and placing of emphasis upon this chief activity, as standing above inferior and dependent activities, political and (in their wake) warlike affairs, should have assumed the highest rank, and that written accounts should have been concerned almost exclusively with the vicissitudes of states, with their foundation, development, decadence and ruin, and with their internal and external struggles. The general opinion or imagination, today as much as ever, holds this to be the only history that counts, holds that it *is* history; every day the common man proves it by looking wide-eyed through the telegraphic and telephonic dispatches in the papers, ignoring all else. To penetrate beyond such specious and gross apparitions to the wells of spiritual life where alone their significance is to be found, there would need to have been a desire for certain kinds of inquiry and an experience of speculative concepts; but the Greeks and Romans were not yet travailed by such a desire, and though in their philosophies they doubtless prepared them they did not yet possess the speculative concepts. Christianity itself was unable also to render this external history any more intimate, in spite of its superior moral consciousness, for by replacing the drama of earthly life by a supernatural drama, it deprived human history of its autonomy and value. Historiography survived in some degree through the height of the Middle Ages only because of the impossibility of wholly detaching man from the world or thought from history; thus a few strands of historical thought were grasped and firmly held. When, in later centuries, the worldly elements became more important, historiography revived, and when worldliness reached its peak in the Renaissance, history regained the level it had reached in the ancient world. It was a long time, however, before history resolutely set about deepening its own range, and the shallowness of military or political accounts of events was in the early eighteenth century ascribed to poverty in the choice of the material. The remedy was sought in turning the historical inquiry on to other sides of life, and in collating the various new histories thus discovered with the political-military history by means of a series of parallel chapters on letters, the arts, the sciences, religions, morals, customs, agriculture, commerce, and so on. Even in our day this kind of historical treatment, though it has been satirized as "pigeon-hole history," is still cultivated because it is pleasing to unadventurous minds who, having panoramically arranged events of history, then think that they have fused them in the fire of thought and reduced them to unity.

The demand at that very time for a "history of civilization" is itself proof that an important moment had been reached in the history of historiography, what was appearing being nothing other than the idea of a new "religious history," no longer transcendental but immanent, which was to resolve into itself the traditional historiography both that of the Augustinian tradition of transcendental religion and that of the other tradition of political history, earthly and profane, but poor in ideal motive. Even the history of civilization was first taken to be a history which either completed or else supplanted the prevalent political history, despising it as being concerned with men and things which the human race had least reason to boast of or to remember—oppressions and slaughterings, tyrants and conquerors—while it neglected the works in which reason and virtue down the ages are fitfully resplendent. This is the touchstone and the contrast which divided the two schools of the "history of the state" and of the "history of civilization," both of which respectively claimed the primacy over the other and the absolute right now of the State, now of civilization. In this controversy the concept of the State, though not subordinate to the moral consciousness, was given an undue and equivocal technical significance or even the position of the primitive and barbarian God hungry for holocausts. On the other hand, the concept of Civilization being separated from the concept of the force of political action, turned into something petty and frivolous as can be seen from the so-called *Kulturgeschichte* in Germany, which frequently became a mere collection of disjointed information about old customs.[1]

---

[1] A fairly wide treatment of these discussions in German historiography is to be found in a memorandum of mine in 1895, reprinted in *Convers. critiche*, I, pp. 201–22.

In order to overcome the difficulty and to restrain departures in wrong directions it was necessary above all that historiography having become allied with a better philosophy, should be conceived as the history of the mind in development, or of the spirit, and that it should re-make the story of events no longer according to external rhythms (seasons of wars as in Thucydides, solar years, lives of monarchs, and so on), but according to the internal rhythm of spiritual life: a design of which, as we have said, only a fanciful and symbolical foretaste was given by the philosophy of history because it was still too difficult a task to execute it effectively; to follow events according to their individuality and detail and to render them transparent as a whole in their various qualities as spiritual acts. Nevertheless even this treatment would not have been sufficient to overcome the contrast between the history of Civilization and the history of the State unless there had been an understanding (and we are still too far from it today) of the concept of the State as being an anterior and inferior moment in relation to moral consciousness, and of this latter as expressing itself by continually influencing and appropriating for its own ends the political power: which could be classically expressed by the old formula of *Platonis Civitas* (Plato's *Republic*), descending from the heights of superior abstractness, to work itself laboriously into *Romuli faecem* (the coarse blood of Rome). In this way the concept of a history which is both ethical and political can be arrived at and justified, a history which examines and exposes the operation and the practice of ethics in politics, the latter being understood to comprise the whole sphere of practical and purposeful action.

Judged by this standard, the historiography which predominated up to the eighteenth century, and which was called "political," is not therefore purely political nor aware of the limits prescribed to it, because it tries to go beyond them by reason of its own claims to the highest plane of history. And, again, by this standard a purely political historiography referring to the lower or anterior spheres outlined above enjoys its own particular rights and its own particular autonomy; and in metaphorical language such an historiography is not without reason often considered as "technical" historiography, because the undifferentiated practical action of which it treats loses its autonomy in the ethical sphere and becomes a mere means for the effectuation of the ethic, in fact becomes its technical instrument.[1]

[1] For the history of these not strictly ethical aspects of human activity, and especially for the history of law, see the introductory section of Jhering's *Geist des römischen Rechts* (1852, 4th edition, 1878), where he condemned the extrinsic character of the usual method used in such treatises, and asked that they should be really "historicized" or rendered coherent by means of a continually established relationship between them and the whole of which they are aspects.

CHAPTER III

Historians and Politicians

THE theory that historiography is born of action and leads to action seems to be in contrast with the obvious comment that writers and experts on history are usually unsuited or ill-disposed to politics, and that political men, however ignorant they may be of historical matters, yet guide the affairs of the world in a way of which the others are incapable. They often smile at them with that wink at the expense of history or of philosophy which we have all noticed, and to which there is no reply except to drop the conversation, and reserve serious discourse upon these serious matters for those who understand them because they love them as we do.

There is always an invitation to look at events as a whole, and not to ferret among the subtleties of thought, extended by the so-called practical men who have not even the faintest idea of the meaning of certain problems (with how much patience one is constrained to hear the unphilosophical rebut the doctrine of the unreality of the external world with the argument that this table really stands outside ourselves; or the refutation of the negative character of evil and pain accompanied by means of similar arguments about toothache being something very positive!). The invitation must be simply declined with the remark that, in the case under discussion, there is no question of looking, but of thinking. Theory is not the photograph of reality, but the criterion of the interpretation of reality, so that it cannot be seen with the eyes and felt with the other senses, just as God (as Goethe says) cannot be personally introduced to respectable professors, because unfortunately "the professor is a person and God is not" (*der Professor ist eine Person, Gott ist keine*).

To proceed didactically and to present in a somewhat schematic way the relationship between historical knowledge and practical action; it seems obvious that what men think on the one hand and what they do on the other will fully correspond, and that the one series continually flows into the other, and *vice versa.* Everything that man does passes into knowledge and everything that man thinks is "reflected" in action.

In reality the reason for the divergence between historians and politicians does not lie in an impossible divergence or estrangement between historiography and politics, but in the specialization of aptitudes and habits in this as in other spheres of life, and therefore in the relative closure of the one against the other: this closure, which may be useful for certain purposes, must occasionally be lifted or suspended, otherwise it may happen that the specializations become separations, and being thus sterilized destroy themselves and the whole of which they are parts.

The mind of the specialized, practical and political man takes up an attitude essentially of "faith," that is, it does not unfold in a live process of production, but takes its stand upon conclusion and result. The moment of faith is always present, even in the inquiring and critical mind; but it is always surpassed by reason of new doubts and new problems, and it is continually transferred from one point to another which is higher and more comprehensive. In the practical man it becomes crystallized, fixed and static, so that truth loses its truthfulness in losing its fluidity, and error loses its falsity by losing its negative strength: or, in other terms, truth becomes in him a thing that is well known, and the well known, as we know, is not the "known." From this very fixed point he moves into action.

This is not the translation or the application of a ready-made and determined programme, but it is a creation which is renewed and which grows with every movement; and it is always a danger, a risk, or an act of courage from which, as is commonly observed, the timid and the fearful try to withdraw, because they would like to have their future actions carefully insured, and, since they can find no such insurance anywhere, they decide to wait until events themselves show them what they ought to do: in other words, to let things happen without them, and afterwards they will have to act at least to the extent of accommodating themselves to what has happened.

In the course of action the belief takes shape among practical and political men, that they really know men and the world, and that historians, philosophers and poets do not know them and live by fancies and dreams. But the truth is that that which they call knowledge is not or (which comes to the same thing) is not any longer knowledge, of which last they possess little enough; and that they do not really know the world and know men, but—which is a very different thing—know how to manage them. They stand, in the course of their practical action which is always a struggle, ready on the offensive and the defensive, but always aware of their aim, which is to dominate others by persuasion and seduction, by caresses or threats, by a violence which will break them, or by the corruption which will undo them. They display their arts and throw their nets and draw into them the docile and the restive, the friend and the enemy: and after that they think they have got to know them well just because they have caught them. But in truth they have not known them and do not know what sort of beings they hold in their cage, nor do they know what is happening in the mind and heart of those they have caught and of the others whom they have not been able to take in. Now and again, and not without disturbance and bewilderment, their hearts become aware of this when faced with a certain unsuspected and insuperable resistance, where forces of another quality are glimpsed, which cannot be broken down either by blandishments or by menaces, which cannot be bought at any price, which can only be acquired by love and with the collaboration of love. The poet, the philosopher, and the historian really know man, and from what they have seen in moments of inspiration and in the peace of meditation, those ideals are born which warm the heart and point the way of action. Even the narrow, partial, contrasting faiths of practical men come from the same fount and represent the different theses and antitheses of ideals in actuation. Here the smile is certainly on the face of the thinkers who have started and guided the dance and now watch from on high the wild dance of the wily politicians, drunk with their dancing and ignorant that the motion is on someone else's behalf.

It is not only that practical men as such do not know, for all their boasting, either men or the world, but they do not even know the reality of their own work, which history inquires into and puts into its place: they are conscious of it, but not self-conscious. In this case also the geniuses of pure politics, the *fatalia monstra*, recorded in histories would, if they relived and returned among people, be amazed to learn what they did without knowing it and they would pore over the tale of their past works as over a hieroglyphic of which they had been given the keys.

So that we can say in conclusion that historical knowledge arises out of action, out of the need to clarify and newly determine ideals of action which have been obscured or confused, and that, through reflection upon what has happened, it permits of such a new determination and new action is thus prepared. From the wideness of the historical vision in which from time to time the mind, regaining consciousness of the whole, reaches to the living God, and from the upflight of the heart in inspiration and in intimate prayer, one passes to practical action, to that action which in its operation is necessarily particular and restricted.

CHAPTER IV

Historiography—Partisan and Non-partisan

THAT intimate link which we have established and very carefully maintained between the impulses of practical and moral life and the problems of historiography is altogether different from that other link between practical ends and historical narratives, which gives rise to "tendencious" or "party" histories.

In these last the process does not start with the practical stimulus and thence by way of a problem defined and resolved by thought attain to that informed consciousness which is the condition of a new or renewed practical and operative attitude; but there is given at the outset a particular practical attitude, the party tendency or programme on the verge of or in process of actuation, wherefore recourse is had among other means of actuation to chronicles and other collections of information about the past, or to true and proper histories which are treated also as mere anthologies of past events, whence images of persons, actions and events are drawn to assert, reaffirm or defend the end which is being pursued. Thus, not only is no historiographical work created, but those which already existed are, by this very act, disintegrated and destroyed. Instead of the past which is present in us because in it *de re nostra agitur*, whose character is scrutinized and its place in the development under consideration determined, we are confronted with images of things, liked or hated, desired or deprecated, to attract or to deter, to persuade or to dissuade us from certain actions or kinds of actions. Such are, substantially, and as a class, the tendency or party histories.

Hence from the historiographical point of view blame must be fastened pitilessly on all of them, for all, some more, some less, some altogether, some in part only, are corrupters and destroyers of historical truth. The most obvious and brazen examples, such as are to be found in clerical historiography, are not easily disguised, and quickly get the reception they deserve. But a vigilant critical sense is aware, even in the most able and cautious of such works, in those which know how to wear the historiographical habit or how to assume the style, even in sections of genuine history books—is aware of excessive or insufficient emphasis, of alterations in perspective, and of things said and omitted, all of which are the means used when practical tendencies work to achieve their purpose. These partisan histories occupy no small place among the volumes which bear the title of history, because there has always been a strong incentive and a pressing need to help the practical and political action of states and churches and groups whose aim is to direct or dominate society, in this way, by means of greater or lesser lies, or, if you prefer, clever inventions. In ancient, mediaeval and modern historiography, their literature predominates everywhere, and even in the nineteenth century, which was called the "century of history," the most popular and renowned historians almost all shared these characteristics to a greater or a lesser degree. Look at Germany, the country from which others sought to learn the arts of research into the past with its methods of observation, its fervid dedication to the task, its abundant and excellent historiographical literatures; here we shall see among the front ranks the historians of the constitutional and liberal party, Gervinus, Roteck, Dahlmann, and among the defenders of the strong State and of military power, Droysen, Treitschke, and Sybel together with the zealots of a "Great Germany" or of a "Little Germany," apostles of German unity, with freedom and for freedom, or without and against freedom; and then the dreamers of a revival of mediaeval manners like Giesebrecht and the Catholic adulators of the pre-Lutheran Germany despising the Germany of the Reformation, like Janssen, and so on. In Italy, too, the chief writers on historical matters in the first half of the century, before historiography fell again into mere erudition, like Troya, Balbo, Capone and Tosti, belong to the liberal-Catholics, the federalists or neo-Guelphists and the others to the Unitarians, anti-clericalists or neo-Ghibellines. In France, the liberals, the democrats, the socialists and the monarchists or other kinds of conservatives were represented by Guizot, Michelet, Martin, Thiers, Mignet, Blanc and Taine; and even if England, by reason of its long and constant political tradition and the uncontested liberty which it has enjoyed for centuries, was in a position to feel the need for defence or offence in these matters very much less, and to enjoy a more spatial and serene contemplation of history because of its wide experience in world policy, yet England, too, displayed various party tendencies in the histories of Macaulay, Grote, Carlyle, and others. And even in that century the voice of communist historiography was beginning to make itself heard in Europe: not restricting itself to a mere episodic alteration of history, while leaving the general lines of the development of civilization almost intact, it vied with the clericals and sometimes outdid them at the game, falsifying everything by putting the struggle for the distribution of wealth into the heart of history, and everything else, religion, morals, philosophy and poetry, into the realm of the imagination.

The idea of a history that is non-party and solely devoted to truth rises in perpetual opposition against party-historiography, whatever the party may be. This is an incontestable and almost too obvious declaration; it has been repeated for centuries in the schools with the Ciceronian words *Ne quid falsi dicere audeat, ne quid veri non audeat, ne qua suspicio gratiae, ne qua simultatis,* etc., but it is confused, it disappears, and is lost in the emptiness and void whenever we arrive at the point of determining how a history which is not an expression of party can be conceived.

The unhappy reasoning which produces this void and loss arises out of the premiss that party histories adulterate the truth because instead of resting content with events as they happen, they judge events; and the conclusion is reached that, if pure and unadulterated truth is to be pursued, there must be abstention from every judgment. This, however, comes to the same as saying that in order to see properly a picture that is badly lit, every light should be put out and we should look at it in the dark. But since historiography is the affirmation and therefore the qualification of the event, and thus consists totally, through and through, in the passing of judgments in every single one of its words, there was no need to grapple with this preposterous demand for abstention from judgment; what was called for was an inquiry whether the judgments of partisan historiography are really judgments, that is logical acts, or not rather manifestations of sentiment. Such an examination would have shown that by expunging judgments from historiography you expunge historiography itself, without in any way checking its opposite and its contrary, partisan historiography. That effusion of sentiments dressed up in the imagery of the past is, on the contrary, left to pursue its way, impetuous and unrestrained, towards usurpation of the field of historiography proper.

But in default of such considerations and deductions there were serious attempts made to write histories void of judgment and of thought. That was only possible in practice when history was rendered similar or identified with the chronicle, even though it preserved a certain dignified literary aspect as of historical narrative. Sometimes a compromise was planned and judgment allowed, but judgment which should be the mean between opposite judgments, that is opposite sentiments belonging to various parties, or it had to lie in the zone where such opposites met and agreed: the result was that one remained inside the sphere of partisan history, but attenuated, extenuated, weakened and rendered insipid. Sometimes also recourse was had to the natural sciences and their exemplary method of perfect scientific objectivity, and a history was outlined and composed which should collect and co-ordinate events just as botany does plants, and zoology animals, describing them without judging them. But this extravagant reversal of the logical relation (that is priority) of history towards classificatory science still did not win immunity from the snares of tendenciousness as can be seen in those typical and almost ironical examples of allegedly scientific historians, Buckle and Taine, and their like, and may God protect men from such objectivity as it was once hoped they would be protected from the "equity" of the Senate of Savoy! Anyway, among the schemes evolved to counter partisan history, the most prevalent were the disguised chronicle, the learned chronicle, or, under another name, philological history.

It was little wonder that these histories of the philologist, so pale and bloodless, should have ended in awakening a new desire for partisan history, filled as that was with vigour and alive with colour: and that people confessed in their boredom and irritation that it would be better to keep or return to this which, being born of passion, could at least give a thrill, and being full of life could arouse lively consent or opposition.

The concealed reason for this bewilderment and these recantations was the reluctance to recognize that since every affirmation is a judgment, and judgment implies category, the constitutive element of historiography is the system of judgment-categories, and consequently that whether we want it or not, philosophy is intrinsic to historiography.

Singular reluctance and singular fear, conjoined with a desperate effort to evade history's own law, of the necessity of philosophizing, that is, the necessity of thorough thinking: perhaps it is like the flight of the soul from God, who still pursues it and makes it his. Curious and almost comic are the ways of escape attempted in these senseless flights, in the search for safety in something that is not thought, in something which is material and external and can never be found, or can only be briefly scented as an illusion. To practise history simply means to judge or to philosophize events: with that end in view it is not possible to remain immersed in events, taking part directly in their formation in the struggle of parties (even if this be a struggle of words or writings), nor is it possible to stand outside them and move as in a void. It is necessary to pass through them, to feel the impact and the agony which they generate in order to stand above them, rising from suffering to judgment and knowledge.

Historiography (which we would call "philosophical," did not this redundant adjective induce the fallacious belief that there is another historiography which is not philosophical), historiography without an adjective, being neither chronicling nor philology nor manifestation of party, is not cold in the way that records and philology are, nor has it the immediate passion of partisan histories which run alongside of movements expressing their loves and hates, but it is at once passionate and passionless, cold and warm. The soul labours here thirsting for light upon the situation which confronts it, and from which it must emerge to be operative work, and it is filled with great joy when the clarity is finally achieved. For then we experience the dissolution of the anxiety of the moral consciousness into the serenity of truth.

Placed like this, not outside but above parties and embracing them all, historiography is by its very nature liberal, but not in the sense of what is called liberal historiography, that is, of the liberals, which, however noble the party may be which it serves, and however wide its outlook, is still just an example of the party historiography and not exempt from the limitations of such. Thus we see it often taking as a measure for all historical epochs the political institutions of a particular state or epoch, and fancifully beautifying that epoch and others which resemble it, while disfiguring or even refusing to notice all the others, finding no trace of liberty or civilization in them. Genuine historiography has not its basis in particular and transient institutions, but in the idea of liberty which would not be either universal or an idea unless so long as the world and history goes on it operates in every epoch and in every section of history, now in one guise and now in another among now greater and now lesser difficulties, at times as the lawgiver and the governor, at times as opposition and rebellion; just as breathing goes on so long as there is life, indoors and outdoors, on the plains and in the hills, painfully or in deep wholesome draughts. If an historical treatise excludes an event by condemning it as irrational and negative, the irrationality and the insufficiency of the treatise and not of the event is thereby demonstrated; for the reason and the strength of historiography lies in being able to find the reasons behind every event and in being able to assign a place and office to each event in the drama or the epoch which is being considered, and which is history.

It must not be imputed against the author that he thinks the kind of historiography of which he is speaking, just because of its philosophical nature, has been manufactured or is waiting to be manufactured by specialized philosophers, or, worse still, by professors of philosophy. It has always existed in the world as a spontaneous production of the human spirit, wherever that spirit has tried to understand the things of this world intrinsically, and free from the disguise of passion. Therefore it is scattered in all the memoirs of the human race, in so-called history books and in books not so called, for ever vitally philosophical wherever there is a serious attempt at the analysis of the logical genesis of its affirmations. It has indeed frequently happened that learned and specialized professional philosophers who are inclined to be the prisoners of abstraction, when once they become interested in historiography render it fatuous instead of promoting it and making it more perfect, thereby discrediting philosophy itself. The spirit which animated the philosophy of becoming and of dialectic certainly led to a fruitful consequence for historiography, lending vigour to its justification of everything that has occurred to the exclusion of any irrational residuum, and to its interpretation of single events and occurrences as necessary components of the whole; and none the less this has on the whole remained in potentiality, or in germ. It has not passed into act, or is only now slowly passing into act, emerging from aspiration to achievement, filling in the preliminary sketch with firm, clear lines.

The increasing self-awareness acquired by historiography in the nineteenth century, and the still further measure of this still to be expected, will not, however, mark the final end of partisan historiography, for the latter, though bearing the name and appearance of history, is not history but a practical stimulant, and as such satisfies needs other than those of knowledge, responds to different situations, and is usually addressed to very different circles of hearers and readers. It is therefore important to observe carefully the meaning and concept of the distinction between the two, but to refrain from undertaking to abolish something which still fulfils a particular and vital function, and which to a certain extent will always be necessary. One can only expect and hope that with an increase in refinement of historical sense and with the consequent growth of culture those circles to which tendencious histories are directed will appear ever more vulgar, and that cultured people will disdain the play of optimism and depression which such works produce by making use of the images of the past.

The concept of historical education has also been, and is even now, taken to have something to do with tendencious histories, as if it consisted in persuasion to be brought to bear on behalf of this or that political faith. They posed as educators of their own people and of the whole of humanity, those historians whom we have recalled, the liberals, democrats, authoritarians, militarists, nationalists, and so on. The old absolutist régimes provided their schools with edifying little potted histories: similar régimes today imitate them and find docile pens ready for the same undertaking. The process is usually useless, or only serves to fashion fanatics or hypocrites or men of slight interior substance who change with every wind. Free régimes take no account of or disdain this so-called education which is no education, and to which the name of "training" should be applied, such as is practised with horses, dogs and other animals.[1] True historical education aims at developing the aptitude for understanding real situations by linking them with their genesis and connecting their relationships; it teaches how history should be read, not idly to fill the memory, nor to over-stimulate the nerves and exercise the muscles, but in order to achieve an orientation in the world in which one lives and in which one's own mission and duty has to be accomplished. This is a true vigil at arms in which there is no use for narcotics or intoxicants.

[1] "Il faut (Napoleon said with candid ignorance) tremper un peu les jeunes têtes des Grecs et des Romains: l'important est de diriger monarchiquement l'énergie des souvenirs, car voilà la seule histoire"; and certainly there was no other history for him (see Caulaincort, *Memoires*, II, p. 281).

The Preparatory and Non-determinate Character of Historiography as Regards Action

It must be clear from what we have said that the relation between historiography and practical activity, between historical knowledge and action, establishes a link between the two, but not a causalistic or deterministic link. The antecedent to action is an act of knowledge, the solution of a particular theoretical difficulty, the drawing aside of a veil from the face of the real; but in so far as it is action it can only arise out of an original and personal inspiration of a purely practical sort, calling for practical gifts. Nor can action be theoretically deduced by means of a concept of "the knowledge of what is to be done," because knowledge is always of the event, not of what is to be done, and that which purports to be such is either nothing less than action or is nothing at all but vain chatter. Action, however much ideally correlated with the historical vision which precedes it and conditions it, is so completely a new and different act that it will in turn provide the material for a new and different historical vision. Therefore we can say that historiography, as regards practical action, is preparatory but indeterminatory.

This latter word recalls the theory of poetry and of art in which the relation between aesthetic contemplation and practical action presents itself in a similar way, for that contemplation renews and prepares the heart by purging it of passion, and ennobling it without directing it in any particular way. If it did so direct it it would not be art or poetry, but would remain or become again practical emotionalism. In truth this relationship is not peculiar to poetry or to historiography, but is common to all theorizing in reference to all practice. In order to arrive at action it is certainly necessary to pass from the world of poetry to the world of historiography, from fancy to judgment, but this step must be followed by another which is no longer historiographical, but would not, however, take the form it takes without the preceding process. Thus a poet, who has deemed a long study of ancient poetry essential to his formation, when he writes new verse finds that it is his own, that it is different and sometimes opposed to ancient poetry and yet it is related to it, and without that relationship and without that preceding discipline, it would not be that which it is.[1]

In this way we are freed from the objection that because historical knowledge does not abolish or alleviate the obligation of each one to see his own needs, in other words to deliberate, determine and execute that which he ought to do, therefore historiography is practically useless, just as by the same vulgar objections poetry would be useless too. On the other hand, we must emphasize that this utility of historiography, as it has just been outlined, consisting in ideal preparation for practical action, has nothing to do with another conception, which in its turn is fairly common and seems at first sight to be based on sound reason: that historiographical knowledge of reality most properly aims at exactly describing the situation in which we find ourselves in order that different kinds of action adapted to the preservation, correction, cure, or strengthening of such situations can be indicated with conformity with historiography. This conception treats the historian like a doctor who diagnoses an organism according to each case, and dictates the hygienic rules which are believed to enhance the good functioning of the organism or the prescriptions intended to free that organism of its pathological elements.

All of this would be all right if the work of history consisted in preserving the social equilibrium and in eliminating the events which disturb it, but since the contrary is true and the work of history is a perpetual creation of new life and the formation of ever new equilibrium, the attitude of the doctor is not at all

[1] See what is said on this subject in *La Poesia* (Bari, 1936), IV, p. 1.

suitable to the actor in history, whose every action is both pre-servation and revolution, constancy and change, preservation which is the starting-point for revolutions, and constancy which is that of change. Therefore every political man who is worthy of the name unites these two moments within himself, not juxtaposed or co-ordinated, but each one reciprocally subjected to the other. This applies to everyone: even those who like to emphasize their opposition to each other as conservatives and revolutionaries, and even when they are considered in their most extreme forms and in their most decided contrasts. Is there any conservative who does not want to innovate in order to preserve with the greatest security, and therefore differently from the way things were preserved in the past, or is there any revolutionary who does not preserve the institutions or dispositions which are necessary to his work, and who does not gradually consolidate that work in institutions and dispositions which he in turn wants to preserve? True it is that the specialization of skill and of social tasks brings it about that the moment of pure preservation of equilibria calls for its own specialists and professionals, but such specialists and professionals are of course not usually called politicians but rather administrators, or more generally technic-ians, who watch over and mend the machine, whether this be an economic, a social, or a State machine, or whether it be a physiological one, in which latter case they take the name of medical men. The confusion and interchange of technicians for politicians; the importance and the decisive preponderance given to the former (to the "experts" as they are called) in matters which require the politicians' intuition, decision and courage; and as the inevitable effect of this change the abstract character of the measures adopted, or, in the case of dangerous delays, the allow-ing of affairs to drift has appeared often enough in the recent history of peoples as a sign of declining mental and political vitality.

Among examples of the technical or medical attitude towards historical reality and of a consequent unilateral and fallacious historical vision and incapacity to act, the most obvious because the most vivid in our memory for the varied notoriety of his work, is Taine: the philosopher, the man of letters, the historian and the counsellor in high politics based on history.

Perhaps by now the clouds of contemporary and national admiration for the character of Taine as an original and profound and vigorous thinker are so far dissipated as to admit of demonstration that he never advanced the critical method in any single field he studied, that he did not confirm any proved truth and discovered no new one, that he sowed no new seeds but on the contrary invented and disseminated not a few paradoxes and paralogisms. It is sad and even displeasing to have to formulate this conclusion when we consider the nobility of the man and the diligence of his labours: it is the same kind of conclusion as one often reaches after examining the copious and mechanical work of estimable persons who have consecrated themselves to art and to poetry when the latter did not want to have anything to do with them, no matter how much they pressed their claim in extravaganzas of originality. Taine was never carried away in his work by the fresh breeze of truth; he was driven on by the tyranny of an idol which he called "science," epitomized for him the figure of the doctor, especially of the alienist and the gynecologist who studied and set out to cure the hysterical and insane women of Salpétrière, which he at one time visited; the whole world became for him a kind of Salpétrière, man a madman and a "patient," healthy only by chance, otherwise a *gorille féroce et lubrique*, who cannot be intrinsically educated by civilization, but only softened and thereby weakened. In his writings on philosophy at the start he dismissed with a flick, as one might use against a mosquito, Kant and the *a priori* synthesis, that is the whole spirit of modern philosophy. He read Hegel without even a suspicion that Hegel is a Kantian who goes deeper than Kant, and that the Hegelian Ideal is an ulterior form of the *a priori* synthesis and of the dialectic contained in that synthesis. So Hegel pleased him extrinsically, and he fitted him in with Condillac; perception was for him "true hallucination" which finds its counterpart by chance in an external reality. He dreamed he would apply the experimental method to philosophy and the classificatory method of the natural sciences to history, to history which, he said, had only just got its first foundation in his own work.[1] However, since such applications were impossible in practice and resisted his efforts (as they have resisted and will always resist similar efforts, whoever makes them), all that he could achieve was the introduction into historical and philosophical problems of a metaphysical presupposition of naturalistic make. He painted fanciful pictures of what he claimed to be historical reality which he viewed as the effect of geographical or racial setting, of circumstances or moments, of *facultés maîtresses* or other mythological entities. This was to be fixed and immutable, and the why or wherefore of any motion or change he did not account for. He wallowed in a muddle of logical inexactitudes, never doubting or subjecting himself to self-criticism. His early literary life was only that of the historian and critic of poetry and of art, but he identified these with the sort of symbolism used in the classifications of the natural sciences; he identified the history of poetry and art with that of the sentiment and practical action, so that the final purpose of his *Histoire de la Littérature Anglaise* was to be a *définition générale de l'esprit anglais*. He converted practical and moral life into a sequence of psychological or, often, physiological and pathological schemes. One of his French critics said of him that although he had written so much literary history, yet he had never understood what a line of poetry was; and indeed he never had any feeling for the poetic quality of poetry. He was revered in academic lecture halls and admired by the journalists who did not understand him but re-echoed his formulae, and—so preposterous were the things he said about art—that he drove artists like Henri Becque to rebellion and irreverence. Taine really does not belong to the history of thought, of philosophy, of criticism, or of historiography, but rather to that of tendencies and cultural fashions, a typical representative of the fanatical interest in the natural sciences, and especially in medicine, which, after 1850, filled a

[1] *Correspondances*, IV, p. 130.

good forty years of European life, accompanied by inane efforts to remodel the whole of culture on a similar basis. Taine's "experimental" philosophy and his historiography degraded to the ranks of botany and zoology had its counterpart in the equally absurd ideal of the "experimental novel" by Emile Zola: these were two fairly similar minds and hearts, and two fairly similar artistic styles, both having the strength but also the creaking, the rhythm, and the monotonous noise of machinery, deprived as they are of mellowness and spontaneity.

Taine, like Renan and other French writers, was recalled to a sense of responsibility and to the duties of the citizen by the painful events of 1870–71. But the distortion of his historical and political concepts were an insuperable obstacle to anything he might have undertaken in the service of his country. The famous preface of 1875 to his *Origines de la France contemporaine* certainly deserves to remain famous, but only as an ingenuous confession of political nullity. He remembers that in 1849 as a voter aged twenty-one he had to nominate fifteen or twenty deputies and to choose among different political doctrines, republican, monarchical, democratic and conservative, socialist and Bonapartist. What should he do? The motive which was valid for others was not valid for him: he wanted to vote according to knowledge and not *d'après ses préférences*. As one might say: choose a wife according to knowledge, and flee from inclination and preferences. And this is certainly not the way to decide to marry. So half-amazed, half-scandalized and curious, he watched how, in spite of his warning, and notwithstanding these preliminary objections which seemed such strong and peremptory evidence, his fellow-citizens in France yet went to vote: "Dix millions d'ignorances ne font pas un savoir." Nevertheless the fault lay in him and not in those who voted according to their own preferences, because those preferences were in fact desires, impulses, needs, and maybe imaginings and illusions, all of which go to make the plot of human action and history, from which new forms of life and also new errors (these too ultimately productive) emerge. But his abstractions bore no fruit, and his practical resolution, self-suspended and awaiting the dictates of science, was condemned to perpetual suspension, since science cannot give an answer to a question that does not concern scientific problems, but is concerned only with practical resolutions.

Being but poorly equipped with self-criticism, as we have noted, Taine did not criticize the question that he had raised: but spinning his ratiocinations from the stuff of the pre-suppositions which he had dogmatically assumed, he arrived at the conviction that the social and political form in which a people can *entrer et rester* is determined by its character, by its past, and must model itself, "jusque dans ses moindre traits aux traits vivants auxquels on l'applique," and that therefore in order to choose a constitution suited to France it was necessary to know the reality of contemporary France, and that since the present is the consequence of past history, it was also necessary to find out how that had been formed. Such an inquiry, in order to be carried out scientifically, had to be conducted *en naturaliste*, with a perfect objectivity and indifference, as if "devant les métamorphoses d'un insecte." As we know this was exactly the opposite method to that of the true historian who participates, taking sides in historical events, and in the very throes of this passion achieves the mental strength to understand history by overcoming his early passion, and having understood it, goes on passionately making history. The historiographical operation which Taine proposed to carry out was an empty one as were also the aims which he laid down for the politician, whom he was desirous to see "diminuer ou du moins ne pas augumenter la somme totale, actuelle et future, de la souffrance humaine,"[1] as though

---

[1] See one of his letters to Lemâitre in *Correspondances*, IV, p. 236. Taine's disciple, Paul Bourget, also faced contemporary conditions in France, and also considered himself (it was recently said in the French Academy by his successor) "Comme un médecin qui étudie un corps de malade et qui veut établir d'abord un diagnostique perspicace. Si le corps avait été bien portant, il n'aurait pas eu besoin de s'ocuper de lui, mais devant les maux qui assaillent de tout part ce grand individu social, tourmenté par la fièvre et ne sachant où trouver le repos, il s'efforcait désespérément de remonter aux sources des souffrances et de lui chercher un remède."

suffering were a mass whose size could be quantitatively measured, and as though man was not always ready to meet every pain for the sake of a love conquest. In order to foster the illusion that this emptiness was not empty Taine foreshadowed its fulfilment, and the effect of long labours which would be seen in a distant future. The book he worked on which was to prescribe a remedy for sick France was to be in his sense *une consultation de médecins*; he said time was required before the patient would accept these medical counsels, there would be imprudence and relapses, and the doctors would above all have to agree among themselves, but they would end by so agreeing, because moral science had finally abandoned the *a priori* method and political notions would filter down from the Academy of Moral Sciences, united with the Academy of Inscriptions to the universities and the thinking public, just as electrical notions had filtered down from the Academy of Sciences, and perhaps these political notions would pass to the Chambers and the Government within a century, and politics would become quite scientific, like surgery and medicine.[1]

Under the inspiration of such propositions the history of the *Ancien Régime* of the Revolution and of the Empire which Taine constructed sets out essentially to be the history of an illness, an illness which he calls *l'esprit classique* of rationalism or illuminism. There is no need here for an exposition or a criticism in order to show that when rationalism (which is on the one hand a perpetual form of the human spirit and one of its necessary arms, and on the other has given its name to a very vigorous and productive epoch of European life) is considered as a disease, the history of civilization in development, the history of the centuries before and after the eighteenth century cannot any longer be interpreted. Taine's interpretation of the French Revolution has several times been criticized, and it would be no use to return to that criticism here. It is only important here to see what were the practical results he achieved after such a long and laborious investigation of the documents of that historical period.

[1] See a letter of 1878, in *Correspondances*, IV, pp. 45-46.

The editor of the last volume of the unfinished work says something about it in his preface. His way of interpreting the relation betweeen theory and practice, history and political life, naturally raised the hope that he would dictate rules and caused people to turn to him (as we have seen them turn to Ranke in Germany in another connection) for opinions on this or that situation, or upon this or that reform. But poor Taine got out of such requests and entreaties, thereby doing much honour to his own modesty, but also making "Science" cut a pretty poor figure, after he had attributed virtues to it which it in no wise deserved. "Je ne suis qu'un médecin consultant," he parried, "sur cette question spéciale je n'ai pas de détails suffisants; je ne suis pas assez au courant des circonstances qui varient au jour le jour." And then, having found that there was no general principle from which a series of reforms might be deduced, he limited himself to recommending not to look for simple solutions, but to proceed by feeling one's way with moderation, accepting the irregular and the unfinished.[1] It was a wise recommendation, but was either too general or too particular and unilateral, if it meant that one method was to be favoured over another or one party over another by one of those *préférences* from which he had tried to escape, believing them to be illicit or dangerous: in fact, it was a declaration of the failure of history by diagnosis and of the pharmaceutical politics which he had proclaimed, and for which he had worked laboriously but in vain.

[1] Vol. VI, pp. xiii–xiv.

CHAPTER VI

The Need for Historical Knowledge where Action is Concerned

IN order to be quite clear about the necessity of the connection between action and historical knowledge it is useful to trace that necessity in the first place, within the history of philosophy and science, in the process of the evolution of new doctrines to amplify and enrich the mind.

This process certainly does not occur when the thread of previous thoughts, inquiries and cognitions has been broken or let drop. On the contrary the method of criticism in the presence of newly proposed doctrines is to discover and determine the point to which the inquiry had already reached, and to examine what advances, if any, the newly-proposed doctrine has successfully achieved. These are inexorable laws which cannot be evaded or laid aside for all the vain labours and efforts of those ingenuous and inexpert people who try to break the chain of history, to jump across it or rise above it, and to consummate a fervent embrace with lovely truth, whom they suppose to be standing and waiting there for the elect and the predestined. Such people are better described as fools, in whose hearts pride of speech, and of writing and fine display, is allowed to lord it over love of Truth. But criticism upholds the law and compels them either to bear its yoke or to leave the field of science for other fields more suited to them. The cult and boast of originality, based upon or buttressed by historical ignorance, gave rise to a noted epigram of Goethe's, who translated the creed of one of those who vaunted his own purity into exact terms by counselling him to call himself simply *ein Dumm auf eigner Hand*, a fool on his own account.

The Need for Historical Knowledge where Action is Concerned

There are branches of literary or bookish production which seem to be condemned to inferiority and to lurk in a sort of scientific "demi-monde," just because they lack a link with anterior research and findings about the subject with which they are concerned: a typical case is so-called "Sociology." Other branches, by reason of the quality and the attractiveness of their material, are especially inclined to win the affection of amateurs who are ignorant of the history of doctrines, as has happened with aesthetics, which because it treats of beauty seems to invite just those people who would be very shy if, for example, they had to dissert on logic, although, whatever they may think, aesthetics are no easier than logic. Except perhaps in certain special cultural circles in Germany in the eighteenth and nineteenth centuries and in Italy in the sixteenth and seventeenth and more recently, the treatment of aesthetics, so far from proceeding by vital and progressive links, has piled up treatises one on top of another, and no one except perhaps the writer took any pleasure in them. French aesthetics are especially deplorable in this respect; it is full of works, each of which starts afresh upon ground which want of knowledge has rendered bare, and which therefore is believed to be virgin ground and is treated as such.

It is true that sometimes we hear ignorance of the works of previous historians praised as a fortunate thing, a *felix culpa*, because thus the object is supposed to have been seen with a fresh eye and aspects not previously observed are noticed. "*Saepius*," Leibniz once wrote, "*aliquid novi invenit qui artem non intelligit. Irrumpit enim per portam viamque aliis non tritam aliamque rerum faciem invenit. Omnia nova miratur, in ea inquirit, quae aliis quasi comperta praetervolant.*" Here, if we notice carefully, it is not ignorance that is approved and admired, but impartiality and mental liberty, which has no dependent relationship with ignorance, and can and must be united with historical knowledge of the precursors. Nor is it possible to believe that the man who seems artless, and ignorant about a subject and discovers new things can really be as ignorant as he pretends and seems to be; for the ways and manner in which a fine and acute mind or a gifted intelligence succeeds in learning what is important about an historical situation and "orientates" itself are manifold.

Sometimes it is objected that in actual fact a pronounced diversity of aptitudes and of work separates the historians of science from the original thinkers; in this case it must first be made clear that by histories of science are not meant records or material expositions of doctrines, or even accurate and intelligent but more or less passive and disconnected and inconclusive treatises, and again that just because the manner in which a thinker is linked with his precursors is often implicit and not explicit, this is not taken for the absence or deficiency of historical character. An original thinker could certainly not respond to the practical requirements of the life of science, of science in its historical development, unless he knew and understood the character and therefore the genesis of that life and development for no original thinker appears to be extravagant or discordant. The truth which he affirms is always at the same time an affirmation of an historical situation.[1]

Just as historical culture is necessary to the life of science, so it is necessary to moral and political life, in which its absence or deficiency leads to an impoverishment, to an inclination to inactivity, to a cowed acceptance of the tyranny of transcendental imagery, as has been observed in certain tendencies among some peoples of the Orient, which has proverbially and by an act of simplification come to be considered, in these matters, as the antithesis of the West.[2]

[1] See *Ultimi saggi*, pp. 263–64.

[2] There is a famous letter, published by Layard in his work on *Nineveh and Babylon* (London, 1853), from a Cadi or Turkish judge to an English traveller who had asked him for some statistical and historical information about the place where he lived, a letter in which the feeling of complete lack of interest about history is expressed so ingenuously as to be almost funny. The reader may be amused to read at least the beginning, which is as follows: "What you ask me is at the same time difficult and useless. Although I have spent my life in this place, I have never counted the houses nor enquired how many inhabitants there are, and as to what a man loads on his mule or what another man rams into his boat, this is none of my business. But above all, as regards the past history of this city, God alone knows what mud and horridness the unfaithful must

Thus the reformer and the apostle of the moral life know and understand, as the statesman does, their time, the maturity of the times, and from that intimate comprehension their activity is born. It is not necessary either that their knowledge of the times should have the shape of a co-ordinated critical process, or of learned and methodical information; it is enough, in so far as they form the directing classes of the people to which they belong, that they should somehow have collected the conclusions necessary to prepare their work. Here also it is an illusion to believe that great and admirable things can be achieved blindly by men ignorant of the present reality and so behaving with greater courage and less piety, changing and destroying furiously. It is an illusion to fear that consciousness of the past takes the spirit out of new things, when the truth is that the more energetically the past is known, the more energetic is the impetus to go beyond it and so progress. This knowledge is life, and life invites to life.

Historical culture has for its object the keeping alive of the consciousness which human society has of its own past, that is, of its present, that is, of itself, and to furnish it with what is always required in the choice of the paths it is to follow, and to keep in readiness for it whatever may be useful in this way, in the future. This high moral and political value of historical culture is the basis of the zealous endeavour to promote and to increase it, of the jealous care used to preserve its security, and also of that heavy censure which falls upon him who abuses or distorts or corrupts historical culture.

have fed upon, before the sword of Islam came. It cannot profit us to look into these things. Oh my soul! Oh my sweet lamb! Cease groping after things which don't concern you. You came among us and were welcome. Go in peace." The letter ends: "Oh my friend! If you want to be happy say: 'There is no other God but God!' Do no evil and so you will not fear either man nor death, for certainly your hour will come!"

TWO MARGINAL NOTES

WE have taken the affirmation of the rationality of every event in a more radical way than it is taken in Hegelian philosophy by showing that the so-called irrational is always, when positively considered, found to be a necessity in a certain particular order; this makes it opportune to recall a false inference often drawn from this phrase, an inference ranging between stupidity and deliberate sophism, sometimes nearer to one and sometimes to another of these two extremes.

A single example is sufficient to illustrate this: it is taken from the Russia of Nicholas I at the time when Hegelian philosophy first gained ground among the Russian intellectuals, poorly prepared and uncritical. A good few of these intellectuals, although they had nurtured revolutionary spirit and conspired with the Decembrists, then began to reason as follows: "Everything that exists is rational. But the despotism of Nicholas I exists. Therefore we must become reconciled with it." No sooner said than done, or anyway tried.

The nullity of this extravagant syllogism is quickly demonstrated by the equal possibility of saying: "Everything that exists is rational. But the hatred and the spirit of rebellion against the despotism of Nicholas I exists. Therefore we must not be reconciled with Nicholas I." With which in practice we come back to where we started from.

The sophism consists in taking the word "rational" in two senses: as "that which has its reason to exist" and as "that which each of us in the certain conditions in which he finds himself, is commanded to do by moral promptings." In the first sense the despotism of Nicholas I and the action of the revolutionary are equally rational, and if, by thinking and inquiring along such lines one has come to understand the existent in its reasons for existence, in other words history, one has not taken a single step towards action, nor has one entered the sphere in which moral consciousness rules. In the second sense, by way of a sleight practised upon the first and an argument with a "quaternio terminorum" a practical attitude has been assumed which is not based on the single voice of moral consciousness; or if this voice should exercise authority in the man who uses these words, it is wrongly represented by him as a simple theoretical conviction: he is thus either (as in the latter case) displaying confusion and obstinacy, or, as in the former, smuggling in a fallacy under the guise of morality. In general, one has to be on guard against those who, instead of referring their actions and their behaviour to an intrinsic and moral reason, appeal to so-called "historical necessity" which, as we know, is too often just the need for one's own comfort.

What has been said about partisan-historiography also needs a marginal note. There is a pseudo-historiography of this kind in the section of historical thought devoted to the criticism and the history of philosophy, or (since this criticism and history usually makes a didactic whole simply called "philosophy") a pseudo-philosophy of a tendencious kind. We do not deny the right of existence in this case, any more than we have denied it to all that other civil, political, economic, or literary pseudo-historiography; but we want it to be judged for what it is, and to be well confined to its own field. Can one prevent the weak-minded or the unthinking from being excited in favour of this or that object, in the name of supposed philosophical truths which are only so in name, and are in fact pretexts for these practical interests themselves? And can clever people be prevented from the abuse of philosophical sentences and from coining others that sound philosophical for the same purpose, with an intent usually not praiseworthy, but yet sometimes for a good cause, when they resort to them as expedients which, for lack of any others, can opportunely avert a major evil with a minor one, that is with a relative good?

This yielding most times to the herd, the eternal and incurable herd, and this tolerance on those rare occasions in which moral conscience warns us not to interfere and not to destroy the deceit which imagination has spun, demand a corrective in the shape of the most energetic and radical intolerance towards pseudo-philosophies, which stain the purity and weaken the universality of the principles and categories of judgment by bending them to practical interests, or by giving them a false aspect of principles and categories of the spirit. It is all the more important that this rigid intolerance should be maintained and exercised, seeing that the great German post-Kantian philosophy was interwoven with political tendencies, and when the Hegelian school followed after 1840, those tendencies predominated and the philosophical matter fell away desiccated, giving place to the Bibles and Khorans of the Nietzsches and the Marxes, to the eschatologies of the Slavophils, and so on right down to the wantonness of present-day philosophy of racialism.[1] Moreover, in our own Italy theories of the State, of morals and of religion, have been enunciated by an irrationalist idealism which are certainly incapable of throwing any light on history, but succeed or claim to succeed in pleasing the men in power, to whom they administer philosophical adulation. In the pages of such servile idealists even the naïve "ethical state" of the old German doctrinaires has taken on a new truculent and brigandish guise. So much for them.

Since we have had occasion to mention Marx again, it will not be out of place to recall here, that modern historiography must not only shake off the subservience to historical materialism or economism into which much of it has fallen, but must also free itself meticulously from everything belonging to that doctrine which may have penetrated its blood and bones, even from that which at first sight seems almost acceptable, but which is in reality part and parcel of the rest and contains the same anti-intellectual and stupefying, not to say stupidifying "virus." No great effort is needed to reject the deduction of art and poetry, and even of philosophy, from the determinism of an economic "superstructure," but far more prudence and insight is required in order to get rid of a conception that history proceeds in accordance with so-called economic classes, their interests, their conflicts, and their struggles. Not that we wish to ignore divisions and contrapositions of this kind, although they are indeed very much less simplified and rigid and constant than this tendencious doctrine usually maintains. But not only morals, even politics become altogether unintelligible unless we go back to the concept of a "classless class," of a "general class," which lays the foundation and rules and governs the State. It will be said that even this is a utilitarian and economic interest, and not ethical and moral in itself; we may agree, but we must distinguish it from other economic interests peculiar to individuals and to their various groupings, and we must consider it as that which is common to all, in the same way as all those in a ship besides their various and conflicting interests share one interest in common, that the ship should sail and not sink. Even when the State is emphatically and passionately said to have got into the hands of a gang or of partisans, even in this extreme case the ruling class cannot, by reason of an inherent contradiction, be altogether a particular

[1] On this subject see *Ultimi Saggi* (Bari, 1936, pp. 241-45).

class, for, it overcomes its own particularity in the very act of becoming the master of the State, and will be constrained to the exercise and celebration of some sort of justice: at least that justice which Don Quixote was astonished to find among the brigands of Roque Quinart among whom he had landed.

In any case, Marxist ideology is one of the most conspicuous cases, especially in our times, of the particular tendency working all the time to introduce concepts into historiography whose origin is passionate and therefore not genuine, concepts which are born of economic and political, moral and religious struggles, and which serve these, but are inept and confusing and sophistical whenever they are transported into the theoretical field. Hence the necessity for patient inquiry into and expulsion of these beings of the imagination which are unfitted to play the part of criteria of interpretation and of judgment.[1]

[1] For an examination of this necessary work of elimination see my remarks on the false historiographical concept of "bourgeois" (in *Etica e politica*, Bari, 1931, pp. 326–38); and a memorandum by V. Travaglini, *Il concetto di capitalismo* (Bari, 1937).

Part IV

Historiography and Morals

CHAPTER I

Moral Judgment in Historiography

In social life there is a continual discernment between good and bad individuals, with various gradations in the goodness and the badness, shading down almost to a point of indifference at which stands the mediocre, neither good nor bad. Everyone discriminates and classifies in this way for his own purposes, and in the case of men who are well known in social life it is possible to get a fairly general agreement or measure of public opinion in the judgment passed upon them.

These judgments, or supposed judgments, however, when closely examined, do not appear nearly as certain as one would expect from the peremptory form in which they are usually pronounced. In fact they all err basically in supposing that it is possible to distinguish truthfully, not between the good and the bad, which are always clearly distinguished and opposed, but between the good man and the not-good man. This second distinction contrasts with common judgment and common consciousness which are perfectly aware that every human creature is both good and bad: this agglomeration of contraries has always been recognized by men of the most upright moral life, and has been expressed by such noble poets as Alfieri, who felt within himself how the dwarf stood beside the giant, and judged himself sometimes an Achilles and sometimes a Thersites.

In the midst of all the habitual loud and impetuous passing of judgments, one hears the murmur of Christ's admonishment "Judge not that ye be not judged," and the man who is accustomed to retire into his own soul finds the words dying on his lips.

Nevertheless the reason why these pseudo-judgments are always being formed and made, and why people cannot do without them, does not lie in the activity of the thinking mind, but in practical necessity, which seeks and finds, by means of these discriminations and classifications, the necessary support and orientation for action which has to be undertaken. In this way the concepts of the probable (which we have already studied) are formed on the data of experience, and though their speculative value is nil, they are in daily practical use. On the basis of this experience one man is judged as being completely reliable and another as being unreliable, and a different attitude is consistently taken up towards the one and the other according to these qualifications. This does not alter the fact that the reliable man may some day prove unreliable either because one's experience of him may have been insufficient for the qualification or because in the meantime he himself has changed. Likewise the man who was suspected of unreliability can put our suspicions to shame and render superfluous and almost ridiculous all those measures which we had taken to protect ourselves against his imaginary perfidies. Meanwhile there was need for action, and owing to the logical and necessary ignorance of the forces which our action had to contend with, and which indeed our action would have variously aroused, there was no other course possible than to stick to the probable and to lend reality and firmness to the characters of individuals, whether observed or imagined, and to assign to each the law which it is believed he will obey. Even the laws which are usually called natural sometimes exhibit similar shortcomings, which become the more frequent when it is the more complicated and more strictly individualized elements in the realm of reality which are being considered, such as the affairs of human society and of man.

The genuine resentment at the wrongness and injustice of some of these qualifications felt by those to whom they are applied, and the feigned indignation which the accused often display in order to cover their action, frequently take the form of a pathetic appeal to what the more or less immediate future will show, and in the case of men and affairs of greater and more public interest, of an appeal to history. History is supposed to be the great High Court which reviews all the troubled judgments arising out of the passions and errors of man, corrects them, and pronounces a final verdict as in a universal judgment, separating the elect from the reprobates. *Die Weltgeschichte, das Weltgericht:* world history, world judgment.

Neither the future nor history can carry this utterly intolerable burden of a task intrinsically absurd and impracticable. First of all it is in fact untrue to say that history suppresses the passions since the passions of contemporaries are certainly propagated in history, and to these must be added the passions of those who come after. But as a matter of justice the passions may always be and always are at every time banished from the mind which exercises as its own function this office of overcoming passion with truth. But the essential point is that in order to realize these hopes and expectations for historiography, the field of the probable where alone these judgments take root and flower ought to be abandoned. Then it is said, in support of a claim for the revision of a judgment, that historiography will in future dispose of information and documents unknown to contemporaries; even this is not exact because if posterity comes to dispose of new evidence and documents it cannot dispose of some others that were familiar to contemporaries; but whether they be old or new, scarce or abundant, no documents can possibly be converted into an inner certainty. There is no need here to insist on a point which has already been clarified, and has anyway been fully proved and exemplified in the controversies which are raised over and over again, but can never lead to an agreement as to the true characters of so many historical personages and the true intentions which inspired them (for example, of Richard III or Mary Stuart, of Ferruccio, or of Maramaldo, of Danton or Robespierre); never so long as what is attempted is to restate and historically or theoretically to solve these questions of a practical character which contemporaries were constrained to set and solve in one way or another as to what was to be expected of such personages in actions about to be undertaken. The Catholic Church follows such procedures, and rounds it off with a sentence of beatification and of sanctification, but only because it suits the Church's end to round them off thus; basing its judgments not only on ever uncertain human evidence, but also upon those supposedly divine tokens, the miracles performed by the candidates (yet even these, in a final analysis, are merely witnessed by the sayings of people, and of wretched enough people, for that matter).

The labelling of men as good and bad is a troublesome enough business in practice and for practical purposes. Surely we need not desire to pursue it and take it up anew in our historical considerations. We can only attain to historiography once we have freed it of that burden which strangely enough is always being pushed on to its shoulders; then historiography, quit of confident yet fragile expectations, and equally free of the suspicion, cunning and precaution which the struggle of life generates, can move in other spheres and seek a different aim.

When the individual proceeds to a conscious self-examination he cannot resolve the question, which is no question, as to whether he is good or evil (though, indeed, he may strive to build within him the coherence of a virtuous character, by treating the self as evil, punishable, and severely disciplinable; or contrariwise to regain courage, esteem and confidence in himself by emphasizing the goodness of intention which has constantly guided him). But the individual, on the other hand, is from time to time to a greater or lesser degree able to sum up his achievement. Unless he were thus aware, the continuity of his activity would not be possible. He thus distinguishes the moral and the non-moral, the ethical and the utilitarian, the dutiful and the merely pleasurable aspects of that activity. The only moral judgment which attains to consistency and significance in historiography is that which is concerned with the character of the achievement, apart from the private impressions, illusions and passions which may accompany it in the mind of the author, or with which contemporaries and posterity enveloped it. As, in the history of poetry, the poetry is important and not the intentions or other concerns of the men-poets, and in the history of philosophy it is the newly-formed and more profound concepts and not the intentions and the passions of the men-philosophers (who, like the poets, often behaved in a contrary and different way to their intentions, yet sometimes, in the midst of inglorious passions and unworthy actions, rose to visions of the truth), so similarly in the history of practical life it is the new political and moral institutions which form the object of judgment and not the intentions and the illusions contributed by their originators or their executors.

Yet while it may not, and ought not, to be difficult to hedge off the intentions and the passions of artists and thinkers from the reality of their works, which these neither contaminated nor touched, it is not altogether easy to see how one can hedge them off in the practical and moral field, where the action is qualified by the intention and the intention by the action, in which alone it enjoys reality. Here, however, the difficulty arises from an incorrect view of the author of the works, whether philosophical and poetical or utilitarian and moral; for he is not an abstract individual in contraposition to and distinguishable from others in the scheme of practical life, neither is he an individuality somehow substantiated. The author is simply the spirit which forms the individual and bends him to its purpose. Thus it sometimes happens that a man imitates an undertaking for his own ends, but in the course of the work he gradually disdains these ends and is seized with a passion for the moral beauty that has been revealed to him and rearranges his work accordingly; or as more frequently happens wicked, selfish or malignant people by rousing reactions through their actions give rise to that moral enthusiasm which they believed they could weaken or destroy, and without wishing to, or even knowing it, they served that purpose. Such occurrences are well known in philosophy and historiography by the name of "providence" (in Vico's sense), or as "the artifice of reason" (with Hegel), or as the "heterogenesis of ends," a less imaginative and less significant term.

This is the truly historical and, in a good sense, the objective approach. But if this approach clears the mind and prepares it or action, it does not encourage action with that stimulus and comfort which is so much desired and required: The venerated images of excellent men and the abhorred images of evil men are always kept alive by means of the anecdote and its use of the probable. Anecdotes provide the paradigms so much required by pedagogues; nay, each one of us has recourse to them in certain moments of internal struggle, receiving from them assistance, comfort, reproofs, rays of hope, renewed ardour, and promises of immortality, of that immortality which is union with the eternal spirit of the good. Such images, as we have already had occasion to note, owe their efficacy to their presumed correspondence with historical reality, and so to their presumed quality of being something more than and different from mere constructions of the imagination.

Now that we have reviewed step by step the process of moral judgment in historiography, it will perhaps be opportune to dispel another cloud that overhangs historiography; the accusation that it is invincibly external, and intrinsically incapable of penetrating to those regions which are more important to us than any others, because "in the sanctuary of the human heart (Droysen writes) only the eye of Him who examines the heart and the veins, or to some degree that of reciprocal love and friendship, can penetrate, never the eye of the legal or historical judge."[1] And again: "To me as an individual truth is my conscience and historiography leaves this to the individual since it cannot with the means at its disposal discover or understand it; for it does not look to the individual according to his truth, but according to the position and the duty he has in the development of the great moral society."[2] Thus we are supposed to have one kind of knowledge of human affairs which is historiographical and another kind of knowledge derived from conscience; and the second kind is supposed to enjoy an intimacy denied to the first. But this cannot be, for, as we know, the story of the individual, his biography, in so far as it is a cognitive act, fully resolves itself into history, since the individual has no reality outside the universal which actuates in him, and is by him in turn actuated.

[1] *Historik*, cit., p. 178 (cf. also par. 20 of the accompanying *Grundriss*).
[2] Op. cit., p. 180.

One could also express the concept in the formula: that historic a knowledge is about the individual as active and not as passive (or which amounts to the same, it is about the passive only in his relation to the active), and action implies the actuation of values or of universals. Droysen himself later very rightly observes: "We do not want to make personal acquaintance with the individual, but we want to inquire into and clarify his historical position."[1] If this is the case, then we must agree that this intimate knowledge, reserved to man's conscience and into which alone the eye of God penetrates, or in certain singular moments the eye of love and friendship, is not only not historical knowledge, but is not knowledge of any kind, not even of the order of truth which belongs to poetry, where the part is always seen as a part of the whole, the human drama within the divine drama of the Cosmos. In effect the so-called intimacy of the conscience is none other than sentiment, poetically and intellectually inexpressive: sentiment which labours and struggles to find its phonic and mimetic expression in the interjection, which in turn expands, becomes more complicated, and takes shape in the effusions of the heart or in the confessions of the patient and not of the agent. God will be the strength of the soul in these labours: love and friendship will unite sympathetically with the patient, giving his support, comfort and direction; but he will not emerge from the obscure intimacy of feeling unless he can judge himself and meditate his own history, which is only his own in so far as it is an integral part of the history of the world.

[1] Op. cit., p. 183.

CHAPTER II

Psychological Historiography

ANYONE who has an historical sense as lively as his moral sense feels unsatisfied and ill at ease, and, indeed, rebellious when examining interpretations conducted by the method called "psychological," according to which the life of a personage is represented as a succession of psychic acts inspired from without, for example through blood or family traditions, associations of images, social surroundings, or sudden occurrences; or, in the case of the history of a people, through dispositions formed in the course of centuries, influences exercised over it by other peoples, the pattern of events, or disasters which have overcome it. The narrative may indeed be closely knit, it may be worked out subtly, and it may penetrate the tortuosity of the mind and depict its lightest shades, and still one feels that this is not true, not seriously human, history.

The principle which lies behind psychological historiography is already evident in that the events which it narrates seem to be provided from outside, that is, explained according to the principle of causation by which one fact is related to another which determined it, and this one in turn to another, and so on. Psychological historiography is not only deterministic but the culmination of all historical determinism, for whatever be the supposed general or ultimate cause of reality and history, it never could operate without being translated into psychic facts. Climate, geographical configuration, original and immutable disposition of the race, means of economic production and distribution, all these and similar inventions would stay lifeless did they not take the form of men's needs, appetites, desires, actions, and illusions; this is most noticeable in the system of historical materialism which interposes the "superstructure" of human ideologies and fantasy between the economic motive power and effectual history.

The motive or the origin of the error through which the deterministic interpretation was introduced into historiography, where it proves to be so inefficient and impotent as to give rise to the rebellion we have referred to, is to be traced back to an abstract consideration of the passive aspect of human action—that is, the spiritual conditions from which or against which there is the revolt and the labour out of which new action is born. Preceding states of mind or actions already accomplished in face of the new actions recede to the rank of mere obstacles or negation; they cannot claim any place for the purpose of activity, thus they only have a position fixed for them as facts attached to a chain of preceding facts. Say you are reasoning according to logic, or calculating according to arithmetic, and you attain a clear and truthful conclusion by process of reasoning, and by the calculation an exact result to the sum. In this case the good results are not attributed to any other reason than the reason of logic and arithmetic itself. But if an obvious error should be introduced into the reasoning, which cannot be justified by reason, attempts are made, while it is demonstrated as an error, to explain it by some cause, as, for example, that at that moment a noise caused distraction, or sleepiness caused a confusion of terms. This is an explanation which on examination explains nothing because a noise need not distract or deviate the mind, but only causes a momentary suspension of the act of thinking, which act can then be immediately pursued again, undisturbed; and sleepiness may induce to sleep, but does not necessarily lead to a combination of words without thought or of figures without calculation. This so-called explanation is tautological, but it meanwhile describes what has happened, and presents events in their particular circumstances, placing them alongside other events which have preceded or accompanied them.

The error in deterministic explanation consists, therefore, in the transference to effective and positive historical thought of the means used to give a fictitious explanation of the negative and, to assert it in its character of negative, which, in relation to the process of activity, then appears as a material fact. Here is the real motive of the dissatisfaction, the uneasiness and the rebelliousness which such explanations provoke. When a man, through the austerity of long meditation, has formed a new theory, or when he has in the purity of his heart achieved a morally inspired action, he hates those people who try to find out "the cause" of his action, and who find an explanation, let us say, in his lust for praise or fame, or in some private spite or vendetta, or even in the good health and prosperity which he enjoys and which is poured out in cheerful generosity; he hates other people who seek "the cause" of the new doctrine only to find it in certain impressions which the author received in childhood, in a particular book which he happened to read, or in some personal success he has aimed at. He is naturally vexed and indignant because this method of treating him is not only riddled with iniquitous insinuations, but is logically incorrect. It could only begin to be correct if it successfully demonstrated that the action under discussion was not good, and that the doctrine proposed was not true; and if the circumstances of the evil and the error could then be differentiated from those of similar evils and errors. The reading of histories of humanity in which everything is said to be the result of external causes, and in which value and nonvalue, truth and falsehood, good and evil, and the beautiful and the ugly are put on the same level, equalized and made to tally with each other, and thought is compared (to use the ill-famed words of naturalists and positivists) to "secretions like urine," and truth with "a chemical adulteration like vitriol" saddens our hearts, and that sadness is shame for ourselves and for that humanity to which we belong, a shame which leads to indignation and rebellion.

Psychological historiography corresponding entirely to the genesis we have outlined is found flourishing among men and in times of little faith where the knowledge of human strength is scanty and the distinction between values and their opposition to non-value is obliterated. Thus in the age which followed upon the age of generous philosophical enterprise, great poetical dreams and struggles for liberty and for the independence of peoples, in the age in which Positivism and Industrialism, both riding roughshod over private and religious life, predominated, biographies and psychological histories found favour, and with them histories and biographies physiological, pathological, psychiatrical, ethnological and anthropogeographical, that is, all of them, in a final analysis associationist, deterministic and psychological. On top of all this a mythology was woven according to which countries and races and even madness, luxury and rape and similar deities, some symbolizing motionlessness, others disorder and annihilation, usurped the part of prime movers of history, of history which is creation and progress. And then, in the second half of the nineteenth century there was a demand for and an attempt to carry out an historiography of philosophy which should describe the psychology of philosophies, which should, in fact, debase philosophy into a private affair; similarly with poetry attempts were made to relate it to the private, physiological and pathological life of the poets, or to their readings of other poets, and to what they borrowed and stole from them. The people who made these psychological histories were idle folk who amused themselves with historical matters prancing round them and finding inconclusive and absurd relations between them: had they been strong, hard-working and thoughtful men with philosophic minds and poetic spirits they would not have done this, but they would have taken things seriously and built constructively.

The principle of determinism has its place and its usefulness in the natural sciences where it is not an explanatory but a descriptive formula concerning certain relationships observed empirically, and therefore concerning certain operations designed to reproduce from time to time certain events which it is desirable should be reproduced, or about whose ways of reproduction there should be knowledge, so that if necessary they may be impeded. But when this principle is uprooted from its proper field and distorted in order to provide reasons and explanations for the reality of history, the principle immediately reveals its incapacity by its entry into the vicious and unending process in which one cause always goes back to another, and from which there is no exit save by debasing all the causes to a phenomenology of an ultimate cause, which is transcendental, and therefore either declared as being unknown, or as being known through an act of the imagination. This principle is incapable of explaining what is positive in human action, and it is just as incapable, as we have seen, of explaining the negative aspect, which it can only describe, because the explanation of that aspect is only to be found in its relation to the positive: in dialectic and not in determinism.

CHAPTER III

Religious Historiography

THAT which we call ethico-political historiography has sometimes, in the course of our search for its sense and outline as we
envisage it, been called "religious history," and it was also said
that every history, or history in its highest forms, is religious
history.

The moral action which transcends the physiological and
economic life of the individual, and bends it and uses it and
sacrifices it to the universal, may indeed be called religious; it
would be difficult to conceive of a religious act of any other
kind. Similarly, that truth which has been conquered by thought
and has become certainty of that conquest, or faith, may rightly
be called religious faith; hence Mazzini's formula "thought and
action" has been called a religious formula, which it is.

But the word "religion" has another more particular and more
technical meaning when it implies that particular faith which is
not born of pure thought, but arises out of a nebulous state which
is intermediary between imagination and thought in which
phantoms borrow from thought an affirmative, that is, a real
character, while thoughts come to be merged into phantoms in
an intermediary state known as "the myth"; action is then no
longer the voice of the moral conscience, but appears as the
prescription and the command of a power and a being outside
man. All the definitions of religion, including those favoured
contemporary definitions of it as tremendous or "numinous,"
can be logically reduced to our definition, which for that matter
has the spontaneous support of every argument that is advanced
within the terms of the discussion.

Religion in this particular sense has always been and in some
measure always will be present in life and in history in the form

of "positive religions," so called to distinguish them from the intrinsic human religiousness of thought and of action. But how can these be treated in an historiography which is not confessional but philosophic?

For one thing, they can be treated in a very different way from the method adopted by the *philosophique* historiography of the eighteenth century which was unphilosophical in presenting them as a congeries of frauds which had overtaken the human race, and of nonsense to which that race had given way: these, as being harmful or superfluous, and as being already or soon to be expunged from human minds through Reason, were made the material not for history but for an account of human importunities and follies which should only be told in a contemptuous, satirical, or comic strain. But these beliefs are an integral part of the history of humanity, and they cannot be torn away without destroying the whole pattern of the history under consideration.

But if they are a part of history, and as such intelligible, they are so only by virtue of the very composite and hybrid nature of the myth, that is, of the rational elements, the mental and moral motives which it contains, of the truths it affirms, and the virtues formed within its enveloping shield through the years of the mythologically graduated "education of the human race" which Lessing defined and clarified. Briefly: in so far as religion is historiographical material it should be treated in the same way as philosophy and civilization, that is, not in the sense of a special historical sphere alongside of these other two, but as an integral part of them, because, if religion contains imaginative elements which are not winnowed out by criticism and not determined by thought, the so-called philosophies (it must be confessed) contain them also, although in smaller or even much smaller proportion: and if religious morality is subject to divided authority, so-called civil morality (it must be allowed) is subject to it and does not arise solely and always out of the moral consciousness. There is error on both sides, but on both sides truth is conceived and goodness is pursued, for the simple reason that there is no permanent dividing wall between the two, but only a movable and dialectical one. This accounts for the conversions and reconversions of the one to the other and *vice versa*; and for religions which sometimes appear more profoundly philosophical than a philosophy, or more morally sublime than those moral systems which are free of all myths. Hence, too, the continued and incessant spiritual and rational activity which pursues its own course right through this process.

There is no doubt, of course, that great concentration and analytical subtlety is required to disengage the speculative needs from religious beliefs which once upon a time represented these needs, or to disengage indications of new concepts, which are threads of gold hidden in imaginative dross, or again to free from religious convention those original creations of the moral consciousness which have since assumed the illusory appearance of a command from heaven or of a miraculous revelation, so that there may be a discernment of those cases in which such beliefs and customs really remain extrinsic and subject to divided authority, and therefore material and utilitarian. If, however, this critical work is not undertaken there would here arise a much graver injustice than that committed by the anecdote, when by reason of passions or vanity or inadequate caution in the use of evidence some person or other is put in the wrong: there would be an injustice against history itself, against its own objectivity and integrity.

In this kind of inquiry the only guide must be reason, which finds and recognizes itself everywhere in the most various forms. That is why it is essential to avoid a method of inquiry into the relations between religious history and philosophical and civil history, now prevalent, which consists in producing a sequence of associative connections and bridges across which certain truths and certain civil institutions are shown as having been acquired, as though in the form of a comedy of errors and a curious dialectic, not logical but psychological. In reality causalism and determinism and psychology which, as we have said, defile historical truth, are introduced here insidiously in a disguised way: an example where this is evident is perhaps to be found even in recent conscientious researches into the relations between Calvinism and the modern Capitalistic spirit, between Calvinism and Liberalism, defaced sometimes by lapses into psychological occasionalism and contingentism.

CHAPTER IV

Ethico-Political Historiography and Economic Facts

THERE is often censure or regretful disappointment expressed because well-thought-out histories of the moral life of a people or an age are said to take little or no account of economic facts.

Such censure frequently arises from fallacious ideas as to the historiographical approach which, instead of pursuing its own theme (in this case the theme of the history of moral life and not of economic history), is expected to furnish information on all the aspects of the life of a people or of an epoch. History is thus confused with manuals or with an historical repertory, just as once upon a time grave imperfections were alleged against this or that history of poetry because it did not contain biographies of the poet or give the editions of their works.

It may be retorted that there is no question here of a desire for repertories or manuals, only for compactness and objectivity. An integral and complete vision, unbiassed, without favouritism for any aspect at the expense of others—that (it may be urged) is what is wanted to raise the historian to the level of the scientist who studies all the works of nature in their entire conjointness and common manifestation. But such an ideal drawn from the natural sciences and imposed upon historiography could never bear any fruit except the repertory or manual.

Historiography is certainly not omnilateral in the sense of attending indifferently to every side. It does not pretend to cover equally all the different countries described by the geographers. When Voltaire and others in the eighteenth century included China and other Far Eastern countries in their treatises they were inspired by a practical, political, moral and religious need, and not by a pedantic external bonhomie; a different need for that would cause interest in some directions to lapse, or to flow in other directions.

Moral and ethico-political history does not ignore economic facts, nor does it ignore the philosopher's speculations or the creations of art, but it does and must take all these things for granted in their specific life, confining itself to a consideration of them solely in so far as, from time to time, that life promotes them, uses them, and surpasses them.

The censures and protests we are considering often, however, proceed from the presumption of that causality which we discussed above, indeed of a transcendental causality to be traced back to a power superior to all others and dominating them all, in this case economic force, held to be the explanatory principle of every human history. In our day this conception of the supremacy of economic activity is most deep-rooted and tenaciously held: economists out of love for their profession and business men have always bowed down to it, but Marx philosophizes upon it and raises economic power to the rank of a metaphysical principle. Thus the ironical question is raised each time that a moral explanation is advanced by moral history, or an intellectual explanation by philosophical history or an artistic explanation by artistic history: are these reality or are they not deceptive appearances reflecting a more solid reality which moves them and makes them sparkle and shine, and leaves them when it so pleases to fall and be extinguished?

If the former type of censure is (as said) to be rebutted by emphasizing the distinction between historiography and the writing of manuals the latter type is to be rebutted by repudiating materialism, whether it be open or masked, whether resolutely welcomed or furtively introduced and operating as a *sous entendu* in historiography. In point of fact this kind of criticism usually, and more or less unconsciously, conceals a tendency to transfer the practical problem from the moral to the economic sphere. Now, in the economic sphere economic problems and never moral ones are resolved. Of course it is profitable and salutary to abolish the social evils occasioned by misery and desperation by means of opportune reforms in economic arrangements; yet even if in the course of such a renaissance the temptation to do bad actions has diminished and the attractiveness and ease of doing good actions has increased, evil has not for that reason been rooted up; it remains in the heart in its ancient or in some newer form. It cannot be conquered with economic means, but solely with moral means. The economist's satisfaction at the success of his measure when it becomes excessive and dilated, making itself full and total, cannot be shared by anyone who knows how serious, painful and terrible is the struggle with evil, and how burdensome, yet ever imperfect, is the desired purification. And in that exaggerated satisfaction there is not only belief or tendency to believe in the alchemy of the transformation of economic facts into moral facts: but since the possibility of vast and profound economic changes depends upon the general progress of things in heaven and on earth, such believers also conclude by expecting from Fortune the formation and promotion of the moral life itself, forgetting that all morality consists in the moral effort which in creating itself creates riches of such a kind as no economic energy can ever produce.

There is another notable instance of confusion between moral and economic history, enshrined in a maxim fashioned during the eighteenth century and still circulating with the authority of a proverb, though the concepts which it utters or conjoins cannot be sustained. This is the dictum that liberalism may give man liberty in the merely legal sense, but not real and complete liberty which is economic—or, in historical terms, that the French Revolution established "formal" liberty, but the proletarian revolution will be necessary to found "real" liberty.

Liberty, however, will always be formal and legal, and therewith spiritual and moral: material or economic liberty is a meaningless phrase. Whatever could it mean? Freedom from material things? Certainly not, for Things—for example an individual's limits in physical and intellectual capacity, his natural inclinations and passions, the greater or less fertility or barrenness of the soil which he occupies, the situation and various reactions of markets, and so forth—such things will always surround the individual, and will always force him to reckon with and come to terms with them, if not to submit and resign himself to them.

We have to face the intractability of things which just will not let themselves be treated by us like the magical objects of the fairy tales. In order precisely to redeem ourselves from this slavery to things, one single way has been found, that of raising ourselves to the moral life, where the very obstacles make themselves instruments of its strength. It may be objected that the above-mentioned formula did not claim impossible freedom from things, that is, from the chains of the real world, but was intended only to affirm the opportunity or the necessity of economic reform in the ordering of property. Very well, let this be granted, but leave alone, then, the "legal," the "economic," the "formal" and the "material," instead of distorting and mishandling these and other philosophic conceptions. And always keep it in mind that, however much we struggle to attain or even to do no more than imagine absolute economic equalitarianism, this is by an inseparable characteristic doomed to be less than absolute. Conscience and moral freedom alone can be absolutely equalitarian, for only in their circle the poorest man who has spiritual value, the *pauper spiritu*, can quietly look in the face of the richest, most powerful and luckiest man in the world, can judge him and treat him for what he is worth.

CHAPTER V

Political Parties and their Historical Character

THE two pronouncements, that history is the history of liberty, and that liberty is the moral ideal of humanity, do not allow of contradiction. They can indeed be contradicted verbally, but only by those who thus deny history or stifle the witness of the moral consciousness, by denying freedom. To the former who, in the name of history, give us not understanding of whatever the human mind has succeeded in creating in every part of life, but heavy incoherent chronicles or mythologies of chance and fate, of irrational forces and obscure material powers, we must simply say that their works are not history, as is indeed proved by the feeling of depression and bewilderment which they induce. As for the latter: We who were born in the light of Italian liberty, and so were wont to read with a smile rather than in wrath the invectives and anti-liberal insults written in the service of the Bourbons, the Austrians, and the priests, never thought that one day we should see these exhibited anew to the world in modern dress; and we are fain to retort not otherwise than with that colourful curse of Carducci: "From thy blasphemous mouth may a green toad fall panting!"

A more special examination is needed of the concept of liberty in relation to action, not now viewed as the criterion of historical interpretation nor as general moral direction, but as determinate action in determinate circumstances. If we very properly omit from our survey of the sphere of practice the eternal Vulgar of mankind—those exclusively intent (or intent in the degree of their vulgarity) upon their private business, upon the means of subsistence, upon comfort and pleasure; and if we consider only true men, animated by the earnest search for the common good and so by the moral ideal—those who effectively carry forward mankind with their work—all such are, intrinsically, representatives of liberty. They vary, certainly, they disagree and oppose each other and fight each other in particular issues, each working according to his own feeling, own experience, knowledge, foresight and hope. But the historical result, which emerges through co-operation, composition and elision from their different or contrary tendencies, is the creation of a new and richer form of life, and thereby involves the progress of liberty. Whatever they may be like individually and characteristically, a single will binds them together, marking them with the same character as "men of good will," working at things lofty and worthy.

The same thing is to be said of the parties which are based upon the variety of men and their problems and tendencies, and designate their changeable groupings. These, provided that they have moral worth and consistency, that is, the will for the common good, and are not mere factions and bands, are also all intrinsically liberal. Indeed, the spirit of freedom accepts them all, wants them, expects them, invokes them, and laments their absence or their inefficacy, and feels that its actual freedom is lacking or rather lessened when that variety and those contrasts are lessened and missing, or tend to cancel out in the inertia of indecison, of docile assent or of indifference.

Now, if this is how things are, how is it that in the past people have spoken, and even now speak, of a liberal party, specifically liberal, which seems to wish to claim for itself the prestige of liberty? Is there then a party which is not an historical formation nor subject to contingency, which champions a philosophical and eternal principle, a philosophical party among political parties, something more and something less than they, and at bottom different, something which therefore does not connect well with them, and like an interloper or intruder, becomes tiresome and may seem even ridiculous?

Nothing of the sort. The liberal party is really a party, because it represents an historical situation, and its name, which, like all names, has good etymological rather than logical reasons, is the name of a political party and not of a philosophical school. It historical character leaps to the eye directly one tries to carry the name to epochs other than its own, because then the discord, the creaking, the empty sound of the name is immediately noticeable. Thirst for liberty, fights and sacrifices for liberty, the glory of liberty emerge from every period of history— liberty "which is so dear, as they know who give up their lives for her." Nevertheless there was no party properly and consciously liberal in the mediaeval hierarchy, nay, not in the freedom of Greece and Rome, nor even in the early centuries of the modern era, when people were working to free themselves from feudalism and theocracy, and fashioning the arms and the rule of the absolute monarchies.

The liberal party came into existence to challenge at one and the same time the outworn and exhausted absolute monarchies and the no less outworn and empty ecclesiastical absolutisms, Catholic or otherwise. Having run through a sort of pre-history in the struggles for freedom of conscience, in the English revolution, in the period of "Illuminism" and in the French Revolution, it took form and consolidated itself after the fall of Napoleonic dictatorship and for a century was the dominating factor in European life. In its days of power, like any other party which wins to office, the liberal party made use of the strong hand: it enjoyed or procured the support of certain economic classes; behaved variously in various countries, from time to time carried out necessary agreements and transactions, customary in the world of affairs and so in the world of political affairs. Yet in so doing it did not lose and squander amid material considerations of circumstances and methods that liberty of which *igneus est vigor et caelestis origo*, liberty which is spiritual and moral strength, operating certainly by means of those circumstances and with those practical methods, but never coinciding with them or resolving itself into them. It was said and it was repeated that, when it had risen to rule and become well established in power, and had passed beyond the danger of counter offensives by the former régimes, the liberal party then lost its splendid virtues, enthusiasm, dash, self-dedication, readiness to fight and

to lose its life for the sake of its soul. And cries of distress and
alarm were raised as its accustomed forms, the well-marked
political divisions of conservatives and liberals, of right and left,
and so on, were seen to disappear and to be succeeded by other
more prosaic divisions on special or economic questions. None
the less it was natural that all this should happen, and that when
the war was over the warlike spirit of the past time should be
laid down with the weapons of war. The triumph of the liberal
party carried in itself, as its logical correlative, the gradual end
of that party itself, which had accomplished its goal, and which
in order to be of further service had to become something else,
had in fact to yield its place to something else.

It was not properly speaking the liberal party—already in
some sort thrust into retirement as the effect of its own victory
—that entered, as they say, upon a period of decadence and crisis.
It was the liberal settlement, which it had advocated and realized
and consolidated, that began to be plotted against, threatened
and undermined by a double range of forces, related to each
other but not identical. In the range of the intellect these forces
were the check to mental, dialectic and historical modes of
thought, modes which had been initiated towards the end of
the eighteenth and the beginning of the nineteenth centuries, and
prevailed in the first half of this latter century, but were now
ousted by positivist materialism, and later by a species of irration-
alism and mysticism. In the range of social affairs the forces at
work were the profound economic changes which robbed
certain classes of importance and increased that of others, indeed
almost dissolved some while bringing others almost newly into
existence or to positions of extraordinary power. This is not the
place to describe a process, which in its essential lines is clear to
everybody's mind, in its past and present development and
acceleration.

Questions badly framed and answers worthy of them, solutions
which solve nothing, and stupid proposals have followed in the
train of this so-called "crisis." The chief and commonest of these
brings into doubt the very principle of liberty, and inquires

whether human life cannot be better conducted by substituting for thought and criticism an instilled and obligatory belief and for the deliberations of the will, obedience—an inquiry shown up by the mere formulation of it as unworthy of further discussion. Many, too, are those who resort to reading of omens to determine whether the future belongs to liberty or to authority or slavery, revealing an anxiety sometimes perhaps not without a hint of nobility. This anxiety, however, directing itself to the solution of a fantastic theoretical problem and vainly circling round it, can but increase to the point of agony and delay recourse to the only means to health, which is to follow the never uncertain path of duty and to nourish in oneself and in others the virtues of liberty.

It is obvious that the great ages of poetry and art are followed, as Dante would say, by the gross ages, and none the less we always long for and desire and prepare with zeal and effort for the coming of the ever-flourishing and classic beauty; so, too, the great ages of thought relax and are succeeded by an age of mere echoers, compilers, or, indeed, by positively forgetful and unintelligent generations, yet the ideal always remains thought, which creates truth, and never becomes not-thought, nor do we devoutly prepare ourselves to become stupid and short-sighted in honour of a stupid and short-sighted century. Not otherwise is it with the ages of liberty, moments of moral brilliance which yield to periods of less splendour and force, of uncertain light or even of darkness and night. In this extreme case we rediscover the meaning of Vico's *cursus* and *recursus*, and of Goethe's saying that God, when he sees a society increasing in wisdom and understanding, but necessarily ever less energetic because less pugnacious, wearies of it, and breaks the universe into fragments to make room for a new creation.[1] Nevertheless, when periods of barbarism and violence are approaching it is only for the vile and the foolish that the ideal becomes unfreedom and slavery; for others it remains that which alone can be called human, the only ideal which always works. We always tend towards liberty

[1] *Gespräche mit Eckermann*, January 2, 1824, and March 22, 1828.

and work for it even when we seem to be working for something else; liberty is realized in every thought and in every action that has the character of truth, poetry and goodness.

Moral action, then, must not be governed by what is about to happen in the near future, or upon what will happen when it happens. For if we suppose that human society enters for one or two centuries, or even for a thousand years, upon a condition of servitude, that is to say of liberty extenuated and reduced to a minimum, of the least possible creativity, approximating to the condition of animals, this incident—an incident as short against eternity as a wink of the eye—does not affect morality, does not interfere with its task, nor change it. This task is ever to kindle liberty from liberty, and from time to time to select the means and materials adapted to this end. And since new adversaries have moved against it, taking the place of those that, like the absolute monarchies, had been vanquished, while others, weary but not extinguished, have again scrambled to their feet, or at least to their knees (like the Roman Church, profiting by the disturbance to offer itself as aider and abettor and to draw rewards and gain), the liberal party, which had been thrust or had thrust itself into retirement for lack of adversaries, today finds the adversaries and with them the ideal conditions for fresh activity.

But at this point the greatest doubts and objections are usually raised, because, it is argued, a liberal party cannot work effectively when the actual conditions in which it was formed and worked in the past no longer exist. For example, there is no longer the same local life and local autonomy, no longer a landlord class which had the capacity and the leisure to take part in the administration and government of public affairs and to pursue political studies, no longer are there industrialists interested in competition and in free trade amongst nations. In place of these, we see everywhere the centralization of administration and government, masses of city workers and agricultural labourers with their respective mass leaders, industrial monopolies, and so on. What such noble minds as De Tocqueville, in the middle of the nineteenth century, and Italians of the Right after 1870, caught a glimpse of as they reflected on the future of liberty, seems now to have happened, and that in an irreparable fashion. The facts have turned against the liberal settlement, and we are invited to resign ourselves to mass governments and to dictatorships, while in our dreams we may long for a "happiness" like that which gleams in the title of a book by Muratori describing the regulations imposed on the natives by the Jesuit missions in Paraguay, as the best which can be hoped for.

Those who make this objection forget, in propounding the material conditions, that the fundamental and sole necessary condition for a liberal party—is the rebirth or oppression or tyranny, whether lay or ecclesiastical, whatever its particular forms may be (demagogy, dictatorship, Bolshevism, and so forth)—the thesis which substantially provokes its antithesis. And they forget it because, unaware or ignorant of its *igneus vigor* and its *caelestis origo*, which we have recalled, they fallaciously posit liberty as a material and economic fact among material and economic facts. Hence it is natural that they consider it finished with the material conditions with which at one time it was bound up and consider that it cannot be restored until those conditions are reproduced.

But why should liberty desert the world, and man descend from being a man to being a slave or a sheep, just because, instead of the few roads and the poor communications of other days, human society has now at its disposal railways and airways, telegraphs and telephones and radio, means of understanding which facilitate centralization of government and business? Or because, instead of individual cultivation of land, we are now adopting or may adopt agricultural associations or even State agricultural institutions; and instead of free trade, trade which is more or less regulated? Liberty has no objection to make, in principle, to these or similar economic changes, if calculation and economic experience, which are alone competent in these matters, approve of them, in the given conditions, as more useful and more productive than others. Liberty objects to and opposes only this: nationalization of the soul, the sale of that which cannot be sold: and for its part it accepts or rejects all economic changes only with regard to this, its supreme principle.

The premises having been thus re-established in their true aspect, the correct conclusion to be reasonably drawn is not that a liberal party has nothing more to do in the world, and is henceforth, as the journalists say, an "anachronism," but rather that it has enough and too much to do because the antithesis of its thesis has arisen. But a liberal party cannot do its work with the same means that it once used, because its antithesis has not the same form that it used to have. Therefore it has to look for new means, and itself, constant in its goal, faithful to its own religion, must renew itself on the practical side, must study other methods of penetrating into minds and hearts, ally itself with other interests, and give life to a new ruling class.

And if someone asks that the programme of the regenerated liberal party should be particularized and that the precise norms for carrying out its intention should be described, the request can be met with a smile at the over-simpleminded questioner. What he would like is to possess, contained in a few short rules, what must be a varied and complex movement finding its way as it makes it and its means to action in acting a labour of good sense, of course, of patience, of practical and political skill, of greater or of smaller scope as it may be, not waiting upon programmes but putting itself into action every day and every instant, because every day and every instant there is work to accomplish towards its own ideal. And (to clear up this assertion by means of an example), in this very instant, the writer of these pages in his way is working and collaborating towards that end, dissipating the clouds of certain bad political reasonings and allowing to flow in with the rays of the sun a little of that warmth of which the need is great. Strong impulses, the opening of new ways to action, resolutions in moments of crisis are more especially reserved for the apostles and political geniuses. There is no reason to suppose that there will be less of these in a world which has need of them, and by its own efforts and labours strives to call them into existence.

CHAPTER VI

Strength and Violence, Reason and Impulse

"STRENGTH" and "violence" are two words, or two concepts, which in common conversation are distinguished and contrasted in accordance with clear-headedness, common sense, or what you will. But the distinction is not always maintained as clearly and securely by the theorists, who not only sometimes use one word for the other (which would be harmless or do very little damage), but sometimes mistake and confuse the two different concepts. Worse still, eccentric minds, unhealthy and morally disturbed souls have directed their admiration towards violence and upon men of violent temperament, transferring to the one and the other the character and prestige which appertain to force; whence is born, as we all know, a plentiful literature which has as its device the remark of Stendhal that we should look for really energetic minds among the guests of the gaol at Civitavecchia. In Italy, D'Annunzio poured out the floods of his image-laden eloquence upon this conception (which, like all his ideas, is not original) to adorn with it the novel, the epic and the tragedy of creative violence and criminality; and if, truly, he has not in the least enriched the world of poetry he has doubtless exercised a certain efficacy of a practical nature (as he could not have done if he had been lifted up in contemplation to the height of serene and divine Poesy), an efficacy in the corruption of feeling, in maleducating and in perverting it.

In opposition to this wrong mode of feeling, which is still in fashion today, we must restore the distinction which common sense makes and develop it in the definition, also agreeable to common sense, which declares that violence is not force but weakness and cannot ever create anything whatever, but is merely destructive, as we can observe in convulsive movements and in the delirium of the sick. Strength on the contrary is a synthesis of the will and is always constructive, even in its most simple form, which is what is usually called power. It rises to its greatest expression in moral freedom, which is continual and constant force at work in the act itself, all the time, though it is more evidently displayed in its character as force, when it is called into play in the guise of severity, harshness, punishment, war and the laying low of the enemy.

In making an historical judgment it is necessary to keep firm hold of this criterion of distinction between force and violence. The former is liberty or prepares for liberty, while the latter does not work for liberty, unless, indeed, it does so negatively, by exciting liberty's opposite or rousing or resuscitating the thing which liberty wished or believed that she had crushed and extinguished. The most serious sanctions of war, the most rigorous states of siege and similar events show themselves to be intrinsically events of liberty or in the service of liberty, when directed towards vigorous resistance to attacks upon the vital necessities of a people or upon the order of a state, yet restrained from encroachments on the life of liberty, or from destruction of its seeds; but rather, indeed, favouring liberty in her recovery and development. English history of the last two centuries offers examples of this, a history of the education of the peoples which it dominates or which are within its sphere of influence for liberty: just as the history of ancient Rome was a history of training for law and justice wherever its power extended. At the extreme opposite stand, to be exact, not the barbarian nations which invaded the Empire in the early Middle Ages, for these, after having through ignorance devastated the works of Roman civilization, quickly went to school to the Romans—but those states which think that they cannot rule and endure otherwise than by mortifying the intellects and oppressing the wills of men, reducing them to instruments; and because men cannot stoop to being instruments so long as they are completely men, the men become automata, who, instead of thinking genuine thoughts, repeat the words of a catechism and instead of performing actions follow prescriptions.

The greatest example of the latter is provided by the Catholic theocracy, especially in certain of its distinctively political periods, such as that of the Counter-Reformation and the Jesuits. It has been and it still remains the model and incentive, affording an arsenal of expedients and tricks, to contemporary authoritarian states, or, as they are usually called in an attempt to veil the reality, "totalitarian" states (which are not instances of total harmonious co-operation, but of comprehensive and total subjection). There is one difference which avails in a certain respect as a justification of the Catholic Church. The Church, placing Heaven above the world, aims only at transporting as many as possible of the sons of men to Heaven, to beatitude, even though it transports them there somewhat or considerably damaged in intellect and weakened in will-power. The same justification is of no avail for these other states, which are in fact worldly and aim at the greatness, the safety and the worldly glory of the peoples which they gather within them, wishing to increase their life, and make more powerful. Yet to sustain their domination they unwisely recur to those methods of the Church which at bottom deny the life of which they boast the fullness and strength. In that contradiction rests their condemnation, which is manifest in their sterility in the spheres of thought, art, fine criticism, inner flame of affection, agreement, reverence, concern for the common good, enthusiasm and moral readiness, no matter how many or what be the efforts and industry and means that they lavish with a view to stimulating (or feigning to stimulate) those things which can only emerge under freedom, the varied works of love. For a time they can and they do make use of the momentum imparted by the previous ages of liberty, of the aptitudes then formed, the accumulated knowledge. Little by little the hoard is exhausted, the fountain dries up, new and able men do not arise, and these same renegades of freedom, who had at first been able to render some service, now through servitude or absence of obstacles lose what was left to them of the ability of other days. Barbarism looms irreparable, and will not be substantially less because it appears, as necessarily happens, in a different dress from that of other times. At every breath of greater liberty lively intellects and alert minds awake and rush to labour, while upon every injunction, every attraction and every promise of reward by the authoritarian states, upheld by violence, they remain stubborn, or do not awake from the slumber into which they have fallen.

Such is the difference between force and violence. An error committed in other quarters is to regard violence as productive —attributing to it the virtue of refreshing and renewing the world by sweeping away old institutions, ideas, customs, and old men. By this standard, fire and earthquake would be reckoned productive and constructive, because after them a new house or a new city may rise, more beautiful than the old. Here, truly, the attribute of productiveness belongs not to the fire or the earthquake, but to untiring human labour. Whatever the circumstances may be in which it finds itself, it never loses heart. It girds itself again ready for the task, and making use of the often sad experiences which it has gathered, makes a better and sounder reconstruction.

Even when violence supervenes to place itself by the side of justice, it does not increase but disturbs and diminishes the effect of justice, arousing against it the wounded feeling of humanity. This is the reason for the tears and affection and admiration for characters, in themselves not deserving of great moral esteem, whom revolutionary ferocity sent to the guillotine. It is also the reason for which prudent politicians recommend us not to "make martyrs."

If, then, the altar erected to violence must be thrown down, perhaps it would be suitable, on the other hand, to restore and renew in our time the altar of Reason—a worship, as is well known, greatly compromised and discredited, indeed turned to a jest and a mockery in reaction against the eighteenth century. In any case, what was usually rejected as reason or *raison*, was not really and in the fullest sense reason, which, in fact, consisted

wholly or in great part in the ideal which was set in opposition
to it.

In the field of theory, or research, and of science there was
often asserted, against reason and reasoning, the value of experience, of documents, of intuition; but reason and the reasoning
which were thus denied were nothing but reasoning upon mere
abstractions, incapable of touching reality, or with empty words,
or upon data which were accepted without being reflected upon,
which therefore did not admit of anything but the affirmation
or negation of an apparent and merely formal coherence. The
documents, the experience, the very intuition which were invoked as means of salvation against arid and sterile reason were
acts of scientific knowledge only in so far as they were reasoned
or thought, and reason has no concrete form of existence other
than as interpretation of experience and of documents, and as
distinction of reality and quality within the indistinctness of
intuition. Outside there remains only fantastic aestheticism or
empty mysticism, which do wrong to experience, to documents
and to intuition no less than to reason.

Similarly, for the tiring, painful and ticklish business of practical politics it was desired to substitute a so-called reason; but
this was just the associative imagination which constructed
schemes of action, and not satisfied with merely thinking of them
as ideas, imposed their execution. This was pre-eminently the
case with the reform of the illuminists and its extreme, Jacobinism.
The consequence was that against political and moral rationalism
were exalted impulse, spontaneity, instinct, boasting of knowing
paths which reason did not know, paths winding and safe,
different from the rectilinear ways of reason which led direct to
crashes and to precipices. Now, what was called impulse, spontaneity and instinct was in its valid aspect nothing but the effective development of the practical and moral life, practical and
moral rationality, that is to say, true reason, not false or superficial
reason. Reason as thought opens the door to reason as impulse
to practical and moral life, and far from pretending to bend this
to conformity with models which by their very nature are

abstract and dead, then says, upon reflection, as Goethe said: "There is an impulse, therefore there is a duty." Moral reason denies only the turbid and contradictory impulse, which for the rest denies and destroys itself. And a great deal of the disgust which is today directed against rationalism is due precisely to affection for the turbid, the sensual, the bestial and savage, to a sort of idolized rebellion of the low against the lofty in man.

If we keep ourselves equally far from today's substitution of wantonness for reason, and from the eighteenth century which put in its place a more or less empty rationalizing formalism, we shall, then, be rendering homage to Reason, to the only reason, which is the light of the universal in the particularity of passion, and we shall restore the word "rationalism" to the honour due to it.

CHAPTER VII

Moral Life and Economic Ordinances

THE hint given above of the indifference of the principle of liberty to the details of economic ordinances is worth further development and clarification for elimination of the perplexities and misunderstandings which are easy enough in this discussion.

It is well to start by rooting out an opinion which, although frequently repeated and with the best intentions, is nevertheless correct neither in doctrine nor in logic. This is that liberty from time to time finds its limits in the moral law or consciousness. But the moral law or consciousness bids us be free, and defines itself by means of freedom, so that it cannot impose limits upon liberty or, in other words, upon morality. Consequently, what the moral consciousness disapproves and rejects as evil is never liberty, but always its opposite, slavery to the appetites and passions contrasted with it which only an overbold metaphor could clothe with the name of liberty.

No more does the relation between the principle of liberty and economics lie in limits set by one on the other: it is not that but a relation of form to matter, where liberty finds in the obstacle which economic life offers it a material to elaborate and to convert into formal harmony. This is not unlike the work done by poetry and art with respect to human passions which are its material; to whose details, as the aesthetic thinkers say, art is indifferent, not taking sides, not refusing any of them out of hand, making all of them into things of beauty. Like art, ethical-political activity—liberty—accepts the economic oppositions which reality from time to time offers it, neither claiming to annul them all, which would be to depart from the realities of human life, nor to have them different from what they are, which would be to change its own nature. Liberty accepts them in order to affirm itself concretely in the given conditions which its work does not abolish but transfigures. This being admitted, what institutions and legal and economic ordinances, among those which seem dearest to it and the most stable through long custom, is not liberty disposed and ready to renounce, when conditions of fact call for it? And it does not in the least feel itself diminished by this renunciation, but rather glories in it. When war threatens our country, the legislative activity or parliament is renounced or restricted, full powers are granted to the rulers, heavy taxes are borne without hesitation, and so are prohibitions of free trading, price control, and registrations; we do not protest against the censorship of the Press and even of private correspondence, we do not claim the freedom of speech which had previously been enjoyed. In such conditions faced in such a spirit citizens feel themselves to be neither enslaved nor oppressed, but as free as or even more free than before. On the contrary, in other conditions, the most trifling of such acts and provisions is felt to be insupportable and to be repulsed as a most serious offence against the life of society. It would be a vain work to attempt to fix the economic and political arrangements that liberty admits, or those she rejects in the incessant, various and diverse movement of history, because, from time to time, she admits them all and rejects them all.

Against this proposition, as evident as it is well founded, an objection is raised which looks no less evident, although it is afterwards seen to be less well founded. This objection is greatly strengthened by the events and debate of contemporary society, and referring to them, it is developed with the irresistible certainty of a *reductio ad absurdum*. Because, it is argued, if liberty admitted economic arrangement of any kind whatever, it would have to admit even communism, which is the most flagrant oppression and the most contemptuous trampling underfoot of liberty. But the point is this: that we have spoken of mere economic arrangements, and communism, which is brought forward as an argument on the other side, is not a mere economic arrangement, but a very different and much more serious thing—a complex ethical-political arrangement appealing to a principle opposed to that of liberty, namely, equality. And not merely to that human equality which all men have in common, however varied and diverse their capacities and professions and conditions may be—that equality which imposes the respect for man by man, pity and justice—but actually to that equality which is found only in the abstract and unreal kingdom of mathematics. This, communism mistakes for a reality or real possibility and strives to realize. (For the sake of brevity I will refrain from tracing the transcendent religious origins of such a conception, which can be very clearly seen in the passage from the Theism of the Hegelian school of the Right to the atheism of the Left to which Marx belonged, and to the idea of Matter as first mover or God, and to the other idea, no less materialistically understood, of "humanity.") Communism strives to realize this ideal, but cannot, precisely because it is abstract. Hence communism is constrained, even against the intentions of its authors, to enter upon the beaten track which every absolutism, every despotism, every tyranny has always entered upon. This is to place one or more rulers upon one side and a multitude of ruled on the other, and to impose upon the ruled a uniform rule of life which treats the latter not as men but as subject material, and makes of society not a living organism but a mechanism. The logic of things does not allow communism to give birth to free representative institutions and freedom of conscience and of speech. The assertions and the promises to this effect which one hears are mere political astuteness, and those chimeras which are usually introduced as liberalism are either monstrous mixtures of ideas or deceptive debating points. Liberalism could not arise except by the effective dissolution of communism, leaving to free discussion and resolution the acceptance or not of those of its demands which are purely economic, as the various circumstances of history allow of them or not.

For the problem of freedom which is perpetually resolved and perpetually recurs is just that of settling human affairs in such a way as at one and the same time guarantee the greatest freedom,

freedom in the closest conformity with given conditions, and the best economic and social arrangements in the given conditions. These are two requirements which are only in appearance two, but in reality form a single need, for we cannot conceive of liberty without some social and economic organization (even the anarchists cannot really conceive of it), nor can we conceive of a society or state without liberty, because it would no longer be human. But there is no other criterion for judgment, no other measure of the utility of economic provisions, and of the equalities and inequalities that they leave or remove, except this of the promotion of liberty; and this is the criterion which should, according to circumstances, lead us to be revolutionaries or conservatives, bold experimentalists or cautious traditionalists. Private property in industry, in land, in housing, or its communal holding in the State, is not to be judged or approved or disapproved morally or economically in itself, but only in relation to that perpetual problem with its ever fresh forms, while it is clear, and for the rest history proves, that these forms come and go subject to the most various changes. Thus claims to demonstrate the intrinsic and continual goodness of the one or the other organization are arbitrary, and the absolutists of private enterprise are no less utopian than the absolutists of communism.

And because we have not excluded the fact that liberty may accomplish revolutions, we must add that the division and antithesis which is usually posed between revolution and evolution does not fit this case well. The revolutions of liberty are accelerated rhythms of its evolution. Hence their character as no mere rejections of the past, but fulfilments, so that they are able to preserve the tradition of civilization and bring to the minds of new generations the memory of their fathers and grandfathers. In contrast, revolutions without evolution are those not inspired by liberty, of which we have already signalized the character: these consequently ignore the epochs of history and of civilization, are estranged from them, curse them and laugh at them, and extinguish the children's memory of fathers and grandfathers, which sustains and comforts and sweetens mankind in labour and in pain.

CHAPTER VIII

Ideal Perpetuity and Historical Formations

We have already said that the liberal party is an historical formation which came to maturity in the nineteenth century, for which
the preparatory period extends from the Renaissance and the
Reformation to Illuminism. This statement furnishes at once the
justification and the criticism of the problem which was debated
and the doctrine which was formulated at the beginning of that
century, on the difference between modern liberty and the
liberty of the Ancients. Principal authors of this doctrine were
Sismondi in the last chapter but one of his *Histoire des républiques
italiennes*, published in 1818, and Benjamin Constant, in a speech
read at the Royal Athenæum of Paris in 1819.

The justification rests in the fact that the idea of liberty which
was then attained summarized within it the long process of the
last four centuries, ennobled by an historical conception which
had previously been lacking, in conscious contrast with the
abstract form which liberty had retained in the preceding century
—a form compounded of Greco-Roman imagery and rationalistic simplification which had given extreme proof of its nature
in Jacobinism and in the Reign of Terror. All this explains how
the liberty, of which these writers were speaking, was felt to be
something really new and proper to the age which was then
opening. But their judgment, in developing itself as doctrine, fell
into the error of confusing and mistaking a problem of chronology
and classification for an historical problem, a determination valid
for collecting and fixing a certain series of events in the economy of
the mind, or in the memory, for a genuinely logical determination.

In the classification of history, that is, in constructing historical
periods, it is not only admissible but indispensable to distinguish
between an ancient and a modern liberty, and more, by means

of subdivisions, to distinguish between other periods and other liberties. We must not, however, allow this deliberate fiction to be followed by belief in it (*fingit creditque*). We must not believe that the two liberties, thus distinguished for the purposes of classification, are really distinguishable. For if within liberty could be discerned two liberties, each with its particular character, it is evident that either one of them would not be liberty, or both would be vague expressions of a single liberty which would be superior and the only effectual liberty. And therefore the differences that these authors adduced, recognizing among the Greeks and Romans a liberty they called political, and among the moderns a liberty that they called civil, adding that one corresponded to the concept of Virtue and the other to the concept of Happiness, and so forth, these differences do not support critical examination. The reason for this failure is that there is no political liberty which is not at the same time civil liberty, and there is not a society which can govern itself by means of virtue without well-being or by well-being without virtue. Those in the academic world who later coldly insisted upon the problem and the solution propounded by the fervid spirits of Sismondi and Constant, lost themselves in sterile and formal comparisons.[1]

Refraining from such overstressing of the divisions of time into periods as would make these a source of logical distinctions and oppositions, we must likewise refrain from believing that in the period or age especially signalized by such-and-such a word is contained the life and death of the corresponding concept. In our own case, we must be on our guard against believing that liberty had its absolute beginning in the nineteenth century, or, if you like, in the eighteenth, or in the seventeenth, or in any other earlier period. Liberty is not a contingent fact but an idea, and scrutinizing it really to the bottom, it is no other than the moral consciousness itself, which, like liberty, is nothing but an incitement to the continuous increase of life, and so in the recognition in oneself and in others of manhood, of the human force

[1] Cf. the paper on *Constant and Jellinek* in op. cit. *Ethics and Politics*, pp. 294–301.

to be respected and promoted in its varied creative capacity. To look for an absolute beginning of liberty, therefore, would be worth as much as to look for a similar beginning of morality, that is, to fall into the phenomenalist or empiricist error of regarding the categories (the good and the beautiful or the Logos and others with their synonyms) as historical, whereas they are not historical facts, but the eternal creators of the facts of history.

In fact, whoever sets out to reach that starting-point is led ever further back in an infinite series, finding as he goes precedents of precedents to the facts that are called facts of liberty. He finds them not only in the centuries immediately before the nineteenth, but in the Middle Ages and in the classical period, and he would find the traces even in the primitive and prehistorical era, among Neolithic or even Palaeolithic man, if the documents we possess admitted of that. Or he would make us see in detail what we already know in general with certainty when (as Vico wished) we make a mental descent from our refined human nature into the primitive, which, however savage and cruel, was nevertheless moved by human passions and by human needs and ideals. How could he not find it there, how could he not find it, in those instances, in the times and in the states of the fiercest oppression if always before us we find men, that is to say, by definition, free beings? The category of humanity and that of liberty coincide, and however inhuman a régime or an age is said to be, it never really becomes inhuman if (as Vico also said) it does not wish to put itself outside the confines of humanity and fall into nothingness.

On the other hand, if one starts with an idea of perfect and pure liberty, one must be ready to find that, in running through history from one end to the other, true liberty is never encountered, even at those times and in those states which are most eminently said to be free. This will happen for the same reason, namely, that liberty is a category, and therefore inexhaustible, while that pure and perfect idea is, instead, the phantom projected into our imagination by our infinite desire, by our moral ardour, by our anxiety for purity and perfection, and it is not to be met with in the world of facts. In this, which is the world of history, liberty is never abstractly perfect, but is there from time to time in such concrete form as may be, and must be recognized and accepted in the given conditions.

It is a strange judgment that ancient liberty was not true liberty, because the social form in which it flourished was founded upon a slave economy. Liberty must be descried in the circle in which it exists and not in that in which it does not exist or does not yet exist. The fact that there were slaves does not destroy the reality of the great works that the free men of Athens achieved in politics, in thought, in poetry, in the other arts, in the whole of culture and civilization. It has been observed likewise that Christianity did not free and made no effort to free the slaves, and that slavery finished when it did finish through the change in economic circumstances which showed it to be increasingly more burdensome and less productive than free labour. But it is not upon this aspect that our eyes must be fixed in the case of which we are speaking, but upon the liberty which Christianity had conferred upon souls, including those of the slaves which were made equal to the souls of other Christians, as all brothers in Christ, and upon the revolutionary character of this principle in the present and for the future.

It is sometimes doubted whether we can acknowledge liberty in the political arrangements and the social customs of the mediaeval Italian cities, since their liberty consisted of privileges in their legal form not unlike those which feudal lords enjoyed. It was restricted to the city, and even to certain parts of the city population, with the exclusion of the countryside. It did not permit or tolerate freedom of speech nor freedom of religion, and so forth. But in spite of all that, the spirit then moved freely in the circle in which it could move, and produced miracles such as had not appeared in the world since the Age of Pericles. Wherever one man or more men recognize fully that some other men are free, a liberal institution arises, however restricted it may be as compared with others; and the curse of despotic states is that liberty is allowed neither to the few nor even to one, not to the one man who is the despot and is even more enslaved than the people whom he rules. The parts of social life not yet penetrated by liberty represent, in all the cases we have recalled by way of example, the materials of future problems; but those which have been penetrated and live a productive life make up effective history, the history which creates values, the history which is advance and progress, and alone is marked by the historical mind which descries it among the shadows and sees it with its shadows, but does not therefore call light darkness.

None the less, while engaged in such a research and in making such an affirmation, the historical mind does not let itself err through inattention, or through naïve admiration at shouts of liberty when these are not of genuine moral inspiration and do not prove their nature by their fertility in civil life. Hence history knows what to think of the "liberties" which the barons, when their sun was setting, tried to claim in the teeth of kings and peoples. These represented private and egoistic interests even when they united in leagues and called each other "brothers" (which they were no more than the members of a band of brigands claiming the liberty of brigandage). And history knows what to think of the "liberty" which the persecuted demand while they are being persecuted, with the secret intention of becoming persecutors in their turn when they succeed in grasping power, as the Catholic Church has always done; or of that allied "liberty" which is the false money scattered by the demagogues of every period, hiding behind the magnification and the invocation of liberty the hearts of tyrants or petty tyrants. These and similar travesties explain how this same word "liberty" has become suspect and satirized, and how those who truly loved it have often been disgusted with it, or have been silent about it through that shame which forbids the vulgarization and profanation of things which we love profoundly.

CHAPTER IX

Religious Piety and Religion

IF religion is necessarily a conception of life with a corresponding ethical attitude, liberalism is a religion, and as such it has been felt and conceived by its followers; as such it has inspired enthusiasm and faith and has had its apostles and martyrs; as such it has been treated by its adversaries who have accused it of being the negation of their particular religions, the heresy of heresies, the ultimate and radical form of the Protestant heresy, and so on. Certainly the liberal religion is a critical religion, feeding on criticism and drawing strength from it, defending and protecting itself with criticism; it tends towards pure truth and rejoices in its possession. But this does not form a substantial difference between liberalism and other religions, which also think and profess truth and the purity of truth; nor does it form a difference that on some sides they remain entangled more or less closely in myths. Myths are imperfect and provisional forms of truth not entirely thought out: in this respect they have the value of symbols, and these symbols and myths persist even in philosophies, although more sparse and subtle, as limits or provisional stops. Therefore the difference that it is sought to mark in this respect would be not absolute but relative, although relatively the detachment is so great as to hide the vision of the gradual passage from one to the other, that is to say, from the so-called religions to the philosophy which is religion.

For this reason liberalism cannot take up the hostile attitude of the destroyer towards other religions. It feels in all of them a substantial identity, a common labour, a common elevation or common effort of elevation towards the divine. Hence the thought, which had already occurred sporadically in ancient times, and became fundamental in the sixteenth and seventeenth

centuries with Socinianism and its derivations, and in the following century passed into practice and custom—the thought that
all religions are varied and diverse forms of worshipping the one
God. But the attitude, which from such an awareness it follows
that liberalism should hold, is very improperly reflected in what
was then called "tolerance" and later "respect" for the different
faiths. Tolerance could well be the psychological attitude of
certain lay and ecclesiastical princes and states, but consisting, as
it does, in a yielding and concession made unwillingly and not
without disgust and scorn, it is not really respectful to the faith
of others. Such a respect, moreover, amounts to a disrespect
towards liberty, for liberty cannot respect what it knows to be
imperfect and fallacious, nor convert the necessary contrasts
between the religions into a static peace, which would corrupt
them. Liberalism, in recognizing the right of other faiths to
affirm and defend themselves and attempt to expand, recognizes
its own right of fighting them in the ways which it thinks most
suitable, whether by direct criticism and polemic, or by allowing
them to criticize and dissolve themselves in that air of freedom
into which they have been drawn and there breathe with difficulty, so that in order to adapt themselves somewhat to it, they
must gradually become ever less mythological and more rational.

The case which has been considered is that of religions in their
character as truths and appropriate moral labours, differing only
as to the greater or less logical perfection of their pronouncements. Here, indeed, takes place a fraternization of the heart
beyond symbolic forms and beyond doctrinal formulae. This is
an old and common experience, whether one goes back to those
Christian and Mahommedan knights who, while they fought,
admired each other and honoured each other (as is written in the
mediaeval romances) for the *haute chevalerie* and for the *bonté*
which they discovered in each other, although divided by Christ
and Mahomet; or in the present day to the not uncommon
friendly and respectful collaboration of free thinkers and humble
men of religion in works of charity, when, although their lips
do not speak the words, all are aware of the presence of *quel Dio*

che a tutti è Giove (the God who is Jove for all), as Tasso liked to call him.

But there is another case in which a more or less mythical and symbolic religion is felt as the enemy to be destroyed by all means, even, when others do not avail, by means of war and bloodshed, because it is the fount of abjection and of moral corruption, the fount of hypocrisy, of oppression, of fanaticism, of cruelty—that which Lucretius perceived in human vicissitudes working darkly so as *tantum suadere malorum*. This is the religion which makes itself transcendent and draws man outside his freedom and his conscience, and submits him to a law which is not found in his own breast, a law from above, but not from that sublime above which is one with the depth, but rather from that above which is a power weighing upon man with threats, or with a kindly smile hiding the threat—a law which, as external, is to be satisfied by external means, or else to be escaped and eluded, and has external ministers in its priests and clergy.

The phenomenological process of transcendence develops through the detachment of the symbol from the idea and sentiment symbolized until it has value and weight in itself, in its quality as a thing perceived and imagined, whence the conversion of the original spiritual *élan* into a materialistic cult. And this business of conversion and perversion is not to be confined to what are commonly called religions, but extends to the very religion of liberty, which sometimes becomes mechanical and material, though much less liable to this than the others, because it is more open than the others to criticism and self-criticism. Still, it needs its renaissances and its rejuvenations, which must often be purchased by serious trials and severe suffering. "Democraticism," radicalism, masonry, are examples of liberal concepts which have become material things, dogmas without flexibility and life, instruments of sects and parties, which do not contribute to the elevation of the intellectual and moral life, nor to the promotion of liberty itself. But certainly the other religions offer more conspicuous and more copious examples by reason of their mythical element being greater. The Catholic religion is typical in this respect, and in this particular sense it would merit the description which Hegel gave to Christianity, of "Absolute Religion," in so far as, being the heir of the Roman Empire and in great part of ancient culture and civilization which it turned to its own ends, it occupies the first place in the systematic conversion of piety into a mechanical complex of beliefs and laws. Therefore, not without foundation, it has often been taxed with materialism and atheism. It has offered and offers the most grandiose and best assembled model for the mechanizations which other oppressive régimes attempt, which have all learnt or are now learning from its institutions and methods, from its method of dominating men through their hopes and fears, from its pitiless persecution with priestly hatred, from its art of weakening minds and making them docile towards itself and incapable of thought and of rebellion, from the astuteness of its greatest artists who were and are the Jesuits. So that today we see religions arising which are in various ways rivals of the Catholics with a rivalry such as the reformed Christian religions did not or could not long display. But such rivals the religions of the Nation, of Race, and of Communism can be said to be. But enough said of them, for everybody is daily forced to hear their chantings and to see their acts of worship, so offensive to humanity.

The very nature of the process which is liberty, its religious process which takes place entirely within, makes it impossible to discern historically the liberal or authoritarian, moral or materialistic character of a determinate action by applying the approximate and extrinsic divisions conventionally traced in the works of man. Only fine sensitiveness and delicate moral and historical intuition allow us to recognize as we proceed the quality of the acts which lie before us—a fact which we must never forget, and it is one of the teachings which is served by the writing of history —if we are not to fall into that fury of partisanship which expresses itself in the famous saying, "Kill them all, for God will distinguish his own." Writing history would be too easy if we could proceed according to the suggestions of names and labels;

and the moral life too easy, if, while accusing others of materialism, we did not first of all accuse ourselves, and did not scrutinize it and watch continually against it within us. Sometimes the words and beliefs and cult of the most open transcendentalism enshrine effective acts of liberty, rich in moral value. Sometimes the formulas of the most intransigent liberty contain the contrary. And just as diffidence about oneself is a necessary moment of moral life, so in the writing of history diffidence about appearances and the unbiased search after the reality of thoughts and deeds done is necessary.

For the same reasons the important part of history which concerns the relation between Church and State is most complex and intricate, and has great need of the attention and discernment of which we have spoken. Church and State may be understood in an ideal manner, as we have already had occasion to observe, as synonyms of the moral and the political with relations of implication and opposition that hold between them; but the Church of which history treats is not religion or morality, nor is the State pure politics. They are two institutions, and in this aspect two political facts or two states, and like all states they are subject primarily to the law of their own conservation, while like all states from time to time their religious and moral consciousness directs and constrains them to lend themselves to moral and religious actions. To consider the State as the work of the flesh and the Devil, in the manner of the mediaeval theocracies, or, on the other hand, to embark upon a delirium of abhorrence for the priestly character, which the eighteenth century enjoyed doing, practising a sort of counterpass or law of retaliation—these are two one-sided and rather crude ways of thought, neither of any more moral and historical value than the other.

There were times or moments in history in which the Church took the part of the moral consciousness against the State, and others in which the State was on the moral side, and the historian must, according to circumstances, hail liberty now in the words and the acts of the Popes and now in those of their lay adversaries. It is all the more necessary to insist upon this, as the Catholic

Church, in modern times, has been usually united to every régime of authority and oppression, and, when it suited, has degraded the concepts of liberty to use as a means of instigating the people to rise against governments disagreeable to it. It has also sucked from liberal régimes whatever it could turn to the service of its own interests, reserving the right to rise against them in league with their enemies when the propitious moment should come. Nevertheless, even in modern times, liberal acts and opinions have sometimes gone forth from within the Church or from the Church itself, because that institution, which is called Divine, is at bottom, and necessarily, a human institution, and while sharing largely in the miseries and the faults of humanity, is not altogether, even in these times, excluded from manifestations of human nobility.

CHAPTER X

History and Utopia

THE liberal conception, as a religion of development and of history, excludes and condemns, under the name of "Utopia," the idea of a definitive and perfect state, or a state of repose, whatever the form in which it is proposed or may be proposed. Such states range from those Eden-like states of the Earthly Paradise, the Age of Gold, or the Land of Cockaigne, to the various political forms of "one flock and one Pastor," of humanity completely enlightened by reason, or by the calculating reason, to a society utterly communist and equalitarian, free from internal and external struggles; from those conceived by the ingenuous popular mind to others reasoned out by philosophers like Immanuel Kant. Utopia, too, is part of the myth, translating into images the full and complete assuaging of the ever-returning thirst of our desires and the resolution of all the difficulties in which we labour. It would remain the mere symbol of this sentimental impulse, if it did not mistake its dream for something realized or realizable, or, worse, did not, as has sometimes happened, gird itself for the perilous and vain attempt to realize it. For example, Campanella towards the end of the sixteenth century tried to build the City of the Sun in his own Calabria, and at the beginning of the nineteenth century the followers of Owen and Fourier tried to carry out their designs for a rational and harmonious life in the colonies of the New World. But other dreams, lacking the broad extent of these, weaving themselves into ordinary life, and seeming plausible, are also utopias and remain mere dreams; for example, the abolition of war in every form, together with the very threat of war, the extermination of superstitions, the definite disappearance of priestly and of secular tyrannies, the discovery once for all of the mystery of the universe, the solution of the so-called "social question," and others.

On account of this negation of Utopia, liberalism, as compared with the various transcendental conceptions which offer a determinate faith and a secure hope in a definitive blessedness, has been judged sceptical and pessimistic: sceptical, because it finds truth nowhere but in the assiduous and unwearying research of thought, and pessimistic, because it similarly denies a state of blessedness which is nothing but a metaphor, and it finds happiness only in the joy of working and fighting, as man always must and can.

In its overcoming of the concept of the fixity of truth, and its removal beyond both pessimism and optimism, in a vision which comprises and binds them together in the unity of life and reality, consists its difference from the illuminism and progressivism and rationalism of the seventeenth century, which was its immediate predecessor, of which the character was so abstractly and extremely optimistic as not to shrink from precipitating a vast blood bath in the hope of seeing the dreamed-of universal happiness of the human race, founded on the triple bases of liberty, equality and fraternity, emerge from it beautiful and perfect. Its concept of progress is also different from that of the seventeenth century, for it does not make it consist in the fantastic increase and the gradual achievement of well-being and of happiness up to a final state of perfection, but simply in the conclusion of what precedes in what follows. (Only in this sense, then, that nothing in history passes away in vain or fruitlessly is there an ascent and a realized progress.) And it shows the futility of rhetorical assertions, even the most seductively deceptive of these, such as that which declared impossible a relapse of the world into barbarism, whereas this is so far from impossible that civilization consists in a continual vigilance and armed struggle against that peril. Equally false is the other comforting conviction that a people, whatever disasters overtake it and whatever its mistakes, does not die—whereas the truth is that a people dies, and when it seems to rise again it does not rise, but a new people that the spirit of the world has created. Which will certainly displease those who believe that we modern Italians are the former inhabitants of Italy, the ancient Romans, the Italians of the Renaissance and those of the Risorgimento, and not, what we really are, a new people with our evil and with our good closely joined to the whole world of our moment of history, a people which is indeed linked, but only ideally, with others that lived on the same earth (or almost the same), when on the civil plane it accomplishes great things as they accomplished them.

By thus bereaving man of the illusion that he can once and for all acquire and permanently possess truth, virtue and happiness, the liberal doctrine deprives itself of two most efficacious means of attracting to itself the vulgar of whatever social order. This accounts for its being assigned another character also, which is both a new title to admiration and a new alleged occasion of weakness: the aristocratic character with which is imprinted its conception and its method, which makes it (they say) comprehensible and acceptable by the few, but without hold on the multitude.

Certainly it is no remedy to counsel the liberal spirit to make good this presumed weakness, by accepting as *instrumentum regni* the illusions which it has rejected and shown to be futile, because if such a thing comes easily to those lay and ecclesiastical régimes which aim at dominating the ignorant swarms and at leading them to their own predetermined goals, and therefore adopt among their other weapons deceit and lying, this is strictly forbidden to the liberal spirit, which aims at liberty, and must educate intellectually and morally. What are nowadays called "mass successes" would therefore be of no use to it. However, does it not perhaps show lack of reflection or blindness to believe that whatever is austere and laborious and exhausting does not work in the world, or works to very much less effect than what is pleasant and comfortable? The effects of the latter are great only in appearance but are unsteady, and those of the former are really great and lasting. This is shown by the creations of poetic and scientific genius, often accompanied not at all or only to a slight degree by the recognition of contemporaries, and none the less constraining the following centuries to most assiduous recognition.

On the other hand, by the recognition of the community we do not mean the echo which follows upon an idea extending equally everywhere, and obtaining an equal response from every part. This notion can also be detected to be one of the usual metaphors that degenerate into utopias. The separation that the culture of the Renaissance had produced between the cultivated and the uncultivated classes has a very particular and relative significance, because neither was there in the preceding age, the mediaeval, with which it is contrasted, the presumed unity. In that age the clergy confronted the lack of culture not only of the peasants but of the upper class of barons and knights. The truth is that a unity in the sense of qualitative and quantitative uniformity is not found at any period; yet, without such uniformity, the unity of social life is always carried into effect. It is effected by means of works of beauty and works of truth, which in their genuine being are produced by the very few and appeal to the few, though others do homage to them without clear understanding, and yet others ignore them and deny them, while all, from the highest to the lowest, receive from them those benefits direct or indirect which they are capable of receiving. Similarly, few are born politicians and very few are born rulers willing and capable of being such. Most men are not politicians but the material of politics and government, whether that absorbed in other loves and other duties, they put their confidence in others and let things go because they do not know how to intervene and act themselves, or that they chatter and shriek and agitate, imagining that in so doing they also are engaging in politics.

The liberal method does not claim to call everybody to politics and the government of the commonwealth, putting them all on the same level, which is the democratic utopia. When people think that they have brought this into existence, it leads to demagogy and tyranny. Thus Savonarola was right when in certain of his gnomic verses he admonished the Florentine people to be contented with the "councils" or chambers, of more or less restricted composition, and not to allow themselves to be ensnared by the mirage of the so-called "Parliamentary assembly," or the gatherings of all the populace in the piazza, because the man "who wants to make a parliament" wants (he said) "to wrest the government from your hands." Nor can the liberal method convert all men into politicians against their nature and against the very nature of things, which does not allow all to be politicians, just as it does not allow all to be poets and philosophers and heroes, but has need of the varied and the diverse and the opposite, of the positive and the negative, to weave the web of reality.

But the liberal method does convert all from subjects into citizens, and gives to all, or to as many as possible, the means of sharing power, whether in government and administration, or by criticism and counsel, or through resistance, direct and in-direct, by means of its various institutions, freedom of speech and of the Press, and of association, of voting and standing for election, and so forth. Whoso wants to make use of these liberties can do so, inspired thereto by civil education directed to this end, and he can take part in the competition and in the political struggle, whose larger or smaller fruits depend upon the quality, more or less good, of the forces in play, and of the men who share in them and handle the method.

A political class, or ruling minority, which knows what it wants, is indispensable to the liberal state as to every other form of state, and the rest follows in consequence. And when it is affirmed that liberalism is depressed, or decadent, or exhausted, and that nobody any longer has faith in its institutions and in its ideals, and that these ideals have lost their plastic force and are reduced to abstract ideas, and that what was a powerful and ruling aristocracy has fallen to the rank of a heraldic or drawing-room nobility, this is but to say that these few, this minority, this ruling class is depressed or decadent or exhausted, and that it must rise again and revive itself, and that if it cannot renew and re-adjust itself to the new events and to changed social conditions, a new generation of men must succeed it, for whom ideals shall be not abstract but effective ideas, and institutions, once more acquiring their content, will acquire confidence again, so that they will compose a new aristocracy, young and vigorous like that of other days. But this ruling class, instead of making an honest recognition of its own fault and its own deficiency, and shaking itself and turning resolutely to its own duty, seems to prefer, as less wearisome and less perilous, to indulge in fancies about the new ideals that the new times have brought, and meanwhile accommodates itself to the changing times, and to the contingent historical situations that have been formed, accepting them as new ideals. Nevertheless, in such talk and activity, an obscure remorse pricks the conscience, and gives an indication of the ever persistent truth that the liberal idea is never outmoded because the moral ideal with which it substantially coincides cannot be outmoded.

Part V

Prospects of Historiography

CHAPTER I

History Does Not Repeat Itself and Does Not Preserve Itself Intact

JUDGMENT (otherwise termed the cognitive act, or historical thought), expressing itself wholly in the formula "S is P," or "I is U," marks the passage from consciousness to self-consciousness, from intuition to reflection, from the image to the concept. Upon the judgment there follows, in swift succession and pursuit, an act of classification, which is directed, as we have seen, to procuring possession of that judgment, or to making it more easily recollected and communicable to ourselves and others. It is plainly recognizable this difference and distinction between the moment in which truth gleams (the light of truth is always a gleam or a flash), and the moment in which we try to fix that light, by means of extrinsic relations, general determinations, analogies and so forth. The theory of this has often been elaborated as the difference between thinking and talking, but this is inexact, for the primitive act of thought is already a kind of talk and animates all speech that develops from it, while what follows and accompanies it is also indeed speech, but speech about classifications. On the other hand, it is observed that those who in their search for truth tend to replace the fundamental act of thinking by classifying, just so far as they succeed in doing so do not think and do not even classify. In the aridity of their minds, forcing two distinct proceedings into one, they lose contact with reality, as we say. Hence the recall to freshness of intuition and to inner concentration, which alone confer the power of attaining the True.

Similarly none can receive into himself and understand an historical narration except he be in a position to penetrate beyond those classifications, even while making use of them as paths; and to renew in himself the original act of judgment, that is, the intuition converted into thought and thereby, together with the original act, renew the memory of the experience of life which was the stimulus of that intuition and judgment.

When the very limited function of classificatory determinations in history is forgotten, there arises the false appearance of history as a continuous repetition of the same acts and vicissitudes, with only the names and the points in space and time changed. A change, this last, which however small and superficial it may seem in the stating, would by itself alone be enough to bring the principal proposition into doubt, for why ever would the names change, if the things did not change, that is, the spiritual conditions? And how could these remain the same in the different relationships that the changed position in space and time carries with it? But the fact is, that in this case we are dealing with a play of illusions, brought about by classificatory concepts, particularly by those of ideal origin, which have by our use of them been rendered abstract and rigid and immobile. We hear the historian of art speak of folk art and civilized art, of romanticism and the baroque, of classicism and romanticism, of idealism and realism, through all times and among all peoples. We hear the historian of philosophy speak of spiritualism and materialism and monism and dualism and empiricism and dialectic. We hear the historian of politics speak of liberty and tyranny, of democracy and demagogy and Caesarism. We finish by imagining and believing that history is a monotonous cycle in which tyranny follows upon liberty, and is later once more replaced by liberty, while materialism is followed by idealism and then by materialism again, romanticism by classicism and then romanticism again, and so on. But the essential point, the characteristic of history, does not consist of the descriptive labels affixed to the events, but the events themselves, each in itself, with its unmistakable physiognomy, in which all past events are stored up, and those of the future are already traceable.

People suffering from those illusions should go to learn from lovers, who are always persuaded that the beloved, and their own love, is indeed a thing new and unique in the world—and in being thus persuaded, are much nearer the truth.

Not only does history not repeat itself, but its products are not transported intact, like objects or instruments which pass from hand to hand, grasped by everybody, and lending their services to everybody. This second illusion is also derived, under final analysis, from the need of ever and again classifying and grouping facts as greater and less, principal and secondary, powerful and less powerful. Such distinctions give rise to the false idea of active and passive operations, active and passive spirits. The correct theory, in this case, is that all works and all spirits are active, and we only call those of them passive of which we seek to deny the existence, or rather we relegate them from one to another form of existence.

The best example of this kind that can be offered is furnished by the so-called "schools," in art or in philosophy, supposedly consisting of one original mind or genius and other secondary personalities, the latter in their work imitating the forms and concepts of the former. Now these others either have their own artistic and philosophic personality, in which case they have their own difficulties and their own solutions, intrinsically diverse from those of the presumed head of the school—or they are mere loudspeakers of his words and ideas, and as such, in art and philosophy they are nothing, and count only outside them, among the social popularisers of works of art and thought, reciters, printers, propagandists.

Therefore schools have no place in the true history of poetry or of philosophy, only personalities which, though described as greater and lesser, are in reality different. For when quality is being considered, there is no sense in speaking of greater and less. Each personality will be there with the work of poetry or philosophy which he was able to create within his own limitations, which after all form his own free domain. The non-poets and non-philosophers who are usually placed in so-called philosophical and poetical schools will instead find their niche in histories of tendencies and social customs, of parties, of slogans, of fashions, and so forth.

Nor can it be objected that, by means of schools and other similar groupings, we are to understand the various affiliations of the ideas and of works of art which are linked one to the others and form chains, each suspended from an initial link. This is also an illusion of classificatory origin which really consists of thinking of something, which from motives of convenience has been placed in order of perspective, as being placed in a genetic relationship. That the great poetry of Homer, Dante and Shakespeare, or that of Sophocles, Racine and Alfieri, may be placed in the same class, does not mean to say that Shakespeare is attached to Dante and Dante to Homer, or Racine to Sophocles and Alfieri to Racine, in an affiliation or poetic causation. Each of these poets, like each of these personages and men of action, is not attached to any particular class of facts in preceding history, but to all that history at once; just as an event is not the work of an individual or of a social class or of a political party, but of all individuals, classes and parties, positively and negatively taken in, those in opposition no less than those in co-operation being collaborators.

The very understanding of a philosophy, the evocation of a poem, are not obtainable except on condition of this activity of the recipient. He preserves their genuine reality in so far as he changes it, he lives it again in so far as he includes it in his own life which is no longer the life of those who produced it, and stopped at that point, and yet is that life, rediscovering it as a moment of its own. If there were not this meeting and exchange between the philosophy which is being re-thought and that of the man who is re-thinking it, between the poem recalled and the soul of the man who recalls it, the words would be echoed but the drama of thought, which is not a matter of echoing voices, would never be rekindled, and in the mere external repetition everything essential would be lost.

A particularly important requirement arises from what we

have just said—that through the similarity of words the dissimilarity of things shall be descried. Let us take an example from the history of philosophy and from concepts of which great use has been made in this book, like this one: that philosophy is, uniquely, philosophy of the spirit, and that of nature, understood as externality, there is indeed a science, but certainly not a philosophy. Such a doctrine might seem to be no more than a renewal of the Socratic teaching—that the task of philosophy must consist in, and restrict itself to, inquiry into the character of the beautiful and the ugly, the just and the unjust, the holy and the impious, and so forth, leaving to the gods the things of nature, which will always remain extraneous to men. The thought, however, which directed Socratic teaching was simply a lively piety and religious reverence, joined with solicitude for correct political and moral behaviour, a very general and distant anticipation of the modern, really humanist assertion, which implies a criticism of the natural sciences.

The doctrine might similarly be identified with the saying of Vico, that true knowledge of natural things must be left to God who created them, and human knowledge must be restricted to the knowledge of history, which man himself makes and therefore understands, if the importance of Vico's theory and its originality in respect to that of Socrates did not lie entirely in his new concept of knowledge as "interchangeableness of truth with reality," although knowledge is in Vico's words still considered incapable of penetrating the so-called world of nature. But our proposition does not reserve the knowledge of nature either for the gods or for the One God. It denies the reality of nature as an entity by defining it as an abstraction, and being an abstraction, as the work of the human mind, which posits it and projects it into an outwardness which is just the mind itself or an aspect of it. The new proposition implies not only Socrates and Vico, but the whole development of thought and of mind up to itself, and something more which is precisely its own thought; when it is willing to make the words of Socrates and Vico its own, it fills them with a content which originally they did not possess, although it may be intrinsic to the things which they were considering.

The examination which might be made of the Hegelian identity of philosophy and history, and of the similar formulas which we have adopted, would lead to the same result. Hegel aimed at resolving history into philosophy by giving it the movement of a system which develops and is completed in time. We, on the other hand, aim at resolving philosophy into history, considering it as an abstract moment of historical thought itself, and its systems as situations historically transient and historically justified, and, like every historical act, of eternal value. And to call this theory "Hegelian" theory and the preceding theories "Socratic" and "Vichian" is a way not only of failing to understand the new theories, but of failing to understand those of Socrates, Vico and Hegel also, which leap to the eye with their characteristic traits only in relation to the new thought, which affirms them and denies them, receives them and completes them.

Unfortunately, both history of philosophy and historical criticism abide in the miserable condition of judging by schools and systems, while the history of poetry has extricated itself or is on its way to doing so in the work of its best and most expert writers. It is certainly a dear and sweet sentiment which, in the labours and anxieties of research, often induces us to refer our thoughts to the great men of the past, and even to read them in their works by unconsciously introducing them there, so that we confirm them by the authority of their names and make them noble with the nobility of these ideal personalities. When, however, we seem just to have most closely embraced those great men, it suddenly happens that we feel that they are statues and we are mortal men, but living, that their words are definitive and ours in formation, that we admire them, but that they cannot satisfy our new and personal demands. Thus the soul of a poet, however infinitely he may love and venerate a poet of the past, in fact separates himself from him by singing a song that the older poet never sang.

We must dissipate the illusions of the repetitiveness of history and of the rigid persistence of its products, generated by the misunderstanding of classificatory concepts; we must on the contrary be fully aware that in history everything lasts only in so far as everything changes. By such awareness we shall spare ourselves from an exaggerated reaction against classificatory concepts leading to the erroneous rejection of the mental categories, the constituents of the judgment; and prevent the judgment itself from being lowered to the level of an act of brute vitality, devoid of cognitive character, while every criterion of value is lost in the darkness of the irrational. The slack conscience which does not react against the ugly, the false, and the bad, and the coarseness of the mind incapable of perceiving the difference between pure concepts and empirical concepts, between judgment and classification, conspire to bring about such degeneration.

Shades of Agnosticism, Mysticism and Scepticism, and the Light of Historical Truth

IT is a matter of common—not to say vulgar—opinion, that we know very little history, and that imperfectly; an infinitesimal quantity, if it be compared with the object which we ought to know. Even those whom we consider the most learned attain but a few drops, and those impure, of the immeasurable historical ocean.

This conviction pairs with another, to the effect that the knowledge of ultimate reality, of true reality, is unobtainable by the philosopher, who grasps only some of its reflections and senses the mystery which presses from all around upon him. Both these ideas are accompanied by the lament that in this finite life the infinite happiness which man desires is unattainable, and that the feeling of unhappiness which makes his heart heavy responds to the darkness which weighs upon his mind. This sophism, one beneath its triple form, takes its force from the incongruous concept of an infinite outside the finite, of a happiness cut off from unhappiness, of a definitive knowledge, a complete and total science—incongruous, because by asserting one of the two terms of a relationship and denying the other, it succeeds in denying and killing the very thing which it wished to assert and exalt. In fact, happiness without unhappiness, thought and science without limits, these things reduce life to nothingness and are fully accomplished only in death.

As happiness is in the instant and not outside it, so historical truth, and with it all truth, lies in knowledge of the particular, in which from time to time the whole is present—not in that of a whole in which every particular would once for all be comprised and exhausted. That would be repugnant to the concept of knowledge as itself, an act of life, and the begetter of ever new life. Nevertheless, even men who are not ignorant of this dynamic character of living and knowing, are seized with melancholy, agnosticism and pessimism before the unattainable knowledge of static totality. Droysen, who was among the very few who really worked with penetration upon the problems of historical gnoseology, closed a course upon the matter, in 1883, by lamenting that historiography did not possess, as did the natural sciences, the experimental method, confined as it is to research so that "even the research which gets most nearly to the bottom obtains only a fragmentary appearance of the past, while history and our knowledge of history are two things *toto caelo* different." "Nor," he added, "are the artifices of imagination, such as the Greeks used, any use. They painted a marvellously beautiful and harmonious image of their past, to which that part of the genuine past which has really been preserved has very little correspondence." But then Droysen continued, "This would discourage us, were it not that we can certainly follow the development of thoughts in history, even if there are gaps in the material. Thus we obtain, not an image of what really happened, but of our conception and of the elaboration of our spirit. And this is our makeshift satisfaction. To obtain it is not so easy, and the study of history is not so joyous as it seems at first sight."[1] The strange duplication of vision, by reason of which, beyond the knowledge which we exercise and possess at every instant—the only knowledge which truly and especially matters to us and is of use to us—we look for a knowledge outside the conditions of knowing, which would be useless even if it were not in itself impossible —to the point of terming this last true knowledge and the other a second-best or makeshift—has rarely been expressed so candidly and clearly.

The idea of so-called "universal history" has arisen from this demand for the impossible. It seeks, precisely, to embrace the totality of history, and in its consequential and logical, if mytho-

---

[1] *Historik,* op. cit., pp. 315–16.

logical, form, a Universal History was at one time expected to include the future as well, finishing with the anticipated account of the end of the world. Such "universal history," however, remains an idea and not a fact, because when executed the universal histories are either just compilations, manuals, and historical repertories, or else under the name of universal histories are really particular (universal-particular) histories, like every genuine history. The mechanical nature of this goal of total vision which universal history aims at, and the relapse of this in practice into an incoherent compilation, is shown up startlingly when, as in the case of certain contemporary works, the universality is forced into a geographical or spatial pattern.

Agnosticism or pessimism about history is aroused not only by the delusive phantom of a mechanical totality which we would see to know, but also by that no less tormenting and deluding problem of "origins of things" to be discovered. This problem, if it is considered seriously, reduces to the first and is a manifestation of it. In fact, the problem of origins (the origin of the world, of man, of civilization, of poetry, of the State, or more particularly of the Hellenic or mediaeval epic, of feudalism and so on; or more particularly still, of a given event or of a given work, such as the Reformation or *Faust*) is nourished by the idea of a totality of facts, in which the first fact is susceptible of being determined, or that which is first in the various series of facts which it may please us to discern. When we have chased away the phantom of "totality" we have chased away that of the "original fact."

Philosophy converts the fanciful concept of the origin of things into that of their ideal origin, otherwise said of their quality. It does not ask how thought or language or morals or religion were first born, but how they eternally come to life, that is, what is their eternal nature. Likewise historiography does not look for the origins of facts, but judges them, and in so doing assigns them an ideal origin in the human spirit. The mysterious nature of origins exists for it only as the very work of passing a sound judgment upon the fact which is present in consciousness, for, if this is accomplished, there is room for nothing else. Whatever is that appearance which is called the "night of beginnings"? Nothing but facts not present in consciousness, and therefore not qualified and not judged, the hemisphere of darkness around light, which would not be light but for that hemisphere, which will be from time to time displaced, as those facts emerge or re-emerge on to our consciousness whence other facts will have dropped away. We know certain poems which are reckoned the oldest in the Italian tongue; before these we are aware of a blank, and we say therefore that the origins of Italian poetry are not well known to us, or are not sufficiently known. But if other poems of more ancient date were found, we still should not have reached the imaginary "origins," and would only know those poems as well.

The same discouragement, which comes from the vain search for origins, is induced by the search for the "cause," whether the cause of this or that event or of this or that work or of the entire course of history, because at bottom the two searches resolve into one another as both depend upon the mechanical conception of totality. Hence the infinite disputes about the "cause" of the decadence of the Roman Empire, of the mediaeval world, of the Renaissance, of the French Revolution, and so forth, which have been fruitless, or if fruitful, not in the respect in which they sought. There is no better experience and no better proof of the intrinsically philosophical character of historiography than its irresistible rejection of every particular assignment of cause which may be persuasively offered.

A different darkness enwraps history when the perplexity is no longer that of extensive but, as we might say, of intensive totality, that is, of the identical and undifferentiated unity, which prevents the beginning of research and of historical knowledge. In philosophy, this kind of unity, intransigent in appearance, abstract or mathematical, in reality, is upon one side a residuum or a reflex of the incompletely absorbed personal God, and so it wearies itself in the sterile attempt to make differences disappear in unity, presupposing them or admitting them surreptitiously. On another side, and more simply, it satisfies itself as well as it can in an alogical mysticism. Similarly, history either disappears for the eye of the mystic who only finds in himself the inexpressible heart-beat of a life which is ever the same; or it is related with the due distinctions, but childishly adorned with unifying images. For example, offering thought which is logical as the unifying principle, the historian will speak of art which is thought, or politics which are thought in so far as they are politics, and so on; or offering matter as unifying principle, he will speak of that movement of matter which is logic, of that movement of matter which is justice and morality, etc.

The most open refutation of abstract unification and of its consequent philosophical and historical sophisms is furnished by the mental process, often recalled and described by us, which always moves, as we have shown, from a need of life. Now, this need is always differentiated, and this not because we cannot, as the proverb says, want two "things" at the same time, for infinite things can be comprised in an act of volition, but because we cannot accomplish two "acts" in the same time. If we think, deliberation is suspended and fantasy at a distance; if we compose poetry, logic and the will are suspended; if we do practical work, thought is no longer thought because it has solidified as a pre-supposition or as a faith, and so forth. Consequently, at the root of every historical research there is always an inquiry *secundum quid*, an inquiry after a determinate quality, moral or logical or aesthetic or whatever it may be. Therefore there is never a history in general, but always a specific history, of art, politics, morals, or philosophy, each of which contains the unity of the spirit. But of this last abstractly considered as outside or above things, it is as little possible to make a history, as (so Hegel said in an analogous case) to eat a fruit in general which is not a pear, a plum, an apricot, or other specified fruit.

The shades of scepticism, equally pessimistic, sometimes alternate in the mind of the historical researcher with those of agnosticism and mysticism, because he sees that the most dis-passionate and most severely elaborated historical constructions, whether his own or of others, even of the greatest historians, once they have been made no longer satisfy, or what is the same thing, do not satisfy completely. They stimulate and constrain to new researches and new constructions, which a similar destiny awaits. But if this fact saddens and frightens him it means that he has not succeeded in making clear to himself the nature of life and death, the relation of thought to life, the growing together of history and historiography, and the eternal working of the past in the present and towards the future, or of rendering his own spirit conformable thereto.

CHAPTER III

Humanity in Fragments and Integral Humanity

IT is also a false view to picture the course of history as a series of actions and of persons, each of which represents only a part or particle of humanity. This is so even if the series is thought of as progressive in such a way that in it the part or particle following is always fuller and richer than the preceding part. Unhappy condition of men if they could not even call themselves half men, nor the hundredths nor thousandths nor millionth parts of men, but were thus infinitely broken up and reduced to less than dust! It is very doubtful whether that part or particle would have the right to call itself human, if humanity is only such in its entirety, in its organism and in its soul.

This manner of historical representation and conception is habitual. In histories of philosophy we see, for example, Socrates discover the definition and the concept, Plato posit their metaphysical reality, Aristotle succeed in bringing it back to earth, Descartes make it internal, Kant interpret it as synthesis *a priori*, Hegel discover that the synthesis or idea is the whole and that beyond it there remains no unknowable reality, and so forth, each playing his part and exhausting himself in that part or partiality. Nor does it serve to say that each of them deceived himself with the idea that in his particular doctrine he possessed the whole: we are not weighing their illusion of being whole beings, but the fact of their not being such. Similarly in civil history it is usual to represent the Middle Ages as the period in which the spirit is thought in a transcendent form, and therefore other-worldly and ascetic, the Renaissance as the initial translation of Christian values into earthly values, Illuminism as the dazzling assertion of earthly values in the form of reason or rationality, opposed in turn to historical reality which diverges from it so far as it diverges from reason. Dialectic Idealism follows as the redemption of historical reality by dint of a profounder concept of reason, Liberalism as the correction of the ancient atomic libertarianism of the preceding age, and so on. Every age thus remains, from this point of view, imprisoned in partiality, which, however superior it may be, remains partiality and does not become wholeness.

The critique of this conception has been given already with the critique of the idea of progress in its double one-sidedness as the *progressus ad finitum* and the *progressus ad infinitum*,[1] because in the first form progress leads up to its own negation, a stasis, and in the second form it is reduced to a wearisome accumulation of particles which cannot ever win to the unity of the creative act. The conception which we are now criticizing depends upon both these one-sided notions, and most frequently upon the first, in which case there is in the historian's mind a belief or hope of a definitive form towards which humanity will have worked and which it will have achieved, or be on the point of achieving. But truth is restored only by re-uniting what should never have been divided, the infinite and the finite.

Such a refutation and correlative affirmation are not enough, however, or, at best, are not entirely clear and persuasive if the bond and unity of sameness and change, of humanity in its wholeness and in its dividedness or specialization are not understood in more detail and more exactly. The two propositions: "Humanity makes itself in its history," and "The presupposition of this history is humanity," are usually presented as distinct and often as contradictory, and yet they must form, and in fact do form, a single proposition.

Humanity in every epoch, in every human person, is always whole. To imagine it deprived of any category whatever of its own amounts to upsetting and overthrowing them all; to think it ignorant of itself and unconscious means that it is reduced to the low level of Nature (that unreality and abstraction which

[1] For the detailed development of this criticism, see *Saggio sullo Hegel*, pp. 144–71.

goes by that name); to long for it to be free once for all from its opposition, its struggles, its dialectic, is a disordered dream, and not a thinkable idea. The common saying that man is always the same is founded upon recognition of this obvious fact, and brings common sense to bear against the beliefs and paradoxes which see in the past or project into the future an essentially diverse humanity, of necessity heterogeneous, superhuman or unhuman.

Nevertheless this sameness of humanity cannot be divided or distinguished from its work or historical development, which would be to posit dualistically one humanity perpetually the same, and another changeable and transitory which attaches itself to the first and accompanies it, but can be separated from it and dismissed. Such a separation gives rise to the illusion of a *philosophia perennis* which lies under and beyond the philosophies that philosophers excogitate and about which they dispute, of a *religio perennis* or "natural religion" which all men have in common, when they are drawn out of their concrete or "positive" religions, as they are called. An illusion, because if we try to formulate that religion or that philosophy, super-historical, eternal and natural, we immediately re-enter the historical orbit with the individuality of its various determinations.

The correct thought is that the wholeness of humanity is not present to itself, and has no being except in the making of it, and the making is never a making in general, but a determinate and historical task. Therefore in the accomplishment of that task, humanity expresses itself in its wholeness, and when other tasks supervene it will express itself in these from time to time, always in its entirety. We must guard ourselves against personifying and subjectifying the bond which is found between the works and their antecedents and consequents, that is, the chain of these tasks, and substituting it for the living humanity which in the course of time has thought them out and realized them. The limit of which one is aware in every man, in every epoch and every work, is not a limit which they have in themselves, a mutilation and misery by which, whether they know it or not, they are affected.

Humanity in Fragments and Integral Humanity

It is nothing but the reference to the process of which the historian treats, when he, in order to clear up the source of a present condition, understands, determines and circumscribes the facts of the past which flow into it and emerge transfigured from it—facts which are "parts," but only in relation to this process.

History to be Written and History not to be Written

WHEN the mind prepares itself for historical reflection and research, what the poet said happens—we climb the peak of the centuries whence our eye dominates countries and cities which were previously seen only sketchily and piecemeal, and aspects of life which were at first veiled by the smoke of action now seem limpid. In so far as we are historians of poetry, what matters to us the practical person of the poet, or the political and moral tendencies to which he was bound, and in which he shared with a great part of his work, when in another part, the only part which has value for us in the aspect we are considering, in the midst of what are called contingent facts (and so they are comparatively) he created a poem which confronts us now as though come down from Heaven, a creation of pure beauty, the only subject of the history of which we are treating? What matters a disputed and confuted error in a doctrine when the doctrine is regarded by the eye of the historian of philosophy? He no longer perceives the error in it, but the truth, not the limit which restricted it and the obstacles against which it stumbled, but its original and fundamental reason, the service which it filled in driving away a greater error, transporting problems to a higher sphere, provoking, as in a logical experiment loyally accomplished and carried to its extreme, the birth of something different and opposite. What matter to the historian blows received and given, shouts raised, outcry of mutual accusations? He sees emerging out of these conflicts the lines of a new political, social, and moral formation, of a new institution with which reality was pregnant, and that this could be brought into the world only by means of this laborious process. All those who, in whatever manner, took part in it, gentlemen and scum, intelligent and stupid, the historian recognizes as positively and negatively (and in ultimate analysis, always positively) necessary, and, speaking historically, he is reconciled with all of them, because "foes' wrath survives not past the funeral pyre" and history is always "beyond the pyre." What is called the "impartiality" of the historian is all one with the disposition to think historically and to relate history, and it is natural and vivid in the historian that sometimes he must guard himself from a certain indulgence in exaggerating the value of those whom he opposed or would have opposed in practical life. Towards these he is sometimes drawn into a generosity which is wrongful, not being really historical, but a perverted repercussion of the practical struggle itself.

Certainly, the disposition of the historian which we have described is taken by itself an intention, a sincere and good intention, which meets with great difficulties in its strivings towards realization as will-power; a progress challenged step by step in its proceeding towards the goal proposed. The difficulties and the hindrances are preconceptions which weigh upon his mind and spirit, old ideas which have not been corrected and enriched in the course of further development, ideas which have remained stagnant, or what appear to be ideas and firm judgments, but are substantially feelings and passions in a state of fixation—in one word, everything that lowers the level of the mind and is mental inertia. Hence the many histories which, in general and in particular, are not true to themselves: histories rendered turbid and opaque by religious myths, by insufficient philosophical concepts, by party idols. These are histories which we read distrustfully, taking care not to rely on their guidance, but to accept it only at points at which the historian's intellect moves free from presuppositions or unconsciously abandons them, and to value them chiefly as an examination from a contradictory standpoint which makes our own ideas clearer and sharpens our pen. The debates of history turn in great part on such questions of Value, as it is called, that is, of standards of judgment and of philosophy, and the others, called questions of Fact, about the genuineness of documents, bulk a great deal less, and in any case depend upon the former. But if this were not the case, if these difficulties did not appear and make it necessary to overcome them, the work of history would not only be too easy, but it would not be work, unless it be work to smash through open doors; would not indeed really take place, as in fact it does not take place in respect of truths of idea and fact not in dispute, which are referred to a common patrimony admitted by all and to a faith which is not disturbed by doubt. Nor should we imagine or expect or hope that the progress of this complicated and intense mental work will lead to a general and agreed philosophical and historical conviction, or to a state approximating thereto, for the challenge and the labour that goes with it are always arising in some new form, introducing difficulty and friction, and only thus can humanity grow. There is never any other fashion or rhythm save this in spiritual progress; it is first accomplished in individual and solitary thinkers or in small circles of kindred spirits and collaborators, until, as a result and not as a process, it issues into general culture, and hence, in the form of myth or of dictum enveloped in religious mystery, it passes at last to what we call the vulgar or the masses.

Yet in other cases it seems that we see the impartiality of the historian replaced by its absolute opposite, by the most resolute and aggressive partiality, and that not on account of a lapse into evil and error, nor with such conscience and remorse as are felt when one abandons oneself to a passion or commits a crime, but with a sure sense of acting rightly, of asserting one's rights and doing one's duty. Then exaltation and abhorrence, love and hate, for the deeds and men that history had carried away beyond this conflict into its ideal city, *civitas Dei*, arise once more and none will listen to the man who reprehendingly calls them back to fairness and true judgment. How can the two different attitudes be explained and justified? How can the two different duties expressed in them be reconciled?

The answer which is usually given is that there is a distinction between past and present, or between the remote past and the immediate past, and that history should be written about the past or the remote past, and not about the present or recent past, where we walk on treacherous ashes which still conceal a fire. This distinction cannot possibly hold good, for to found a logical distinction upon a greater or less chronological distance is to offend sharply and jarringly against reality. For, on the one hand, if a deed is a deed, and, as the old Italian saying has it, *Cosa fatta capo ha*,[1] the origin of a deed is found in its character, and one can and does write history about it, though it may belong to an instant which has scarcely passed; while on the other hand, love and hate, exaltation and defeat, in the case which we are considering, do not reveal themselves only in the history of our own generation or of the preceding one, or of the last fifty years, or of the last century, but as everybody knows and perceives, they ascend the whole stream of history and invest it all with their fury, taking sides with Cato against Caesar, with Socrates against Athens, or, if so be, with Saul against Samuel, or the reverse, for these are personages not less living than those who lived a few years ago, or who are still living nowadays. For that matter, this solution, inexact in its logical formulation, is on the right lines in interpreting its temporal distinction between remote past and recent past or present as a metaphor for the ideal and conceptual distinction between the time for the writing of history and the time for action, that is, between the attitude of knowing and the attitude of doing, which follow each other in a necessary nexus, but are nevertheless not to be confounded.

To introduce the time for the writing of history into the time for action, to take up the attitude of historical thinkers when in fact we are acting in a practical fashion, would be empty effort if it were not in its turn a mode of action, a fillip administered to ourselves, an attempt to discourage the adversary and force him to renunciation. It is a mode of action in which we do not make use of history, for history cannot be "made use of," and can only

[1] "What's done's done." (Translator.)

be thought, but we endeavour to prepare and produce the varied feeling that arises from the vision of good and evil, of triumph and defeat, of safety and peril, of salvation or certain perdition, and to this end we have recourse to the evocation of facts which have happened or are said to have happened. This practical process, which arises spontaneously in uncultivated minds and in the undisciplined and uneducated, is artificially cultivated in applied rhetoric, and is indispensable when time, place, or persons do not allow of other means for increasing energetic action. But for that very reason it is obvious that the philosopher and the historian ought not to and cannot share in it; they ought not, out of respect to their cloth, and cannot, on account of the difficulty for them of such unaccustomed action, which being repugnant to that cloth, would in any case be cold and failing in persuasion. Besides, the philosopher and historian, and the man who is philosophically and historically educated and disciplined recognizes and distinguishes the hour for knowing and the hour for doing; he knows, like every other man, when it is his business to risk his own person, as a practical man, and refusing to falsify the writing of history by turning it into a practical struggle, he refuses similarly to falsify the practical struggle by turning it into historiography, procuring for himself and others a cowardly moral alibi. The deliberate sophism which interchanges "historical serenity" and moral weakness or servility, is so miserable as not to be worth refutation—scorn is enough.

History is about the past-which-is-present, action is of the present, and imagination of the future; imagination, mother of hopes and fears, which the historical inquirer keeps at a distance and the man of action rejects, playing with it only in the pauses and lapses of their thinking and acting. When imagination weaves a fable, or traces the lines of a story projected into the future, we have so-called prediction or prophecy, "the memory of times not yet born," history of the future, of which the substance is the imagination itself, lacking any logical foundation. And when it seems that historical forecasts assume the bearing of logical truth, or receive confirmation from events, look at them more closely and you will see that they are neither forecasts nor historical, but merely the deductions and reasonings of concepts, economic, moral, or whatever they may be; necessary consequences from premises and not effects or facts, which come into the world only by the work of the will, which is free by definition, and necessary only because so and not otherwise have they been willed and realized.

CHAPTER V

Historiography and Naturalism

It may seem somewhat strange that in our discourse of historiography we have not entered into discussion or refutation of concepts which, in the second half of the nineteenth century, were of such prominence, for example—taking some at random —"environment," "influences," "races," and similar ideas, but have scarcely so much as mentioned them by the way. The reason is that having excluded the concept of "cause" from philosophical and historical thought, and having taken our distance from every form of naturalism, the refutation of the particular concepts deriving from it was implicit and the demonstration could be taken for granted.

Let us take, for example, the concept of "environment," which in that era had so much prominence given to it, not solely in the literary hypotheses of Taine, who saw it, powerful and imperious, together with "race," moulding every part of history, whether political, social, artistic, or philosophic.

This is definitely a naturalistic and determinist concept, and retains for us, as such, no utility whatever, and in this matter we must behave in a more radical manner than did Hegel, who attributed to it a maximum efficacy in the life of animals and a minimum in that of mankind. "The animal," he said, "lives in sympathy with its environment; both its specific character and its particular developments depend upon it, entirely so among many animals, more or less among all of them. In man, such bonds of dependence diminish in importance the more cultured he is, and thus the more all his creation of life is placed on a liberal and spiritual foundation. The history of mankind is not dependent upon revolutions in the solar systems, nor the vicissitudes of individuals upon the position of the planets."[1]

The truth is that the environment always has its reality and power over men as over animals, but only in the same way that all the past, all previous history has its power, and therefore only in relation to the new action and the new life which is created, in unbreakable unity, and outside such a relationship it is unreal, fantastic, an impotent abstraction, to which it is wrong to attribute the power of determining life and action.

If this criticism now seems somewhat obvious, it is more difficult to recognize the infiltrations of naturalistic concepts into history and to guard against them. Keeping to the example we have chosen, "environment," we find that this oft-repeated saying, that a philosopher of genius takes up and resolves the problem entrusted to him by the society of his time, upon which so many others have previously laboured, reduces itself to this idea of "environment" unless, indeed, it is no more than a figurative manner of speech. And it is the same with the idea that a poet of genius in his song interprets the feeling of that society or of many kindred spirits who had tried to give it poetic form. "Society" in this case represents the environment, and the philosopher or the poet is supposed to work as its chosen mouthpiece. Now, the song of the poet coincides wholly with the individual passion which moves the poet, and its form is ever new like its content; similarly the problem and the solution of the philosopher coincide in a real unity. It is possible to discourse about the need fulfilled by that song and by that theory as of something which already existed in a widely diffused manner, but if we look closely at the appearance of this asserted common and general need, we see it disappear and change into the reality of problems and solutions which were never exactly this theory, and of expressions which were not this particular new song, or into the reality of events, actions and passions which were things in themselves and not some other thing or things supposedly brought to a complete or final form.

[1] *Encyclopaedia*, par. 397, note.

And we realize, then, that these ubiquitous appearances of problems offered to thought, which finally by the aid of our philosopher receive an answer; of rough sketches or material offered to the imagination, which finally perfects the former and accepts and elaborates the latter; of imperfect attempts to do what is later done to perfection, are due one and all to the action of the new thought, in arranging these scattered problems and solutions in their place in a system, and that only on that account it seems almost as though they had preceded the new thought and generated it. Similarly the new poem, by rising above preceding expressions and poems, makes them re-echo in it, thus bringing about the illusion that it already existed in them in the form of a need; and the new event gathers past events into itself, preparing those of the future.

Thus we also dissociate ourselves from that historical conception which a witty English writer called the "firemen's chain"—the firemen, drawn up in single file, swiftly pass from hand to hand the bucket of water to throw on the flames to extinguish the fire: the hands are many, and the bucket is one, but it is carried continually nearer to the task which has been assigned it. Against such a doctrine, in relation to art and poetry, Leo Tolstoy protested. Warning us against such supposed genealogical series as that of Balzac-Flaubert-Zola by the reminder that every genius begins again from the beginning and is born only of himself.[1] Against a similar view, in respect of the history of philosophy, protests are nowadays raised insistently: "In no other case," I read in a recent monograph on Hegel, "has the history of philosophy been so roughly treated in its psychological and historical relations of dependence as with the pretended line of descent: Kant-Fichte-Schelling-Hegel. In no other case have the relative originality and the independent development of personality been so sacrificed to a scheme of logical construction apparently simple and luminous."[2] The problems of Fichte are not those of Kant,

---

[1] See Croce, *Nuovi saggi di estetica*, p. 168.

[2] T. L. Haering, *Hegel, sein Wollen und sein Werk* (Leipzig-Berlin, 1929), I, pp. 56-57. The arbitrary nature of this affiliation had already been noticed and

nor the problems of Schelling those of Fichte, and so on, and if the later seem to arise out of the earlier, it is because the later thought is richer and contains the earlier.

Also to be referred to the naturalistic concept of environment in its fixity and abstractness is the whole of a certain false theory of art and poetry. This theory is eager to deduce works of art from the Neo-classic, the baroque, the romantic, and so forth, that is to say, from environments and traditions which have no real existence in art other than in particular works, or in particular minds. In these the environments are no longer merely themselves, but the individual minds or works, poetic if these are poetic, prosaic if they are prosaic, and outside them existing only as other works of art or other determinate acts of knowledge, of practice, of morality, of custom, or whatever they may be.

refuted in 1890 by Lucien Herr in his article in the *Grande Encyclopédie* on Hegel: it may be consulted now in Herr, *Choix d'écrits* (Paris, 1932), I, pp. 117–19.

CHAPTER VI

Nature as History, not as History Written by Us

BOTH in everyday and in learned thought it is usual to deny without hesitation that nature has an historical character, nature being understood as the complex of beings inferior to man. This denial is explicable only as a reflection of certain religious views, or of a most un-Franciscan scorn for natural beings, or of the false belief that these beings are not living but mechanical, and so on. The denial is logically unjustifiable, for (given that reality is mind which is becoming or history) a part of reality which is not history cannot be conceived, just as, on the other hand, when an historical character is attributed to nature, it is inconceivable that its history should develop mechanically and not spiritually.

For the same reasons the division usually made between the history of mankind and the history of nature is inadmissible. An assignable distinctive criterion is lacking, and both, in an homogeneous manner, belong to the single spirituality and the single history.

And if so-called nature, too, is spiritual and historical, it is necessary to agree (however paradoxical the affirmation may sound) that it cannot be without awareness, in its own fashion, of what it is doing, that is, awareness of its history. How would it have brought itself about, and how would it continue to do so, without feeling and thinking and desiring and willing, without labours and satisfactions, joy and sorrow, without aspirations, without memories? No doubt foolish pride may greet this affirmation with disdain and scornful smiles; but this is the same pride that, proceeding along these lines, denies—although it may not confess it openly—human awareness to primitive men, and next the lower classes or to foreign peoples, and at last even to one's own neighbours of the same social group, until the proud man is disposed to believe that he alone possesses this awareness as a privilege.

But this historical awareness which is in their very life, this unwritten history, is recognized from time to time by the beings whom we call natural. We could, by completing and correcting a saying of Vico, say that they know it because they have made it and are making it—not that God, as Vico said, knows it thus, but the natural beings themselves, animals or plants, or whatever they may be, know it—but men do not know it, because they have not made it and are not making it.

They do not know it, do not want to, and cannot know it, and it remains for them a closed book, for a reason which shines forth clearly when we have abandoned the idea of historiography as the passive notation of a reality detached from us, and have accepted the true idea of historiography as a theoretical problem arising out of a need for action and correlative to this need. Man does not reconstruct, think or write the history of natural beings because their needs of action are not his; and similarly even in the history of human beings he is uninterested in some parts which are too remote from his present and living interests, just as, while following one of these interests to a determinate end, he provisionally disinterests himself in others, and therefore is not actually in position to construct their respective history.

One of the many questions often proposed and never answered, because badly proposed, concerns the starting-point of human history, which is sometimes stated to be with the invention of writing, at other times with the formation of the State, at others with the appearance of individuality, and in other manners. It has occurred to no one that it begins every time that the need arises for the understanding of a situation in order to act. The other ways of determining the beginning are in fact arbitrary because sought for and found in things which are extrinsic, or have been made so.

If our knowledge, our effective and full knowledge, consists in this, what are called cognitions about natural things are not properly cognitions, but abstractions executed upon the living reality of the world. Being abstractions, they are the product of a practical operation, in which things are stamped and marked in order that they may be found again and used when necessary, not in order that they may be understood. Rather does that very act of abstraction make them unintelligible, external things, soulless objects, blind forces without the spirit which moves them. They become things which are ordered and classified, placed in relationship among each other, measured, calculated, and not known at all.

Such is the operation of the so-called sciences of nature. We are not maligning them when we define their method and aim as we have defined them. The students of the sciences do not themselves define them otherwise, when they assert that they stick to appearances and phenomena, putting essences and noumena aside, and saying that beyond phenomena lie the unknowable and mysterious. In fact, beyond them or below them is history, which has been known by the being who should know it when he should know it, but has been forgotten by and unknown to us in so far as it does not matter to us that we should know it.

Either it does not matter to us provisionally, or it does not matter for an indefinite time. It does not matter provisionally, as in the case in which, while we are engaged in stating and solving an historical problem about a particular situation of our life, the other situations relapse, for the time being, into merely indifferent things upon which we perform the abstraction which materializes them, renders them external, classifies them, measures and calculates them, which does not prevent them from once more becoming from time to time the object of historical problem and thought. Or it does not matter for an indefinite time, as in the case in which things have been so far surpassed by us and removed to such a distance that they do not revive, and presumably will not revive, as problems and solutions of ours. An example of the first case is offered by the so-called positivist or naturalistic sciences of spiritual facts, such as the classifications of psychology, of linguistics and grammar, of the moral virtues, of legal and political forms, which from time to time dissolve and give place to the concrete, the individual and historical. An example of the second case is given by the so-called natural sciences, such as zoology or botany. These have at their foundations an historical character that man will never feel or think again within the limits of what can be foreseen, because in order to feel them or think them again he would have to abase himself to a subhuman level, as sometimes he does abase himself in certain conditions considered pathological, in which he re-acquires sympathies and correspondences with natural things or beings, such as he does not possess in the ordinary state of sanity and will lose again when he returns to sanity.

Each various attempt to know historically, that is, to know in their intrinsic nature, natural things can but substitute for the knowing process some process of the imagination. This may simply be that things are animated by the imagination as in the fables about animals and all the others in which things are given sense and life. Or it may be that we dream of entering into familiar relationships with them by means of a supposed magic art and power. Or it may be, finally, that as in certain philosophies of the Romantic period, they are converted into categories of a metaphysical order.

A particular method of this last imaginative transfiguration was notably accepted in the age of Positivism by reason of its apparent independence of religious beliefs. It consisted in taking the classifications of natural beings that the natural sciences make, and arranging them in series from the most simple to the most complex—rather like the Days of Creation—and giving such a series an historical colour by making use of tautological formulae, such as "evolution," "passage from the indistinct to the distinct," "struggle for existence," "survival of the strongest" (or of the fittest). Thus a pseudo-history was shaped which, basing its argument on having discovered the genesis of animal-man, joined itself to human history in a single series, from the nebula which was regarded as the beginning of the life of heaven and earth to the political and social forms of Europe in the nineteenth century.

In the same way in which this conception of natural evolution succeeded the philosophy of nature of the Romantic Age and was substituted for it, so the history of humanity, which was its continuation, succeeded the philosophy of history and replaced it. A new positivist and naturalist historiography was installed, which destroyed all genuine historical sense and all lively and powerful historical thought.

At the Seventh Congress of German Historians, held in 1903, the voice of the economist, Friedrich von Gottl-Ottilienfeld was raised against this type of historiography, conspicuously represented in Germany by Lamprecht. He energetically denied the community and even the affinity of the historian with the geologist, of whom the former has as his object events (*das Geschehen*) and the latter stratifications (*die Schichtung*), and thereby refused to admit the continuity which had been asserted of the evolutionary history of nature with the history of humanity. He resolutely required the "emancipation of historical thought from the naturalistic," and the pretended history of nature (which evolutionism constructed and which historians had too heedlessly accepted and struggled to continue by fastening human history to it), he dubbed "meta-history," considering it a formation analogous to the ancient "metaphysics."[1]

The criticism of Gottl-Ottilienfeld did not then take root, nor was it lucky later among German historians,[2] who were as yet entangled in naturalistic concepts, but it was nevertheless an

[1] The memorandum presented to the Congress of 1903 is now reprinted, with introduction and long explanatory appendixes and discussions, in the author's volume *Wirtschaft als Leben, eine Sammlung erkenntniskritischer Arbeiten* (Jena, Fischer, 1925).

[2] The author says so himself, pref. op. cit., p. xx: "Bei uns hat der Vortrag auch später wenig Beachtung gefunden, mehr dagegen ins Auslande, genannt sei nur Benedetto Croce," See *Teoria e storia della storiografia* (3rd edition, Bari, 1927), pp. 163–70.

arrow which hit the bull's-eye and remained firmly stuck.[1] After that, this pseudo-history should have been recognized by the intelligent for what it was, a pseudo-history in two senses (if I have argued correctly): it is false history in general, and false history of nature. For the latter has certainly a history which is appropriate to it and not false, immanent and not transcendent, not "meta-history," and if this does not usually figure as history to man's mind that is for want of a stimulus, for want of practical importance and significance: and being therefore a dead history, it lends itself to the mechanical and determinist treatment which the positive and natural sciences give it.

[1] An anticipation of the criticism of Gottl-Ottilienfeld might be glimpsed in Hegel, who said that it was "an unsound representation of the old and of the new philosophy of nature to consider the progress and passage from a natural form and sphere to a higher one as a production furnished with external reality, which, however, to make it more *luminous*, is then pushed back into the *obscurity* of the past. . . . Misty representations, ultimately of sensible origin, such as the birth of animals and plants from water or of more developed animal organisms from lower, etc., must be entirely excluded from philosophical consideration." (*Philosophy of Nature*, Part II, *Encyclopaedia*, par. 299, note.) We must, however, note that Hegel denied the historicity of nature, and following the method of the philosophy of nature, kept to the conception of it as a "system of grades, of which the one issues necessarily from the other, and is the actual truth of the grade from which it results," conformably with the dialectic of the Idea. Not only, therefore, was the concept of the historical character of nature foreign to him, but his criticism could not have the significance and value of that made by Gottl-Ottilienfeld in very different conditions and with different reference. We must remember that the continuity of evolution from nature to the history of man is the assumption of the *Ideen zur Philosophie der Geschichte der Menscheit* of Herder. This also was treated with feeling and imagination, but not critically, as its contemporary Kant showed in his review of that book (see *Works*, edition of the Prussian Academy, VIII, pp. 43–66).

CHAPTER VII

Prehistory and History

THE point we have already cleared up about the historical character of nature and "meta-history" or "history of Nature," which does not represent it in the least because it is a naturalistic classification upon a scale of ascending magnitudes by means of which the series of classes so constructed is given a false imprint of historical development, makes it easy to understand and settle the disputes which have arisen about "prehistory."

When the studies thus named began to grow in extent and importance, a sense of mistrust, of estrangement and even of scorn could be noted among historians. (The witty remark, attributed to Mommsen, about that "illiterate" science is well known.) They were heard to demand that it should be excluded from what is properly speaking history. But others replied that if history is the science of men in the development of their activities as social beings, carried out in conformity with the principle of psycho-physical causation, there is no reason whatever for excluding prehistory, in which this social aspect and these activities are already manifest, from history proper.[1] It is true, they conceded, that "a knowledge by averages and types" is better adapted to the facts about primitive or inferior peoples, and that a useful division of labour counsels us to entrust prehistory to a special science—ethnography or ethnology—because professional historians are not familiar with the knowledge and the methods which it requires.[2] This concession let it out that prehistory was indeed viewed as a natural science, with superimposed historical or meta-historical embellishments. Thus the

[1] E.g. see the defence of this thesis in E. Bernheim, *Lehrbuch der historischen Methode*, pp. 44–52.
[2] Op. cit., p. 46.

reply amounted simply to the affirmation that natural science and the principle of causality can be extended, if we like, to all the facts of all times and all places, which, however obviously the case, did not advance the argument at all, because it did not penetrate the motive of the repugnance which the historians felt towards prehistory.

On the other hand, the historians, ensnared in varying degree in the same naturalistic concept of history, could not rebut that reply, because they were not in a position to give the well-founded reason of their feeling, and in so doing to limit it and prevent it from becoming excessive and capricious. The secret motive of their repugnance was that in the facts, as prehistory offered them, they could not usually catch a glimpse of any bond with the problems of human life, whereas these are linked still by a strong body with the histories of Greece and Rome, and with at least some parts of the histories of the East and of Egypt. Prehistory presented itself to them as a collection or even a mere prospectus of information, the material of innumerable conjectures, and often of pure imagination about things which remained external, indeterminate and inanimate because without an echo in our soul. They therefore turned their backs upon it as upon that other natural or philosophico-naturalistic science, sociology, with which they saw prehistory marching in good accord, or even identifying itself.

But here it is necessary to mark the limit of their negation and the point at which repugnance should give way to the opposite attitude. When a particular question of genuine historical quality arises in relation to those prehistoric zones, prehistory becomes history, as does any other congeries of facts which lies provisionally inert. When Vico began his research, far beyond the range of the usual superficial ideas, into the nature of language and poetry, or of the State and religion, it occurred to him in a flash, as in a vision or presentiment, that these forms of the spirit must have been, in the primitive ages, furnished with an energy, a body, a power which was later attenuated or mingled with other and diverse things, becoming more hidden and less visible. And he had to force himself, as he said, to "descend from our refined human natures to "natures savage and cruel," primitive and prehistoric, "which we cannot in fact imagine and only with great difficulty are permitted to understand." We do yet understand, because there is a trace of those dispositions from a remote age in the lowest depths of our being, below our "refined nature." In this way Vico, among the very first to make use, for this purpose, of the method which was afterwards called comparative, used it to support the evidence which he discovered in his spirit, and which he set his mind to interpret.

But, certainly, to convert prehistory into history is not everyday's task, nor is it everybody's work, and if we have wished to show, with the reference to Vico, in what this conversion really consists, it has been in order to clear away the illusion that it is enough to place (as is done in manuals and universal histories) a chapter of prehistory, perhaps preceded by another chapter of history of "Nature" or of "the Earth," immediately ahead of Oriental History. This is a type of prologue now often seen in many treatises of the kind, which fails to enliven the intellect, nay it mortifies the mind, which asks from history the noble vision of human struggles and new food for moral enthusiasm, but receives instead the image of fanciful animal and mechanical origins of mankind, and with it a sense of discomfort and depression and almost of shame in finding ourselves the descendants of these ancestors, substantially like them—notwithstanding the illusions and hypocrisies of civilization—and brutal as they were. We do not feel thus about the ancestors whom Vico assigns to us, although he calls them "big brutes," for they have at the bottom of their hearts a divine spark, and fear God, and raise altars to him; through him they feel shame awake, and found marriage and families and bury their dead, and through that Divine spark they create language and poetry and the first science which is the myth. In such a way prehistory, where it happens that it is really raised to the level of history, remains human and does not make us relapse into naturalism and materialism.

CHAPTER VIII

Chronological and Historical Epochs

"HISTORICAL EPOCHS" bounded chronologically and counter-signed with a concept or a general representation, or with the figure of some personage or other symbol, are divisions of use to the memory, legitimate to this end and even indispensable as is proved by the fact that they arise spontaneously and cannot commonly be avoided. When, however, their origin and purpose is forgotten, when they stiffen into concepts or philosophical categories, they no longer serve to make the memory of history easier, but rather to compress it, deform and mutilate it, and so, indeed, to make its truth forgotten.

This is met not only in the extreme case of the so-called "Philosophies of history," hybrids of abstract philosophy and distorted historiography, but it can also be observed in a tendency of many historians, to start with an "epoch" fashioned in this mode, and therefore to expound real history—political, moral, religious, literary, or whatever it may be—as though they were carrying out a programme contained in the title conferred upon the epoch. In it the individual persons and actions and works are posed as if the persons were employees of the epoch, and the actions were tasks assigned to and discharged by them. Hence the difficulty frequently felt with persons and works more openly resistent to the reduction of their being to the epoch in which they have been inscribed, and the qualifications, often disparaging, which they receive, such as "retarded," "anachronistic," "hetero-clite," "isolated." Sometimes it is even judged well actually to omit mention of them, because while they lived and worked, they did not see to it that they lived and worked conformably to the pigeon-holes of which the future historian disposes for their location; so they must pay the penalty of such lack of foresight, by remaining shut out of historiography, even if they had a place in history.

Similarly, from forgetfulness of the practical origin and empirical use of divisions by chronological periods arise inextricable controversies about the character of this epoch or that, for example, of the "Middle Ages" or of "humanism" or the "baroque" or "romanticism." A vain attempt is made to arrive at elaborate definitions which will embrace all the facts contained in these chronological partitions, whereas the real problem, in these cases, is to define the universal forms and modes of the spirit which the titles indicate. These cannot be confined within chronological limits, but by their nature are extra-temporal. The definitions obtained should then be used in order to understand certain aspects of the facts gathered into the framework of the relative chronological epoch, which aspects are the objects upon which the real interest of the historian is directed. It even happens that we witness the personification of the "centuries," under their numerical designations, and we watch the determination and deduction of their characteristics and modes of working and disputes about these things. Sometimes this is carried so far as to be laughable, as when, in the last part of the nineteenth century, the division *fin de siècle* was formed and had its vogue, being used as a substantive and also adjectivally, to describe a presumed ideal and moral content, so that it almost seemed to become a norm for action and behaviour.

But while historians often feel the rigidity of these conceptualized compartments of time, and the incapacity of such epochs to embrace and explain the facts to be understood and judged or described, yet instead of rejecting outright the mistaken proceeding of conceptualizing the epochs, they try to correct it, amplify it, and adapt it. Hence they speak, for example, of "transition periods" as though every period and every moment of it were not transition, and perpetual creation of new life; or they distinguish epochs into "organic" and "critical," towards which distinctions the same reserve is to be made, that every epoch is organic and critical at the same time. Sometimes the rebellion is made on correct grounds, but the formula with which it concludes is not correct, as in the case of Ranke. He protested against the treatment, usual in philosophies of history, of one epoch as a mere passage to the following epoch, agitated through and through by this aspiration and suffering in its awareness at once of one-sidedness, imperfection, and deficiency. Against that he emphasized the positive and self-contained character of each epoch; but, in so doing, we can say that he expelled one mythology by means of another, that of restlessness by the other of satisfaction, breaking the immanent continuity of the course of history by the idea of a transcendent God uttering a word in each single period.

The truth is that, when we bring thought to bear on history in its concrete reality, we always pass beyond the sphere of such chronological divisions into periods, which are not valid for such thinking, nor ever will be, in spite of corrections and variations and modifications which may be introduced. Their use is simply what we have said it to be, and it is not permissible to abuse it. From the index, which is by design schematic and a skeleton, we must pass on to reading the book; from the announcement and playbill we must enter to watch the play itself, which is not for the sake of the bill, but the bill is for the sake of the play.

In this direct intellectual intuition of the real and concrete, not chronological or extrinsic, process of the Spirit, which is history, "epochs" (without which the process would not be thinkable, or would not be at all) are certainly to be distinguished. For its unity consists only in the variety of its determinations, its infinity in the finite things in which it is unceasingly realized, its universality in the individuations which it is ever surpassing, and of which it is ever producing new forms. Its epochs are, then, itself, that is, its works with which it fully coincides, and in which everything consists. Each of these works is at the same time closed in itself and open towards others. It has been said sometimes in protesting against a mythological personification that "the genius of an epoch is nothing but its men of genius."

The saying is more profound and rich in consequences than the state of mind which has usually accompanied it. When lit up by the light of intellect, and subjected to criticism, the chronological epoch vanishes, leaving place for the numerous real epochs which it had covered with its veil—that veil which was transparent in its first and simple uses, but often made dense by lack of reflection and mental laziness, and transformed into a heavy opaque fog.

Historical thought recognizes these real epochs, these individual works, not the abstract and unreal—recognizes the true and not the fictitious. In Italy, where the sense of poetry and art is lively and has a long tradition (so that even today, in somewhat unfavourable times, it persists as best it may), we have worked hard to conceive and realize a history of literature and art; not such a history of metaphysical idealism and positivism produced in rivalry by dint of compressions and contortions, not an arid sequence or a fallacious dialectic of epochs and schools and extra-aesthetic or pseudo-aesthetic tendencies, but something like a choir to which one may hearken and direct the mind's attention; an eternally living choir of harmonious voices, in which each has its unrepeatable and personal timbre and all are in accord in the constancy and unity of eternal poetry. The man who still pauses to ask whether Dante expressed the fourteenth century or the age of the Communes or the Middle Ages, or Ariosto Humanism and the Renaissance, or Tasso the Counter-Reformation, and Foscolo the Napoleonic period, and so forth, or whether Homer expressed the unification of the Greek stock, and Sophocles the religious feeling of Athens, and Virgil the Roman consciousness of Empire, is still far removed from the true and individual standpoint of history of poetry and of history in general. We need not add that such an interpretation which reduces poetical geniuses to the rank of supporters and publicists and mouthpieces of particular, practical or supposedly practical interests, makes them poor, narrow, and indeed not poetic, and shows a scant feeling for poetry, or entire lack of it, in the man who is satisfied with it. The new conception of literary and art history meets and will continue to meet with opposition and misunderstanding, but it will in the end prevail, or, which for us is the same thing, it already prevails and reigns in us and effectually governs our judgments.

All other histories must, like the history of poetry, release themselves from mechanical subjection to chronological periods, exercising and moving themselves and freely unfolding the fullness and richness of their individualities. This process, which is in part just begun, in part already well advanced, can be observed in the studies of history of philosophy, as of political, civil and moral history, in conformity with the historical nature of the modern mind and with its logic which is the logic of the concrete. The generalizations and abstractions, mistaken for truth, gradually yield before the truth of the individual which is the real universal, the living God.

Nevertheless, we hear it objected against the individualizing conception of philosophy-history that works which are thus interpreted and qualified and described one by one, lack the unifying bond which used to join them, and must, perhaps indeed in a new form, somehow be restored. The objection may well arouse wonder, because to interpret and judge an individual work among other individual works necessarily implies its being gathered into the unity of a process which is composed of all of them. The work is therefore linked to the whole and in definite relationship with all the other works which have preceded and followed it. There is therefore no place for any other bond, for it is not possible to join together what has already strongly and indissolubly joined itself. But the wonder ceases when we observe that, at bottom, what is desired and demanded are handy groups and handy chronological divisions, and the pleasure they give with their apparent orderliness; and on the other hand, what is feared is the being deprived of this support and aid to memory and imagination. A thing which is not at all our intention. We have wished only to put historians on their guard against the confusion of chronological periods with real periods, and against the false judgments and false problems, as tiresome as they are insoluble, derived from this confusion, and we wish to insist on emphasizing the capital truth, that if to think is to think historically, to think is, always and solely, to individualize.

CHAPTER IX

Natural Species and Historical Formations

BY way of a quip, we could say that the concept of "race" does not find fortune among the "thorough-bred" historians. And the motive of their disdain and of their cold and silent rejection is due here also to the character of individuality which belongs to historical truth, and, as we have shown, to every genuine truth. A fact which we are pleased here to present in the words of Machiavelli: "If anything pleases or teaches in history, it is that which is described in detail."

The historian knows and marks well the formation of common modes of feeling, thinking and doing, in human societies and in their various moments, times, epochs, or whatever we may call them, modes which differentiate them from those of other moments, times and epochs. Italians of the age of the Communes, for example, are very different from Italians of the Counter-Reformation and of the Spanish domination, and all differ from the Italians of the Risorgimento. The very aspect, the air, the physiognomies of these three social communities confront us, sharply distinct, in the portraits remaining to us of the men who represented them. And yet neither the historian nor the ordinary talker (except in certain metaphorical and emphatic expressions as when it is said that "a new race seems to have arisen," and so forth) make use, in these cases of the word "race." For these communities are historically individual, and therefore arise, modify and dissolve or resolve themselves, whereas race seems to be distinguished from the course of history and to stand above it or intervene in it like a natural force and entity.

It seems so, but in fact when we try to discover or determine it as a natural force we never succeed in grasping it in the real world. In reality, "race" cannot be detached from the so-called "environment," that is, from historical conditions, nor can it be fixed and described as constant, because it changes with the changing world. Neither can the supposed different races be distinguished radically, because they have always mingled and still mingle, so that regarded from the imaginary standpoint of purity, they all appear impure or mixed. The foundation of that extra-historical concept of race is not "physical," as believed, but "metaphysical," nay "mythological," referring to a God who created human races fixed like the fixed species of other living beings, those species which even the historicized natural science of the nineteenth century considered variable.

Of course such fixed races, which criticism denies and of which history is ignorant, are passionately asserted, championed, assailed and defended in political struggles, but this merely proves that their reality is constituted by passion and imagination, and not by truth—it consists in a phantasm and not in a concept. Idols of passion as they are, they can be brought to truth only in one way: by showing through what ideal process they are generated and by treating them at the same time historically, that is, by unfolding the history of the individual works and events in which they have played their part.

Their ideal genesis is due in the first place to the practical need for classification, which in this connection leads to the grouping of men according to empirical ties of place, family, language and so forth, forming varied groups, from the larger and largest which cover one or more of the five parts of the world to the small and smallest which are limited to the narrow confines of a city or a village. Into such groupings by external and superficial characteristics are then introduced determinations, also empirical, but of a psychological character, referring to moral, intellectual, artistic, technical, practical and other aptitudes of the particular groups. So far there is nothing to which we need object, for the purpose and intention is and remains that of serving the understanding and the memory, which draw advantage from divisions into classes, let us say, of French, Germans, English, or of Indo-Europeans, Semites, and Turanians, and also from the psychological characterizations which permit us to say, roughly and generally speaking, that the French are logical and tend to the abstract, the Germans speculative and dialectical and tend to the concrete, the English observers and experimentalists—or, again, that the French are impetuous, the Germans methodical, and the English both prudent and bold, and so on. It must, of course, be understood that since these are classifications, we must expect to see them contradicted from time to time and rendered out of date by changing and developing reality, and to find ourselves forced to signalize distinctive characters differently from the way in which this was first done, if they are to retain any use whatever. And another warning should not be overlooked, though it has often been overlooked. It is that these classifications, made *pour parler le monde* and not *pour le juger,* will not serve as criteria of judgment, because in judgment we must qualify a work in its individuality, as a human individuation of the human universal, so that there is no sense in judging it according to a fictitious universal, an abstraction, a pigeon-hole which we have constructed for our convenience. For example, it is no use to say that this work is intellectualistic because it is French, or profound and speculative because it is German, or realistic because it is English. We should not do honour nor justice to Dante by defining him as Italian, to Shakespeare by defining him as English, to Socrates by defining him as Athenian, to Kant by defining him as German, because if these definitions had, as fortunately they have not, real content, we should succeed in withdrawing from these men, together with their own personalities, the universal humanity of which they are heroic figures.

With these reserves and these warnings the concepts of race and other characteristics of nations, countries, regions and towns will maintain themselves quite innocently in their modest function as aids to memory. But they lose their innocence and become quarrelsome and malign when those descriptions of aptitudes are qualified positively and negatively as good and evil, useful and harmful in relation to the ends of our activity. It is not in the least necessary, if one desires to observe this passionate transformation at work, to turn the eyes towards the great loves and great hates, often lasting centuries and sometimes thousands of years, of whole peoples, who celebrate themselves as "chosen peoples," nations or races "superior" in respect to others or to all others, pointing out one particular people as their perpetual antithesis or their hereditary enemy, and keep on their guard against another, alone or with allies, because they regard it as not to be assimilated, divided from themselves in mind and soul, following interests adverse or strange to them. It is not necessary, we were saying, because the same process can be observed in miniature, limpidly and completely, in the frequent case of two neighbouring towns, of which one—or both—is full of the feeling of its own superiority and of its own arrogance, and sees in the other its "hereditary enemy" and the stranger which cannot be "assimilated." Thus, understood as powers of good and evil, the classificatory concepts of race link up again with the imaginative naturalistic idea of race, and like it also acquire a sort of reality, but only metaphysical and mythological.

Such a process of passion and imagination, which history conceives and represents as a fact among facts, is for the politician a material which he handles and uses for his own ends, as was seen in the last war and continues to be seen in the unpeaceful peace which has followed. But the moral man, the religious man has the different duty of always defying what is often called "the race" prejudice, to fight it incessantly and continually re-establish the consciousness of a single humanity, which the division into races, transmuted from classificatory into real, disturbs, and if it could, would destroy by means of the incurable separation and of the reciprocal foreignness which is introduced. If the Jew Ezra separated his own people *a populis terrarum*, the Jew Jesus, rising to common and universal humanity, recognized in the Samaritan the man *qui fecit misericordiam*, as neither the priest nor the Levite had been able to do among his people. In the moral life, not Ezra but Jesus is here the Master.

CHAPTER X

Poetry and Historiography

THE relation of likeness and difference between poetry and history was already established and defined in a celebrated place in the *Poetics of Aristotle*, Chapter IX. The Aristotelian position and definition allow us to measure the great advance of the human mind from the Greek conception of the life of the mind to our own, the modern conception.

In Aristotle, the highest and perfect knowledge, because knowledge of eternal and necessary universals, is philosophy; and the nearest to it is shown to be poetry. Poetry, representing according to verisimilitude and necessity, tends more closely to the universal than does history, which diverges strongly, turning to the particular (according to the Aristotelian example, to what Alcibiades did and suffered), thereby showing itself to be less philosophical and less austere than poetry.

But just as modern truth has gradually freed itself from the chains of Greek and then of mediaeval transcendence, the modern theory of logic has withdrawn philosophy from heaven or from the peak on which it practised its sterile contemplation of the Ideas. It has invited and constrained it to descend towards the earth, while, in the same act, it has withdrawn history from its lowly function as a collector of anecdotes, a chronicler of what happens, and has raised it towards Heaven or the peak of the Ideas, making it meet philosophy half way, embrace it and mingle with it into a new spiritual personality. At the same time, modern aesthetics has advanced, destroying the traditional doctrine of poetry as a superior form, or more public form of philosophy, like the latter founded on universals or ideas, and has distinguished it both from philosophy and from history, assigning it a sphere which is certainly theoretical, but is neither logical nor historical, and may be called the sphere of fancy.

Such is the end of a revolution slowly and laboriously realized, which certainly has its precedents and its roots in the same difficulties with which the Ancients struggled, but nevertheless, when the extreme terms which we have pointed out are considered, appears a complete reversal. It is right to take account of its deep significance, because concepts and modes of judgment still persist today which habitually and unconsciously are bound up with the ancient conception, surviving but no longer properly living in the world of the living.

To understand profoundly the new relation between poetry and history, we must set out, in both cases, from the practical and moral life and from its dialectic of action and passion. Action, as new life realizing itself, is in the same act death and passion, springing life and dying life. Anxiety, effort, the weariness of this eternal nexus of life and death, of joy and sorrow, of pleasure and pain, mingle in an aspiration for repose; that is, not really for the cessation of life but for life which should be a true repose, action which should be action without the torment of passion. This cannot be called contradictory and absurd, since it is not a logical affirmation but an aspiration, and therewith a relief which action wins for an instant. But that aspiration may also acquire hardness and consistency, expanding into an ideal towards which one aspires, an ideal that, being contradictory and absurd, is not really an ideal, but as we are more frequently accustomed to call it, a dream—the dream of blessedness.

It is a dream which takes the various shapes, now of an idyll of simple life and placid work, among the pure joys of home, in the peace of the country, often modelled upon the image of the good old times—or times thought good because old; now of sweet, intoxicating or ecstatic love; now of a state of Paradise, of something surpassing the human, of peace attained in the Divine; forms which sometimes combine with one another, whence love is coloured with religion, religion with eroticism, and similarly the idyll, and so forth.

Nor is the dream dreamed by all in the same manner. There are those who dream it as believers or even as fanatics, as if it were an ideal which could be realized, and they pass hastily to unfortunate attempts to realize it. And there are those who dream it with the awareness that it is a dream, but let themselves go the way of pleasantness, in moments of idleness, tiredness or emptiness, and yet, letting themselves go, they do not give themselves up to it, being always ready to draw back and return to the one Reality. But except in the case, or in those instants, of credulity and fanaticism, all know and admit that this dream, common more or less to all men, belongs to human frailty, and is a sort of weakness. For this reason, it has no rôle in education, like the positive modes of human activity. No one has ever thought of providing an education in dreaming. Rather does the work of education fight it, curb it, and dismiss it as far in the background as possible. The stigma of unhealthiness, which is impressed upon our dreams, finds confirmation in the shame with which they are usually denied or hidden or veiled by those who experience them, and in the blame meted out to those who have the habit of communicating them to other men, to whom we should give information not about our passional disturbances, but about our collaboration in the work of society. Besides, egoism and evil have been discovered and acknowledged in the depths of these dreams, in the desires for life in another world no less than in the idyllic and erotic. And with evil, with the desperate wish and search for an unattainable satisfaction, there creeps in a sense of languor and a desire for dissolution.

But how comes it that what in real life is regarded and punished as madness and sickness, forms an object of admiration, exalts and elevates the soul, becomes beautiful and pure, when expressed in poetry? Works of poetry have always aroused suspicion and repugnance, even disgust and scandal in ascetic minds, who saw or caught a glimpse in them of the world, the flesh and the Devil. I remember that Herbert Spencer (who in my youth was acclaimed as a philosopher) condemned them all or nearly all, epics and Greek tragedies, mediaeval romances, Shakespearian dramas and works of modern art, because full of battles and blood and inferior sentiments. But by dint of feeling and judging in that way we are, for lack of poetic feeling, held back or thrown back on to the brute matter of poetry, where it is natural that we find only the dream, disturbed, sorrowful, tormented, wandering, of unattainable bliss, for there is nothing else to be found there, nothing but love-sorrow, eternal inspiration of poetry, in its full sense which is of Heaven and Hell, of pleasure and pain united. Action itself, even the most heroic, does not lend itself to be the material of poetry except in so far as it is the passive suffering of action and the melancholy and tragedy of action. And even if there are makers of verses, of pictures, of music, who do not free themselves successfully from the material of poetry, and do not sing but to some extent live their dream, true and complete poetry has the power of rendering the impure pure, the disturbed serene, precisely because such poetry is not "dream" (as is often said, meaning that such is its material), but the overcoming of the dream, a dream with eyes open, a passion illuminated by the light of truth upon the background of the infinite and in harmony with the whole.

This liberation from the fierce fang of passion, and the form of knowledge which represents it, and which is in fact intuitive, is not enough for the formation of action, but is its necessary presupposition, and as it were a first step. We must go further, and not only bridle the tumult of passion and prepare for the acceptance of life and of its law, which is law of industry, moral law, but prepare ourselves for definite and particular forms of activity, for definite and particular duties. We must therefore know the situation in which we find ourselves, the point which the history of the world, which is the history of each of us at every instant, has reached. The inner act, in which we attain this form of knowledge, no longer intuitive but logical, is the judgment; and judgment and historiography are, as we know, identical in quality as in extension.

Poetry and history are, then, the two wings of the same breathing creature, the two linked moments of the knowing mind. A third wing, more powerful than the two in this relationship, there is not because it would be of no use, and it is of no use because it does not exist; philosophy is a moment of historical thought, as a concept is a moment of the judgment, and outside this it has no life—for those piles of abstractions which take the name of philosophy in treatises and in scholastic dissertations cannot be considered living. The requirement of something above both may take an appearance of life in the effort to pass beyond the universal-particular of historical knowledge and to sink back into mere historically undifferentiated universality, purely ideal and super-historical. This effort, however, leads back from thought to imagination, from historiography which is criticism, to poetry. Thus more than once, in the history of thought, to the question how we can attain the Absolute, the reply has been to designate poetry and to make Art the speculative instrument *par excellence*. In this solution the ancient Aristotelian concept bloomed again—that poetry is more philosophical than history, more philosophical precisely because philosophy was conceived to be non-historical and history as non-philosophical.

CHAPTER XI

Historicism and Humanism

HISTORICISM is creation of appropriate actions, thoughts, or poems, by moving from present awareness of the past; historical culture is the acquired habit or power of so thinking and doing; historical education, the formation of this habit.

To bring the characteristics of the historical attitude into clearer light it is helpful to compare this word, "historicism," of recent origin and various and changing meanings, with an ancient word of which the use recurs throughout the centuries, although its meaning also varies (as for that matter, does the meaning of all words)—"humanism." The comparison will help us to understand both concepts, and may be followed by an identification of both in the formula that historicism is the true humanism, that is, it is the truth of humanism.

In fact, the universal principal of humanism, both of that which in the ancient world has its greatest example in Cicero, as of the new which flourished in Italy between the fourteenth and the sixteenth century, and of all those arising or artificially constructed later, consists in the reference to a past to gain light from it for one's own work and action.

The fact that certain more or less defective concepts and historical limitations, of varying importance but always arbitrary, meet with this principle does not affect the principle itself. It merely confirms the necessity of the correction of those errors and narrow views which historicism has gradually accomplished. Let us begin with the most serious or best known case. Humanism has been accused of immobility and servility. Against it there have been revolts and revolutions on the ground that it had adopted the concept of imitation and had exalted the past (the particular past which it had a liking for) as a model.

But in practice it was the imitators, the *servum pecus*, who were guilty of servility, not humanism itself, nor the humanist conception of imitation which was a first attempt and approximation, though certainly insufficient, at affirming the bond of the past with the present, of history with action. In this respect, imitation, in the humanist sense, was not a mere copying or repetition. It was imitation, but also variation, competition and renovation, or in other words an imitation not of the thing but of the method of the thing, and this, if it is considered well, amounted to a substantial correction of the concepts of model and imitation. For the man who varies and competes and outclasses something works afresh from his own wits and does not cling to a model, or (which is the same thing) does not cling strictly speaking to the model, but to law which it exemplifies, and therefore he attains to the eternal founts of the Spirit, or to its eternal categories. Thus a glimpse was caught of the problem, but it was not well stated and not resolved as historicism later resolved it by throwing a light on both the dependence and the independence of the present with respect to the past, and of the new work with respect to the works which compose the history of humanity.

And then humanism only gradually enlarged its vision of the past as competent to give light and guidance. Cicero and other Romans found this guide in Greece, considered only, however, in its cultural relations; the new Italians found it in Greco-Roman antiquity, the Germans at the end of the eighteenth century in Greece as it really was or was believed to be—in the Greek spirit as something above or opposed to the Roman (and they sometimes also amplified it into Aryan or Indo-European humanity). To all this were opposed, in the rebellions to which we have referred, the proposal and the cry that one should *se délivrer des Grecs et des Romains*, and should take as model the great moderns or indeed reject any model whatsoever. Still it was gradually agreed that the poets and writers and artists of modern times should take their places by the side of the Greeks and Romans, and modern languages and literatures played their part in humanist education. But humanism, however great the

316

concessions it made, never arrived at the conclusion which historicism affirms: that the past which enlightens our determination and action is the whole history of humanity, which from time to time becomes present again in us. It was an impediment to such a conclusion that the past to which the mind was directed had been conceived as a model, for this consequently implied the choice of certain times and certain peoples to the exclusion of others, and ultimately the choice from among this primary selection of certain particular works according to one's requirements and personal predilections.

A third accusation which is commonly made against humanism is less just. This is the view that because it had asserted itself chiefly in poetry, literature, the fine arts and architecture, it lacked awareness of connections with the rest of history, scientific and religious, political and moral. In truth, there was a humanism analogous to this literary humanism in the modern period, all admiration and calls to imitation of the great deeds and the great personages of Greek, and especially of Roman, history. Its support and instrument (among others) were the *Lives* of Plutarch, and in general the books of the ancient historians. Oriental and modern history, like their respective poetry, literature and art, succeeded only slowly in claiming their place beside the ancient, although, on the other hand, there were explosions, half romantic and half barbaric, such that even today, with our own eyes, we can observe denials, aversion and scorn being levelled against Roman history, and the exaltation in its place of an imaginary history of the most ancient Germans, whom a bold invention joins to Greek civilization, hailing them as authors of the latter as though it were one of the many admirable works which the Germans, with the liberality of a most humane people, have generously given to the world; authors, too, of other similar works which they will give to it, if only the world will let them do as they like and will accept their rule.

The fact that the names of some of the most celebrated humanists are those of mere men of letters, closed or only slightly open to politics and philosophy, is not enough to limit humanism, as it manifested itself in history, to the history of literature and art alone. If there were fanatical lovers of Homer, there were similarly fanatical lovers of Brutus—some of them were seen in the Italian Renaissance and some in the French Revolution. However this may be, historicism, which refuses to recognize any limitations in time and space, also denies those of a qualitative character, and understands as history all history, that of action and thought no less than that of literature and art.

If these corrections brought by historicism purge from humanism the dross of its literary origin and let the fundamental truth shine forth, from another point of view we can see how, in this developed form, humanism now resumes the office which it so signally filled in its first age of greatness, that in which the Middle Ages were decaying and the Renaissance flourishing. Humanism was then a movement towards earthly and worldly life against the transcendent and ascetic idea, and its embrace of Greek and Roman culture had this intrinsic and pregnant signification. Certain contemporary artificial theories, constructed by Catholic or Catholicizing writers and by paradox-mongers who try to represent humanism as though it had been born in the service of Catholicism and of the Roman Church, a sort of rebirth of the thought of the Early Fathers, are so riddled with sophistries as to forget the meaning of the very words they use. For the thought of the Early Fathers itself made use of the pagan literature and poetry which had gone before, and had existed as pagan and not Christian, and similarly the Catholic Church took what was to its advantage from the literary forms which came into honour with neo-paganism, that is, with humanism—this was practised first with a certain simplicity and ingenuity by sincerely pious writers, and continued to the pitch of perversion by the political astuteness of the Jesuits. Humanism in its origins seemed only a movement of impatience against scholasticism and a hymn of joy to classic beauty, working principally in the field of art. But upon its rise there follows closely the eager progress of culture and of thought, which renewed philosophy and all the moral disciplines, ethics and politics and the theory of art, and scientific methodology. The heir of this great labour is historicism, which contains in itself liberation from transcendence of all kinds, affirmation of moral, political and economic life, emphasis upon passion and poetry, rejuvenation of intellectual and moral life, dialectic which is its new logical instrument. Without these conditions and parts it is not possible to think history truly.

Finally, if we note in humanism—already in that of past ages—but much more outstandingly in that of our age—an indifference or aversion from the natural sciences, physical and mathematical, the sign of a sort of war which from time to time is rekindled between humanists and would-be scientists, and in general between the cultivators of the mental sciences and those of the natural sciences; the sign, too, of educational controversies between the humanist school and the real or technical school; this indifference or aversion attains its justification and at the same time its purification in historicism, because it did not really aim at the discredit and overthrow of the adversary—the mathematical, physical and natural sciences—but was, and is, only a mode of self-defence against the superfluous adornments of determinism and materialism, which are commonly woven around the sciences and drew strength from their name. Reality is history and is only historically known. The sciences certainly measure it and classify it as is necessary, but properly speaking do not know it, nor is it their business to know its intrinsic nature. The claim to dignity of the *Studia humaniora* over against the *Studia realia* means nothing but this; and nothing less than this, but nothing more is endorsed, for its part, by historicism.

By resolving humanism into historicism, not only do we penetrate into its essential motive and understand the part it played in the history of the European mind, but we also close the door to the bad use often made of it when it comes to be restricted to certain particular tendencies or would-be tendencies, whether literary or moral or religious. Even the so-called Hellenizing German humanism had not and could not have the character, vigour and fruitfulness of that humanism which closed the Middle Ages and opened the modern period. For this German humanism of Winckelmann and of the Wolfs appeared when a more direct and profound knowledge of things Greek and Roman was certainly possible, and with the fresh interpretation a renewal of their spiritual power, but the foundation of the *regnum hominis* which had been founded long before and was growing stronger and expanding magnificently, was no longer possible. And contemporary programmes of humanism appear vague and tangled and perplexed just because that idea is too closely bound to mere classical philology, and its representatives. lack the knowledge that in order to be thought and seriously realized, the humanistic idea must necessarily be identified with historicism, which is the humanism of modern times, and adequate to modern times. As for the so-called "humanism" asserted and vaunted in some schools and sects and petty circles of aesthetes and decadents—in which truly it is not easy to find either the *homo* or the *vir*—we can, in the present discussion, neglect it without harm.[1]

---

[1] It is worth while here to recall a typical passage from humanism to historicism, because its particular importance has not been noticed or understood. It is the passage which may be observed in the youthful development of Hegel for which his writings of that time, now published and studied, serve as documentation. He passed by degrees from a first pagan form for which the ideal was Greece, and for which Christianity was abhorrent, to the historical acceptance of Christianity, to the recognition of what it contributed which was new and superior to the Greek, and which remains as the foundation of the modern epoch. He passed, that is, from humanism to *Weltgeschichte*.

Index

Achilles 207
Acton, Lord 68
Alexander 48, 104
Alexander of Macedon 96
Alexander VI 48
Alfieri, Vittorio 61, 207, 268
d'Annunzio 235
Ariosto 94, 304
Aristotle 37, 76, 97, 138, 149, 278, 310
Attila 164
Augustine, St. 49, 96

Bacon, Francis 33, 138
Baggesen 81
Balbo 180
Balduino, F. 121
Balzac 290
du Barry 118
Bayle 97
Becque, H. 191
Bentham 84
Bernheim 129, 129 fn., 298 fn.
Bernini 109
Bismarck 93, 95
Blackwell 71
Blanc 181
Boiardo 94
Borgia, C. 166
Bossuet 96
Bourget, P. 193
Bruno, G. 118
Brutus 119, 318
Buckle 182
Burckhardt, 100 et seq., 114, 125
Burke 71
Byron 118

Caesar 47, 48, 104, 285
Campanella, Thomas 29, 134, 256
Capone 180

Carducci 81, 227
Carlyle 181
Casanova 118
Cassirer 70, 72
Cato 285
Caulaincourt 186 fn.
Cavour 83
Charles of Bourbon, King 39
Charles IV 94
Christ 48, 59, 207, 248, 251
Cicero 181, 315, 316
Cola di Rienzo 94
Columbus 118
Commodus Pertinax 28
Comte, A. 149
Condillac 190
Condorcet 71
Constant, Benjamin 245, 246
Copernicus 68
Cosimo de' Medici 166
Courier, Paul Louis 15
Cousin 59
Cromwell 118

Dahlmann 186
Dandin, G. 130
Daniel 142
Dante 26, 155, 166, 231, 268, 304, 308
Danton 209
Darwin 79 fn.
De Maistre 74
Descartes 40, 74, 115, 278
Dilthey, W. 86 fn., 88 fn., 99, 100 fn., 137
Don Quixote 203
Droysen 133, 133 fn., 137, 138, 180, 212, 213, 273

Early Fathers 318
Edward III 94

Erasmus 52
Ezra 309

Falier, M. 94
Faust 274
Fergusson 71
Ferruccio 209
Fichte 20, 80, 81, 82, 290, 291
Ficino 115
Flaubert 290
Fonseca, E. de 125
Foscolo 118, 304
Fourier 256
Frederick II of Prussia 96
Frederick William I 96

Galiani, Abbé 29
Galileo 118
Genghis Khan 164
Gervinus 180
Gibbon 68, 71
Gieselrecht 180
Goethe 36, 44, 55, 71, 75, 76, 78, 80,
    118, 122, 125, 167, 196, 231, 240
Gottl-Othlienfeld, F. von 296, 297 fn.
Gresélrecht 98
Grote 181
Guglia, E 86 fn., 90 fn., 91 fn., 92 fn.,
    93 fn.
Guicciardini 170
Guizot 181

Haering, T. L. 290
Haller 74
Hartmann, E. von 102
Hazard, P. 70 fn.
Hegel 20, 38, 40, 53, 59, 71, 76, 78,
    79, 79 fn., 80, 81, 82, 96, 110 fn., 143,
    145, 166, 196, 211, 253, 270, 276, 278,
    288, 290, 297 fn., 320 fn.
Heine 81, 97, 98
Herbart 38
Herder 71, 80, 82, 167, 297 fn.
Herodotus 100
Herr, L. 291
Heusser 84 fn.

Hirsch 98
Holy Fathers 118
Homer 76, 268, 304
Humboldt, Wilhelm von 89, 90, 129,
    137, 167
Hume 71

Janssen 180
Jessop, T. E. 72 fn.
Jesus 48, 59, 207, 248, 251
Jhering 174 fn.
Judas 48

Kant 40, 80, 81, 110 fn., 115, 118,
    137, 165, 190, 256, 278, 290, 308
Kierkegaard 103
Köpke 98

Lamprecht 296
Layard 198
Leibniz 71, 75, 197
Lemâitre 193
Leo 97
Leo X 52
Leopardi 91 fn.
Lessing 71, 220
Linnaeus 90
Livy 170
Lorenz 86 fn., 91
Louis XIV 93
Louis XVI 92
Löwith, K. 101 fn.
Lucretius 252
Luther 26, 52

Macaulay 181
Machiavelli 70, 76, 166, 170
Mahomet 251
Manzoni, Alexander 47
Maramaldo 209
Marcel Etienne 94
Marcus Aurelius 28
Marie Antoinette 112, 118
Martin 181
Marx, K. 53, 83, 149, 202, 224, 243

Marx, R. 109 fn.
Mary Stuart 209
Max, King of Bavaria 93
Mazzini 70, 94, 219
Meinecke 66, 66 fn., 67, 68, 71, 72, 72 fn., 74, 75, 76, 78, 80, 82, fn., 83, 84 fn., 91 fn., 135
Menger, K. 84
Merimée, P. 119
Michelet, *History of France* 24, 59, 181
Mignet 181
Mommsen 298
Montaigne 33, 119, 122–23
Montesquieu 71
Möser 71, 74, 80, 82
Muratori 97, 233

Napoleon 26, 48, 61, 92, 118, 157, 166, 186 fn.
Napoleon III 93
Nebuchadnezzar 142
Nicholas I 200
Niebuhr 97, 102, 156, 157, 158
Nietzsche 105, 107

Oersted 146
Oken 90
Omodeo 74 fn.
Owen 256

Percy 71
Pericles 104, 248
Petrarch 115, 128
Pharsalia, Battle of 17
Philip II 48
Pico, G. 115
Pius V 96
Plato 38, 73, 76, 97, 173, 278
Plutarch 118, 119, 317
Polybius 17, 76
Pompadour 118
Pompey 17, 48

Racine 268
Ranke 46 fn., 66, 78, 79, 80, 85 et seq., 104, 106, 107
Raphael 109 fn.

Rembrandt 108 fn., 109 fn.
Renan E. 128, 192
Renouvoir, *Uchronie* 28
Richard III 209
Riehl 104
Robert of Anjou 128
Robertson 71
Robespierre 81, 209
Roland, Mme 125
Roteck 180
Rousseau 71
Rubens 109 fn.

Salpetrière 190
Samuel
Sanctis, F. de 73, 73 fn.
Saul 285
Savonarola 259
Schaumann 81
Schelling 80, 100, 290, 291
Schlegel 80
Schopenhauer 102
Schornfeld, W. 110
Schulenburg, W. von D. 100 fn., 104 fn.
Segni, B. 167
Severus 102
Shaftesbury 71
Shakespeare 76, 155, 268, 308
Sismondi 245, 246
Socrates 37, 38, 48, 166, 269, 270, 278, 285, 308
Sophocles 268, 304
Spencer, Herbert 312
Stendhal 235
Stewart, D. 137
Sybel, H. von 156, 158, 180

Tacitus 49
Taine 181, 182, 190, 191, 192, 193, 193 fn., 194, 195, 288
Talma 166
Tasso 252
Thiers 93, 181
Thucydides 170, 173
Tocqueville de 232
Tolstoy, Leo 290

Tosti 180

Treitschke 180

Troeltsch 84

Troya, Carlo 25, 180

Turgot 71

Valla, L. 112

Vertot, Abbé de 15

Vico, *Scienza Nuova* 17, 35, 40, 60, 71, 72, 73, 73 fn., 74, 78, 79, 82, 113, 118, 142, 143, 211, 231, 247, 269, 270, 293, 299, 300

Virgil 304

Voltaire 71, 96, 118, 223

Vospiscus, F. 120

Wagner 134

Wetzold 99 fn.

William IV 92

Wilmans 98

Winckelmann 71, 320

Wolf 320

Wood 71

Zola 30, 192, 290